T0329943

How to Keep Your Research Project on Track

How to Keep Your Research Project on Track

Insights from When Things Go Wrong

SECOND EDITION

Edited by

Keith Townsend

Professor of Human Resources and Employment Relations, Department of Employment Relations and Human Resources, Griffith University, Australia

Mark N.K. Saunders

Professor of Business Research Methods, Birmingham Business School, University of Birmingham, UK and Visiting Professor, Gordon Institute of Business Science, University of Pretoria, Johannesburg, South Africa

Cheltenham, UK • Northampton, MA, USA

Published by
Edward Elgar Publishing Limited
The Lypiatts
15 Lansdown Road
Cheltenham
Glos GL50 2JA
UK

Edward Elgar Publishing, Inc.
William Pratt House
9 Dewey Court
Northampton
Massachusetts 01060
USA

A catalogue record for this book
is available from the British Library

Library of Congress Control Number: 2024942856

This book is available electronically in the **Elgar**online
Business subject collection
https://dx.doi.org/10.4337/9781035332724

MIX
Paper | Supporting
responsible forestry
FSC
www.fsc.org   FSC® C013604

ISBN 978 1 0353 3271 7 (cased)
ISBN 978 1 0353 3272 4 (eBook)

Printed and bound by CPI Group (UK) Ltd, Croydon, CR0 4YY

Contents

PART II   GETTING DATA

PART III   GETTING IT TOGETHER

Editors

Keith Townsend is Professor of Human Resource Management and Employment Relations at Griffith University, Australia. His research spans a wide range of areas including a focus on frontline managers, employee voice, industrial relations and human resource management and work–life balance. These broad themes are brought together with an overarching approach to better understanding the complexities of managing people within the modern workplace. His research has been published in journals including *Human Resource Management Journal, Work, Employment and Society* and *British Journal of Management*. He has also published a number of research methods books, including *Method in the Madness: Research Stories You Won't Read in Textbooks, Handbook of Qualitative Research Methods on Human Resource Management: Innovative Techniques* and *How to Keep Your Doctorate on Track: Insights from Students' and Supervisors' Experiences*.

Mark N.K. Saunders is Professor of Business Research Methods at Birmingham Business School, University of Birmingham, UK and a Visiting Professor at Gordon Institute of Business Science, University of Pretoria, South Africa. He holds fellowships of the Academy of Social Sciences, British Academy of Management and the First International Network on Trust. His research interests include research methods (in particular participant selection, and methods of understanding organisational relationships) and human resource aspects of the management of change (in particular trust, and organisational learning). He also has an emerging interest in small and medium-sized enterprises. His research has been published in journals including the *British Journal of Management, Human Relations, Human Resource Management Journal, Journal of Small Business Management* and *Social Science and Medicine*. He is editor of the Edward Elgar Handbooks of Research Methods series. He has also co-authored a number of research methods books, including *Research Methods for Business Students* (currently in its 9th edition), *Doing Research in Business and Management* (currently in its second edition), *Handbook of Research Methods on Trust* (currently in its second edition), *How to Keep Your Doctorate on Track* and *Handbook of Research Methods on Human Resource Development*.

Contributors

Neve Abgeller is Asssistant Professor in Organisation, Work and Employment and Undergraduate Dissertation Coordinator at the University of Birmingham, UK. Her research interests include, but are not limited to, trust and distrust, research philosophy and methodology, and culture.

Samreen Ashraf is Principal Academic in Marketing in the Department of Marketing, Strategy and Innovation at Bournemouth University Business School, UK. Her research areas include multiple identities, digital identity, financial services, trust repair, religious influence on consumption, sustainable consumption, and consumer behaviour.

Carol Atkinson is Professor of HRM at Manchester Metropolitan University Business School, UK. Her research interests focus on employment quality, in particular in the adult social care sector and for older workers.

Hugh T.J. Bainbridge is Associate Professor in the School of Management, University of New South Wales, Australia. His research interests focus on workforce diversity with a specialisation in the experience of employees who, in addition to their job, also provide informal unpaid care to family members with disabilities.

Helena Barnard is full Professor and Academic Head of Doctoral Programmes at the Gordon Institute of Business Science, University of Pretoria, South Africa.

Timothy Bartram is Professor of HR Analytics and Head of Department HRM in the School of Management, RMIT, Australia. His research is in the area of HRM in healthcare, Indigenous Men's Sheds and disability in the workplace.

Rebecca Beech is Lecturer in Marketing, Oxford Brookes University, UK.

Polly Black is Associate Teaching Professor in the Department of Communication at Wake Forest University, USA. Her research focuses on consumer behaviour and consumer trust.

Ilenia Bregoli is Associate Professor in Management, Department of

Economics and Management, Università degli Studi di Brescia, Italy. She considers herself a pragmatist and in her research she uses mixed methods.

Mollie Bryde-Evens is Lecturer in Ethical Business and Responsible Management at Liverpool John Moores University, UK.

Kenneth Cafferkey is Professor at Sunway University Business School, Malaysia and Programme Leader of the Masters in HRM. His research is on High Performance Work Systems, HRM System Strength and employee perspectives and experiences of HRM.

Jillian Cavanagh is Associate Professor in the Department of Human Resource Management, School of Management at RMIT, Australia. She's an Associate Fellow of the Higher Education Academy (Indigenous), Associate Editor for the *Asia Pacific Journal of Human Resources* and on the Editorial Board of the *International Journal of Human Resource Management*.

Kate L. Daunt is Professor of Marketing at Cardiff Business School, Cardiff University, UK. Kate enjoys eating biscuits.

Hetal Doshi is Adjunct Professor of Sunway University, Malaysia and the CEO and Organizational Psychologist at O-Psych Sdn Bhd.

Dawn C. Duke is Head of Researcher Development, Africa Research Excellence Fund (AREF). She leads the team that delivers professional development opportunities for biomedical and health early career researchers across Africa.

Jane Glover is a Research Associate, at the Centre for Women's Enterprise, Leadership, Economy & Diversity (WE LEAD), University of York, UK. Her research interests lie in small family firms with a particular focus on rural firms. Jane conducts qualitative research using multiple approaches including interviews, participant observation and documentary analysis.

Colin Hughes is Head of the Graduate Business School, Technological University, Dublin, Eire. His research focuses on trust building in virtual sales teams.

Peter J. Jordan is Professor of Organizational Behaviour at the Griffith Business School, Griffith University, Australia. Peter's research interests include emotions in organisations, team performance and psychological entitlement in organisations.

Stefan Jooss is Senior Lecturer in Management at UQ Business School, The University of Queensland, Australia. His main research interest and focus is human resource management, specifically in the areas of talent management, global mobility and future of work.

Alex Kevill is Lecturer in Enterprise at the University of Leeds, UK. His research interests include dynamic capabilities, micro-enterprises and social entrepreneurship.

Catheryn Khoo is Professor in Tourism and Hospitality at Torrens University, Australia. Her research focuses on women travellers and family tourism, and often, qualitatively, from an Asian perspective.

Jerome Kiley is Senior Lecturer in the Department of Human Resource Management in the Faculty of Business and Management Sciences of the Cape Peninsula University of Technology, Cape Town, South Africa.

Jennifer Kilroy completed her PhD at NUI Galway, Republic of Ireland, while working full time in a HRM position in a multinational firm. She continues her practitioner life while publishing from her PhD findings.

Wojciech Marek Kwiatkowski is a Doctoral Researcher at Alliance Manchester Business School, University of Manchester, UK.

Amanda Lee is Senior Lecturer in Human Resource Management at the University of Derby, UK and Chartered Fellow of the CIPD. Prior to a career in academia she worked in retail, construction and the NHS.

Qian Yi Lee is a Postdoctoral Research Associate at the Australian Catholic University. She is a qualitative researcher with expertise in frontline management and performance management research. Qian is currently working on three projects on employers, employment services, and job quality/good work.

Rebecca Loudoun is Associate Professor at Griffith University, Australia. Her research and teaching focuses in the areas of human resource management, industrial relations and health and safety management.

Aoife M. McDermott is Professor of Human Resource Management at Aston University, UK and adjunct faculty at the Centre for Work, Organization and Wellbeing, Griffith University, Australia. She is particularly interested in the employment relationships of health and social care employees.

Hannah Meacham is Senior Lecturer in the School of Management at RMIT University, Australia. Hannah's research focus is on the inclusion of workers with intellectual disabilities within mainstream workplaces, along with the workplace wellbeing of home care workers in the aged care sector.

Sameer Qaiyum is Senior Lecturer in Strategic Management at Liverpool Business School, Liverpool John Moores University, UK. His research interests are in the areas of strategic management and innovation.

Céline Rojon is Professor of Business Psychology at CBS International

Business School, Koln, Germany. Her research interests include work performance, assessment, selection and development, research methods and cross-cultural studies.

Mark N.K. Saunders is Professor of Business Research Methods in the Birmingham Business School at the University of Birmingham, UK and a Visiting Professor at Gordon Institute of Business Science, University of Pretoria, South Africa.

Heather Short is Associate Lecturer and Practice Tutor, Faculty of Business and Law, The Open University, UK. She has worked in multinational organisations and runs her own small and medium enterprise (SME). Her research interests include e-learning and SMEs.

Vivienne Spooner is Faculty Lead for the MPhil programme with a specialisation in evidence-based management at the Gordon Institute of Business Science, University of Pretoria, South Africa.

Rohit Talwar was a Teaching Fellow in Marketing at the University of Birmingham, UK. His research focused on consumer experiences generated by interactive installations in public spaces with a postmodern lens.

Andrew Timming holds a PhD from Cambridge University in the UK and started his academic career lecturing at Cambridge, followed by academic positions at the University of Manchester, the University of St Andrews, the University of Western Australia and RMIT University.

Keith Townsend is Professor of Human Resources and Employment Relations in the Griffith Business School at Griffith University, Australia.

Kiran Trehan is Pro-Vice-Chancellor for Partnerships and Engagement and Director of the Centre for Women's Enterprise, Leadership, Economy & Diversity (WE LEAD), University of York, UK. Kiran is a key contributor to debates on critical approaches to enterprise development, leadership and diversity and how it can be applied in a variety of small business and policy domains.

Catherine L. Wang is Professor of Entrepreneurship and Strategy at Brunel Business School, Brunel University London, UK. Her research interests are in the areas of entrepreneurship and strategic management.

Jenna Ward is Dean of the College of Business and Law at Coventry University, UK and Director of the Art of Management & Organization. Jenna's research focuses on exploring emotionality within organisations, organising and managing by prioritising marginalised voices.

Adrian Wilkinson is Professor at Griffith University, Australia. His research interests span industrial relations, human resource management and employee voice.

Carol Woodhams is Professor of Human Resource Management at the University of Surrey, UK. Her specialist research topic is in the general area of equality and diversity, especially gender and intersecting pay gaps

Deisi Yunga-Godoy is Assistant Lecturer and Researcher in the Education Department at the Universidad Técnica de Loja in Ecuador. She earned her doctorate in teacher education from Eötvös Loránd University, Budapest, Hungary.

1. The more things change, the more things stay as they are!

Keith Townsend and Mark N.K. Saunders

The Horse and Groom is a friendly Cotswolds country pub that has consistently won UK 'best public house' awards since 2009.[1] The quality of this Bourton-on-the-Hill pub is hence a perfect starting point for this unusual research offering. In the autumn of 2016 we sat in this country pub after a day of working through a significant and important revision of a research methods article. As we enjoyed a pint of beer, an award-winning dinner and exceptional service, we discussed the differences between textbook research methods and the realities that all of us in the field face on a day-to-day basis. Previously, we had both embarked on publications that drew on the realities (see for example, Saunders and Lewis, 1997; Townsend and Burgess, 2009), but felt that there was scope for something new. Something that was both practical but based in real-life experiences.

As a fellow researcher we are sure you can appreciate the excitement that grew throughout the course of the evening as we discussed the possibilities that would become this edition. 'There's so much that goes unwritten', we would lament; 'we're doing our students a disservice by not telling them', we would declare. 'So let's do something', we agreed. It was then that we embarked upon a journey that started the same way that many top research publications start ... on the back of beer mats (Figure 1.1).

Our plan was literally written on the back of 'beer mats', with the key final stage 'Talk to Fran tomorrow' as one of us had a meeting the next day with Francine O'Sullivan, our commissioning editor at Edward Elgar Publishing. One might be forgiven for thinking pubs, beer mats, chats with publishers – doesn't sound all that 'scientific' or high-brow. Perhaps not, but it does reflect the broad experience of reality while not paying enough attention to the many hours of subsequent planning, discussions, reviewing and commenting on drafts that we were about to face.

The chapters that were in that book were based upon our realisation that research projects do not always go smoothly. In all honesty, we would argue that they rarely go smoothly. But we are employed to perform research from conceptualisation of worthwhile projects to the completion of these projects

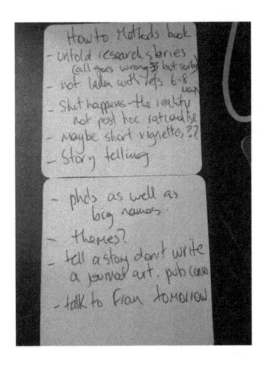

Figure 1.1   Horse and Groom research proposal

including dissemination to a range of different audiences. This book hit a chord with researchers, and we subsequently collaborated on a book titled *How to Keep Your Doctorate on Track* (Townsend, Saunders, Loudoun and Morrison, 2020) focused primarily on advising and supporting doctoral students through the rollercoaster ride of completing their studies. Following the success of these volumes, we embarked upon this contribution – *How to Keep Your Research Project on Track* (second edition).

So here we are – doing research – and we are not making judgements on whether 'doing research' is particularly difficult, or particularly easy – it just is what it is. And we as researchers must find ways to jump through a myriad of invisible hoops and over a plethora of hurdles of unknown heights. So planning is important and the knowledge and understandings we can glean from textbooks and journal articles on research methods are an important part of that planning. But, and this is an important 'but': these textbooks and journal articles rarely are of help regarding what do you do when your research project goes off track, usually offering only sanitised accounts. This book we hope will address this important, and usually hidden, aspect of research.

For this edition, we have asked many of the contributors to the first edition to freshen up their chapters, and brought in new contributors with new ideas, all providing their own inside accounts in the form of 36 contributions – 20 chapters and 16 vignettes offering revealing insights and highlighting their own lessons. We believe these will give hope to the early career researcher, the PhD or Masters student, and at the same time provide the 'old timers' such as ourselves with some reinvigoration.

Contributors were given strict instructions. This is not to be a theory driven, literature-soaked piece of work. Much like the book's inception, we would tell the authors to imagine you were at a pub or a coffee shop and relaying a story to a friend. Keep it informal, keep it light, but tell it as it actually was and have some lessons for the reader to take away.

We have divided the book into four sections. Maintaining the informal theme, the sections are 'Getting started', 'Getting data', 'Getting it together' and 'Getting finished'. Within each section we have chapters followed by short vignettes, all of which tell tales of researchers facing real-world problems or not quite getting things right in the first instance.

In the first section, 'Getting started', we draw on expert experiences in the 'not-so-straightforward' manner in which research projects develop and progress. Carol Atkinson leads the book with her chapter (2) 'How to develop research projects' and recounts her experience with trying to balance the researchers' interests with some form of broader, social good. How does that feed in to a system that is supposed to start with identifying a problem from literature reviews? Céline Rojon gives some insights in Chapter 3. There are many 'types' of literature reviews, and her chapter, while focusing on the use of systematic literature reviews, also offers insights into traditional narrative reviews, providing some important insights to keep the researcher on track.

The next two chapters in this section focus on the interactions between PhD supervisors and students. In Chapter 4 Jillian Cavanagh, Hannah Meacham and Timothy Bartram explore a number of important themes where all parties within a PhD team must be working together to ensure the success of the research project and in particular successful completion. As part of this they reflect on a few different matters, for example: the differences between the literature review and a theoretical framework; academic writing styles; and key challenges in different supervision styles. Polly Black then, in Chapter 5, outlines a supervision saga that happens all too often: when a supervisor and student are forced to go separate ways, but the PhD and research project must go on and a new supervisor found! New supervisors, indecision, uncertainty, and a completely different approach to feedback … all at a time when the PhD student is at their most vulnerable. The final chapter in this section draws on a topic that may very well be outdated before it's even written – whether or not to use Generative AI. This rapidly moving area is important for academics, and Jerome Kiley provides some thoughts on the issue.

We round out the first section of the book with two vignettes. The first of these (vignette 7) is from Deisi Yunga-Godoy who explores a number of issues in coming up with a research question, including the importance of communication and evaluating rather than acting immediately on every piece of advice. Our final vignette (8) in this 'Getting started' section comes from Hugh Bainbridge, explaining why a researcher with career development in mind needs to differentiate between 'reply' and 'reply all' in an email [editor's note: Keith feels Hugh's pain here having engaged in a similar faux pas].

Once a research project moves from the 'getting started' phase, 'getting data' is often the next hurdle where researchers and research projects can come unstuck. Neve Abgeller opens this section with Chapter 9, titled 'Epistemological odyssey: a journey of self-discovery', offering what she refers to as a journey of self-discovery 'from clueless despair to confident revelation'. Ideally, researchers should have some sense of their epistemology prior to collecting data because this drives many of the decisions around the data that will be collected. However, as Neve illustrates through her story, an epistemological position is something that emerges over time and may not fit neatly into the typologies offered by textbooks.

In Chapter 10 Mark Saunders provides us with the first of four chapters focusing on the realities of data collection. Theirs is a panicked description of an online data collection process that began to spiral into desperate territory as questionnaires were not returned and email requests to respondents did not meet the intended people. Not only were their numbers not flowing back in, but the legal threats were arriving! However, as you will read, their research was eventually completed successfully, and lessons were learned. Next, in Chapter 11, Heather Short offers insights about undertaking interviews and, reflecting on her experiences, asks why research participants may be less than truthful. Heather questions whether she was either willing or able to hear the truth and, quoting George Bernard Shaw, asks whether she and her research participants were 'separated by a common language'?

The fourth chapter (Chapter 12) in this section comes from Kenneth Cafferkey and Hetal Doshi, who demonstrate through experiences using case studies that access and data collection do not come without the difficulties of interference from practitioners. Practitioners may prefer researchers to ask the questions the managers want, not the theoretically derived research agendas that we seek to deliver, emphasising the importance of having the right access for the right question.

Getting data is one thing, but in the business-related fields of applied research we are often reliant upon collecting data from people in organisations for whom our research project is not their biggest problem. Our contributors provide seven vignettes for this section; the first of these (vignette 13) comes from Polly Black, who reveals why, when she was developing qualitative interviews, a pilot study was really necessary. Wojciech Kwiatkowski provides a story in vignette 14 that many researchers will appreciate, a tale of feeling strung along with the endless promises of physical access to collect data 'soon' that never comes to fruition. What do you do? When you do get access, can you be sure that it will be maintained?

Vignette 15 comes from Keith Townsend, who found himself in an interview with a recalcitrant employee, unwilling to offer anything to the research project. Given the project had reached the theoretically important point of saturation (see for example, Townsend, 2013), the researcher decided that there was little point in persevering with the interview. Perhaps a different decision would have been made at a different point of the project, but that's why context is so important in the social sciences. In vignette 16 Catheryn Khoo wasn't going to take any chances with not having enough data collected, so she worked very hard in offering incentives to garner participation. Great idea until her examiner questioned whether the incentives were 'too lucrative': read her vignette to find out how she responded! Following this, we have Colin Hughes's vignette (17), which provides some hard lessons learned during his doctoral research when being a researcher can often feel like being in sales. His vignette offers five valuable steps for the researcher to keep in mind when undertaking projects with practitioners. Before we move to the next section of the book, Qian Lee describes in vignette 18 being placed in the unenviable position of a senior manager continually rescheduling interview times before inviting a second interviewee in to the meeting. Sometimes split-second decisions must be made in data collection!

In our simple progression of the perfect project, we've managed to get started, got the data, now it's time for 'Getting it together'. Our first chapter (19) in this section brings an old joke in to modern academia. People interpret things differently, so this is something to be mindful of when you are interpreting your qualitative data, according to Rebecca Loudoun and Keith Townsend. What seems like a sensible idea at the start of data collection proved much more complicated for this project as the researchers found many people interpreted, and therefore responded to, the interview questions differently.

Sameer Qaiyum and Catherine Wang have contributed a conversation-style chapter (20) exploring issues of quantitative data analysis and issues associated with learning new statistical techniques. Sameer tells of times 'in the dark' and at least one 'wild goose chase' on their research project and the importance of thinking 'outside the box' when you are faced with problems of analysis. He also highlights how quantitative data analysis can be a messy business and that the associated learning is ongoing. And just when you think you have the analysis all covered: the writing – what if it doesn't just flow from the fingertips? We've all had those days in front of a white screen or written and deleted a sentence 17 times. In Chapter 21 Dawn Duke offers some insights for getting the writing part of your research project back on track 'when the words just won't come'. Emphasising that we all struggle with writing at some time [editors' note: we certainly both do!], she shares stories of researchers struggling with writer's block and, importantly, what helped them overcome this. Dawn also offers a series of excellent quotes, including fiction writer C.J. Cherryh musing: 'It is perfectly okay to write garbage – as long as you edit brilliantly.' Good advice for anyone struggling with a blinking cursor!

The last two chapters in this section come from Carol Woodhams and then Vivienne Spooner and Helena Barnard. The Woodhams' contribution tells of the benefits that can be gained from shifting our thinking from performing our research 'on' organisations, to researching 'with' organisations. Spooner and Barnard's contribution comes in the form of a consideration of the golden thread – that mystical 'thing' that winds itself through our research and indeed, careers, holding everything together in a somewhat (hopefully) logical package.

Our vignettes in this section tell cautionary tales. Ilenia Bregoli reveals her affinity with feelings in a Led Zeppelin song about betrayal as she transitioned from paper to computer software for analysis (vignette 24), highlighting the need to really understand the analysis method used. In contrast, Rohit Talwar's story in vignette 25 emphasises the importance of making regular and frequent back-up copies. His cautionary tale of coffee and electronic devices tells of how a poorly designed coffee mug destroyed over three weeks of data analysis and associated writing. When you have your work written, sometimes it needs to be presented to humans and, according to Kenneth Cafferkey, that doesn't always go smoothly, particularly if one of your audience isn't really a 'people person' (vignette 26). Jennifer Kilroy, rounds out this section (27) and reminds us that sometimes the space for our research comes in the most peculiar places; nevertheless, we can often find these spaces when we plan well.

Well, the project seems to have gone well until now; we've got started, got the data, we've got our analysis completed and we've even got some writing done. Time for 'Getting finished'. Getting finished sometimes requires wonderfully difficult conversations about authorship; just ask Kate Daunt and Aoife McDermott. Or better still, read Chapter 28, where these authors explore the complicated politics of authorship within academia, considering questions such as on what basis to award authorship and in what order and, crucially, what to do when things go wrong. Apparently, biscuits can solve almost any problems. These interpersonal tribulations are nothing compared to the internal struggle many of us feel when we pass our work to others for feedback (and that's before those pesky editors and reviewers!).

In Chapter 29 Amanda Lee provides us with an account of coming to terms with detailed feedback. More specifically, Amanda was convinced that one of her supervisors thought she was incapable of writing (which, when you read the chapter, you can see she is not) and struggled with managing her feelings, reactions to the feedback she was receiving, and her supervisor! Amanda embarked on a useful process of keeping a reflective research journal to help work through the difficulties that, as many of us can appreciate, affect motivation and confidence. Most of us develop 'thicker skins' as we progress through our career, but it is important to remember that the feedback we receive is rarely about us as people, but about the work that we've presented – an important distinction to make.

All the world is a stage, Shakespeare tells us, and academia is certainly verging on a pantomime sometimes. In Chapter 30, presented in three scenes, Kiran Trehan, Alex Kevill and Jane Glover explore issues associated with securing and maintaining research projects for researchers at different stages in their academic careers. For each career stage they reveal the messiness and complexities of keeping research projects on track and how, despite things going 'wrong', you just have to keep moving forward. We mentioned those pesky reviewers, didn't we? Well, Chapter 31 comes in with a whack at editors too. Townsend, Wilkinson, Timming and Loudoun recount some difficult to understand and explain reviews and editorial feedback they've received over the years.

There's no question that the world has changed with the advent of 'smart' devices, phones, laptops and tablets. Billy Bragg has a lyric in a song voicing concern about 'smart bombs in the hands of dumb people'. Let's be more optimistic about the smart devices in the hands of educated people and, as Samreen Ashraf shows in Chapter 32, embrace what the 21st century has to offer with tales of social media use as both a means of support and to enhance the development of research projects. From here we bounce between chapters and vignettes to the end of the book. In Chapter 33, Mark Saunders gives us some thoughts about rewriting in vignette 33. Drawing from an interview with John Lennon published in *Spins* magazine, Mark reveals how, like song writers with their lyrics, we write and rewrite each publication. Mark presents the process of development of a journal article (that the editors wrote together – see Saunders and Townsend, 2016) that lived through 22 drafts before even being presented to a journal editor and which was finally published after 41 drafts. It may surprise readers to know that this introduction has also gone through a fair number of drafts ... maybe we should have done one or two more?

In vignette 34 Peter Jordan reflects on his experience with research students who claim to be 'over it'. Over what, Peter contemplates ... the writing, the process, the research, the idea of research as a career perhaps? After reading the trials and tribulations of our fellow researchers (and ourselves) in this introduction you may have started to wonder why on earth we even do this job and question whether we should be 'over it'.

For this edition, we have added two additional contributions that step a little further into the career of the academy researcher. After reading the trials and tribulations of our fellow researchers (and ourselves) in this introduction you may have started to wonder why on earth we even do this job and question whether we should be 'over it'. In this regard the chapter by Mollie Bryde-Evens and Rebecca Beech offers a potential way forward. They offer a toolkit for developing resilience arguing that we need to develop a proactive, dynamic and engaged version of resilience centring on the ability to learn and progress when faced with challenges. Stefan Jooss tells us of his experience moving countries while trying to maintain the contribution to existing research projects and collaborations, and our final chapter is an interesting contribution from Jenna Ward. Jenna tells of her experience following a managerial pathway with success, only to realise that this means she is far from what initially engaged her in a research career.

You may be thinking, 'surely it's too difficult?' But the enthusiasm we had as we developed the idea for both the first edition and this volume was matched by the enthusiasm of the contributors who were not only excited about the project and their chapters but also wanted to tell what they considered to be the interesting tales of when things went wrong and offer insights from their real research experiences. That's why we do research, because although it rarely goes smoothly, it is almost always exciting and interesting. The reality of doing research is that 'shit happens'. Things will never go perfectly. But we have a job to do, so we draw on the dozens of researchers who've found out that when things go wrong, you will learn, and you will be able to get your research project back on track!

NOTE

1.   There is a photograph of the pub on the back cover.

REFERENCES

Saunders, M.N.K. and Lewis, P. (1997), 'Great ideas and blind alleys? A review of the literature on starting research', *Management Learning, 28*(3), 283–99.
Saunders, M.N.K. and Townsend, K. (2016). Reporting and justifying the number of interview participants in organization and workplace research. *British Journal of Management, 27*(4), 836–52.
Townsend, K. (2013, December). Saturation and run off: How many interviews are required in qualitative research. In *ANZAM Conference 2013* (pp. 1–17).

Townsend, K. and Burgess, J. (2009). *Method in the Madness: Research Stories You Won't Read in Textbooks*, Oxford: Chandos Publishing.

Townsend, K., Saunders, M.N.K., Loudoun, R. and Morrison, E., (2020). *How to Keep Your Doctorate on Track: Insights from Students' and Supervisors' Experiences*, Cheltenham, UK and Northampton, MA, USA: Edward Elgar.

PART I

Getting started

2. How to develop research projects

Carol Atkinson

Research is an integral part of most academic careers. For many, it is the thing that 'gets us out of bed' and keeps us motivated at work. But while it can be a source of great fulfilment and satisfaction, it can also be overwhelming – where to start and what to do? – and rarely goes as smoothly as the neat, linear process laid out in research methods textbooks. In this chapter, I discuss how to generate ideas for research projects that meet the twin priorities of interesting us and also being important in other ways, be it economically, socially and so on. I also discuss how to tackle the inevitable pitfalls that research projects bring. So be reassured if you are already experiencing some of these dilemmas: you are not alone. Also take comfort from the iterative, dynamic nature of research which presents opportunities to revisit, rethink and navigate these challenges.

GENERATING IDEAS

There are many different ways to generate ideas for research projects and I discuss these in what follows. One influencing factor is whether the research project is being funded, and if so, who the funder is. Many projects are externally funded, most commonly being contract research or research council/ charity research. Contract research, funded by a range of government or commercial organisations, often tightly specifies the 'idea' or focus of the project. Research council/charity research may also do this, but more usually sets general parameters that you can submit proposals within. While your research may not attract external funding, if it is undertaken in university (or other research organisation) time, it is effectively internally funded and you may need to take account of organisation priorities or strategies when deciding on your research project. For example, I work in the *Decent Work and Productivity* research centre at ManMet Business School and this focus guides our project ideas. In very early career, PhD study is often supported through scholarships which may specify a particular focus, although it is often possible to hone the focus of study, and research assistant/associate roles are usually attached to pre-specified projects. Within these constraints, however, there is still lots of scope to come up with ideas for great projects, and below I outline five ways to do this.

Curiosity

Or in other words, what interests you? Many of us start our research careers by doing a PhD. While it might not seem like it at the time – a PhD can be a long, arduous, sometimes lonely journey – it is also a fantastic, perhaps unique, opportunity to study something that you are deeply interested in. It is also *your* project, with no tricky team dynamics to navigate (see later section on challenges!) other than a supervisory team to 'manage' (for ideas on this, see Atkinson and Townsend, 2020). But once you complete your PhD, or get your first lectureship after a research assistant/associate role, how do you decide on a programme of research?research assistant/associate role, how do you decide on a programme of research?

An obvious place to start is with what interests you. How will you decide this? And will you have to research it for the rest of your career? Curiosity is often stimulated by two things: academic study and personal experience. Thinking about your studies, what has fascinated you? This could be from either undergraduate or Masters' level study to guide your choice of PhD topic, or from your PhD to inform your research projects. What have you enjoyed, what do you think is important, what gaps in knowledge do you have a burning desire to fill? Reviewing the literature and techniques like mind mapping to identify topics of interest and develop a conceptual framework are important steps.

Alternatively, what personal experiences have led you to think that we need to know more about a certain topic? Many of my research ideas have emerged this way. While doing my Masters' degree, for example, I was the management development manager of the IT division of a large UK bank. I wrestled with how to provide career development opportunities for IT specialists and this became my dissertation topic, leading to the establishment of both management and technical career pathways. Some time later, I had a role in a small firm and saw the very different challenges in that context when compared to a large organisation. In my thirties, I decided to move into academia and do a PhD. My choice of topic: the psychological contract in small firms. Actually, I was fascinated by employment legislation and how it impacted the psychological contract, but (spoiler alert) see below for how this was just too big an idea. To return to the 'do you have to research a topic forever' question, no of course not! Although again, see later for the pitfalls of changing research focus. Ignoring my own advice on this, later in my career and drawing again clearly on personal experience, I developed an interest in older women's careers and, in particular, workplace experiences of menopause. Although these research ideas came from personal experiences important to me, literature and research evidence were still central to identifying what we know, what the gaps are, what we should research in these topics and so on. A solid theoretical under-pinning is essential however the research idea is arrived at.

Collaboration

What are your colleagues interested in/researching? Is it something that interests you enough to collaborate with them? Collaboration is important, especially in your early career as it can provide an opportunity to work with more experienced colleagues and learn from them. Don't let being a junior academic hold you back from suggesting collaboration. If you have recently finished your PhD, you will have much to offer, including an up to date and in-depth overview of relevant literature, novel findings and new ideas. Don't underestimate the contribution you can make.

An important consideration though is your current focus versus your col-leagues' focus. Ideally there would be a close match, but this isn't always so and the question then is whether to change tack. That will depend on many things, for instance, how much your current research interests you, the mileage left in it and so on. But do bear in mind that being the only academic in a department with a particular interest can be a lonely place in terms of lack of mentoring, team-working opportunities and so on. But do make sure that your colleagues have sound ideas and good track records before making any change in topic!

If you are isolated in terms of your research focus in your own institution, think about building cross-institution collaborations. Your colleagues may be able to help with introductions, but also focus on doing this for yourself. Publishing high-quality papers in reputable journals, attending conferences, taking on roles in learned societies, reviewing journal articles and so on are all important ways of building a name for yourself in a particular field. Conferences are also a great way of generating research ideas and, while they can be expensive, many now offer online attendance which is more cost-effective. Building your name in an area may lead to invitations to collaborate with others or, at the very least, mean that your attempts to build collaborations are taken seriously. Cross-institutional projects are also usually more likely to be successful when applying for external funding.

Real-world Problems

There is increasing emphasis, in the UK at least, on research that has impact, that is, brings about change in the world beyond academia. This perhaps explains the growing interest in research design approaches, such as engaged scholarship (Van de Ven, 2007), that co-design and co-deliver research with a wide range of stakeholders outside of academia. Academics work with these stakeholders to identify their problems and conduct research that aims to solve them. This requires a set of skills that is relatively new to many academics and also the building of robust networks with policy makers and practitioners who can be drawn into idea creation. It is then a good idea to build these networks from the earliest stages of your research career, but this is something that is often overlooked in research methods training or PhD programmes of study. Ask yourself: 'if I needed to ask a question of a practitioner in my field, who would I contact?' If the answer is, 'I don't know/don't have these contacts', then action is needed!

I am perhaps fortunate in having had a career in industry prior to becoming an academic and so have long had strong policy/practitioner networks. Certainly, this has been central to the research ideas and projects I have undertaken, as the following two recent examples demonstrate. First, we wanted to put together a proposal for the Economic and Social Research Council (ESRC) on creating good employment, a key focus for our research team, and reached out to our networks to work with them on determining the focus of the project. Ultimately, we settled on how to develop management skills so that managers understood how to create good employment via a Good Employment Learning Lab.[1] Our strong networks meant that we had two sub-learning labs, one for a place-based approach in Greater Manchester, and one for a sector-based approach in adult social care. In the UK, research funders are increasingly requiring a partnership-based approach, again meaning that strong networks are central to identifying research ideas. This is evident in the second example, where, at the time of writing, I am part of a bid to the National Institute of Health and Care Research (NIHR) responding to a funding call that seeks to create five-year partnerships to promote research into the health and social care workforce. This specifically requires academics and sector partners to work together to identify and solve workforce problems.

As you can see, there is a growing emphasis on policy maker/practitioner collaboration to ensure that real-world problems are addressed and change enacted. Building strong networks are central to this, so it's a good idea to build these at an early stage of your career.

Emerging Trends

It is important to pay attention to what is happening in the world around you. There are many research projects now on matters that simply did not exist earlier in my career. Some of these result from developments in technology, such as artificial intelligence (AI), some from changing societal norms, for example, a shift over recent years to greater emphasis on equality, diversity and inclusions and yet others from matters such as climate change. These, and other trends, have created new research opportunities and more will follow given the global pace of change.

So, how to spot these trends? The networks discussed earlier are important, but so are the press and other media, friends, family and colleagues, and a general awareness of what is going on in the outside world. Funding bodies can also be important sources of information. For example, the ESRC has strategic priorities including climate change and sustainability, improving health, well-being and social care, and using data to inform decision making. This would suggest these are going to be important future trends. If emerging trends interest you, be prepared to move into new areas. For example, AI and employment research barely existed only a few years ago and, if of interest to you, may require you to change your research focus. You'll need to consider the balance between new interests and moving away from something that you are known for, which is covered in more detail below. But certainly, in your early career, it is important not to confine yourself to an area that is of dwindling interest to you and miss out on exciting new fields of research.

There is also an ever-increasing emphasis on inter-disciplinary projects, as recognition grows that the grand challenges of our time will not be solved by working in disciplinary silos. Think of how your research could intersect with other disciplines to add a richness to it. In my research, I am broadening my adult social care employment focus by working with both clinical colleagues and health economists. Here, we are looking at how to redesign care worker roles to take on health care duties and conducting an economic evaluation of this to consider its effectiveness. Again, ask yourself, who do I know outside of my own discipline and how could we meaningfully work together? Think about how to build networks and connections. For inter-disciplinary work, it might be easier to start in your own organisation using its infrastructure and then extend to other institutions from there.

Serendipity

You'll have seen by now that my research interests have developed across my career. I've already explained how curiosity driven by personal experiences led me to an early focus on small firm employment relationships before later moving on to older women's careers and menopause transition. You'll also have noticed that arguably my largest and most impactful research is around employment in adult social care. This was the result of pure serendipity, otherwise known as good luck or good fortune. A former student who worked as a consultant in the sector intended to apply for a contract research tender on investigating care worker pay and wanted the gravitas of working with a university. They approached me and asked if I would be interested in joining them. While there was some relevance from my small firm research (as many care providers in the UK are small firms) and an emphasis on job quality, largely it was just an opportunity seized. I was only two years out of my PhD, I'd had a small British Academy funded project on small firms but was ambitious and wanted more, larger funded projects – and this fitted the bill. I was fortunate that what was only an emerging issue at the time has gone on to become a national priority with many associated funding streams – but I took risk on a new area that simply presented itself and it has paid off. Such opportunities do need careful consideration, but my advice would be never to turn them down out of hand.

So far we have discussed how to come up with ideas for research projects. Some might say that this is the easy bit! Seeing ideas through to a successful outcome can be very challenging, and we move on now to discuss how to deal with this.

NAVIGATING CHALLENGES

Across my career, I have worked on many projects and I think that it is fair to say that none have been entirely straightforward, unproblematic and a joy to work on at all times. Though I do want to reassure you that most have been largely enjoyable and had successful outcomes! Nevertheless, you will inevitably face challenges in the projects you work on, and below are some thoughts on what these might be and how to address them. The focus here is mainly on the personal skills needed to navigate challenges in both generating ideas and conducting projects, working on the assumption that research design has been robust!

Stay Focused

Standard advice to early career academics is to decide what you want to be 'known' for and pour all your energies into that. Making yourself known for something is doubtless good advice in many ways. It helps with identifying collaborators, winning funding, building a social media profile and so on. It can, however, be at odds with some of the ways of developing research ideas laid out above such as curiosity, spotting emerging trends and serendipity. Plus, what if you lose interest in the topic that you have focused on in the early part of your career? There is always the opportunity to change tack, but do think carefully about doing so, its costs and benefits, and perhaps try to evolve your interests gradually rather than undertake a sudden change.

It is a delicate balance of focus versus changing interests/emerging opportunities. That said, you may be looking at my research profile and thinking that I am not practising what I am preaching – and you would be right! While I have largely, and gradually, moved away from small firm research as my career has developed, I still have very active research streams around both employment in adult social care and menopause in the workplace. These both interest me greatly, but are very different and I can testify to the difficulty of maintaining both. You will have an easier, if not necessarily more interesting, time if you can focus on one area. But never do that to the point of feeling stuck in a rut or missing out on great opportunities.

Problem Identification

Research projects encounter many problems and identifying and addressing the root causes of these will need strong problem-solving skills. Here are a few examples that I have experienced across my career – yours will probably be different, but these may give you some pointers on what can happen and the skills needed to resolve them.

- Unrealistic expectations: engaged scholarship is incredibly powerful, but one of the drawbacks to having lots of people in a room who are passionate about a topic, but not necessarily expert in research, is the difficulty in creating realistic expectations. The Gender Pay Gap in medicine project was a great example of this. We had unions, associations, doctors, policy makers and so on as members of the steering group, which was fantastic. But all had a view on what the project should comprise and it was in danger of trying to solve every problem in the employment of doctors. Fortunately, we had an amazing steering group chair who ensured a tight focus on project objectives and stopped us wandering too far from these with frequent use of a phrase I grew to love: let's not try to boil the ocean. Pay attention to developing your leadership skills – whether you are a team leader or member, these are important to influencing how the project operates and setting realistic expectations.
- Team dynamics: this is often one of the biggest issues in a research project and (for obvious reasons) I am not going to offer specific examples here. Only to say, choose your collaborators very carefully in the first place, develop your people skills and don't be afraid to take advice from more senior academics or human resource specialists if needed. While you do hear some horror stories, these are fortunately relatively rare and I certainly have never yet had a project that has failed due to team dynamics – but some have needed more careful management than others.
- Unclear boundaries: the project is simply 'too big'. For my PhD, I collected data on the impact of employment legislation on the psychological contract in small firms, but I just had too much data. After wrestling for lengthy periods with how to fit it all into an 80,000-word thesis, at 120,000 words

I had to recognise what I had been trying to ignore: something had to go. My final thesis focused only on the psychological contract in small firms as a pragmatic decision to get to the end of the process. But I did publish journal articles from the other data, so all was not lost. Do draw clear boundaries around your project to avoid similar experiences.

• Time: always be realistic when allocating time in research design. It is easy to fall into the trap of promising to do far more than the time costed into the project allows and this creates many pressures. If this has happened, and time allowances can't be renegotiated, you will need to decide on project priorities and ensure that you deliver those.

Adaptability and Flexibility

All projects experiences snags, and sometimes bigger problems, at some point. From demanding funders, to tricky team members, from access difficulties, to data that doesn't adequately address the research questions, and a host of others. The trick here is to be adaptable and flexible – what changes are needed to improve things, how can you bring these about, how can you influence these changes? It's time to rely on your personal skills to ensure an effective project is delivered – and alongside adaptability and flexibility, resilience and perseverance will be needed. Think about ensuring that you have worked on developing these personal skills at an early stage of your research career.

Getting Support

Finally, remember that you don't have to do it all alone and that strong support networks are invaluable. These can include mentors, peers, for example, colleagues and fellow PhD students, external stakeholders and so on. They can fulfil a range of functions, from simply being there to offer advice, right through to joining the team to give support. In the same way as you should start to build external networks to support engaged scholarship at the beginning of your career, it is never too early to start building academic support networks. Your PhD supervisors might become trusted mentors, fellow PhD students can offer a safe space to bounce ideas around, colleagues might join teams to help resolve problems. The key is to ensure that you have strong networks and that you are not alone in trying to resolve research project difficulties.

CONCLUSIONS

In this chapter, we have discussed both how to generate research ideas and projects, and how to navigate challenges that may arise. I'd encourage you to try different ways of idea generation, build networks in academia and beyond and draw a balance between being focused while remaining open to new ideas. It is impossible to lay out here all the challenges you may have to navigate – they are too many and too varied – but some examples have been presented. While you will inevitably experience some of these, or others, along your research journey, take consolation that many can be avoided by robust research design, and others can be addressed using effective personal skills. Most projects will have a successful outcome so ensure that you enjoy the journey that your research career will take you on.

NOTE

1.   Good Employment Learning Lab, Manchester Metropolitan University, https://www.mmu.ac.uk/research/projects/good-employment-learning-lab.

REFERENCES

Atkinson, C. and Townsend, K. 2020. Whose doctorate is it anyway? How students and supervisors can work well together. In Townsend, K., Saunders, M., Loudoun, R. and Morrison, E. (eds), *How to Keep Your Doctorate on Track*, Cheltenham, UK and Northampton, MA, USA: Edward Elgar Publishing, 36–42.

Van de Ven, A. 2007. *Engaged Scholarship: A Guide for Organizational and Social Research*, Oxford: Oxford University Press.

3. On the path to enlightenment? Reviewing the literature systematically – or not

Céline Rojon

INTRODUCTION

As researchers, we all have to do literature reviews all the time for our research projects. Whenever we start out on a new study, or we write an article, we try to make sure that we know what others before us have found and we need to demonstrate that we are aware of the main issues discussed by the scholarly community. Having that knowledge also means we will be in a better position to articulate the contribution we hope our own research will make. So, in sum, as researchers we should all have (plenty of) experience with doing literature reviews. Well, I too thought I had experience with doing literature reviews, from having studied for a BSc and an MSc, when I started out on my PhD, some years ago now. Was I wrong? Perhaps not, but I did find that undertaking a literature review for a PhD, and subsequently doing literature reviews for other projects that I was working on, was quite a different ballgame to what I had been used to. In this chapter, I reflect on my experience with conducting literature reviews. As much of my experience comes from doing systematic reviews, this is what I will be drawing on mostly, with particular reference to my very first systematic review, which I did for said PhD, but I will also give some insights into 'traditional' narrative literature reviews.

DECISIONS, DECISIONS, DECISIONS: WHICH TYPE OF LITERATURE REVIEW TO USE

When I started my PhD I did not fully realise there were different types of literature review. I was, of course, aware of the need to review the literature critically, but not of the various different types of literature reviews to choose from. Indeed, although it may seem that knowing about more types might make the decision harder (much like in those restaurants that have lengthy menus!), it is actually helpful as the different literature review choices enable different research aims to be addressed or can appeal to different populations. Like many researchers I was aware of what I now know as the narrative literature review. This is the traditional way of reviewing literature on a given topic and is still very widely found, typically summarising the current state of knowledge about a particular topic and making reasoned arguments (being critical) regarding what is known and not known. Whilst this is a pretty flexible approach that can be undertaken in various different ways to suit the researcher's needs, allowing them to explore their own ideas, I found there are also several disadvantages. It is often seen as being subjective and non-transparent with no clear methodology – or at least not one that is made public to the reader – and the potential for the researcher to focus on their 'preferred' pieces of literature (or journals, or databases …).

Before I now say a bit more about the systematic review, which is the type of literature review I personally know best now, I think it is worth highlighting that aside from narrative and systematic reviews, there are also other types of reviews that merit consideration; the ones that I have encountered most in our subject area are realist reviews (also known as realist syntheses), meta-analyses and evidence syntheses. I found Booth and colleagues' recently updated book (2021) to give a comprehensive overview of these and other types of reviews.

Over to the systematic review then. Having been successfully used in medicine/health-related sciences and education for decades, this type of literature review made its debut in Business and Management about 15 years ago and has since started to become rather popular. Those who like systematic review methodology, including myself, claim that it can address some of the disadvantages encountered with traditional reviews. As much of this chapter is about systematic review, I will leave the discussion of my experiences – and why I found the process frustrating at times, but generally very useful – until a bit later. At this point, I will just give one of the most frequently cited definitions of systematic review methodology in our subject area, so as you have an idea of what it is: 'Systematic review is a specific methodology that locates existing studies, selects and evaluates contributions, analyses and synthesizes data, and reports the evidence in such a way that allows reasonably clear conclusions to be reached about what is and is not known' (Denyer and Tranfield, 2009, p. 671).

SYSTEMATIC REVIEW: WHAT IS THE BIG DEAL?

Perhaps you are wondering why to bother with doing a systematic review when you could 'just' be doing a regular narrative review? Well, let me talk you through the advantages and disadvantages of systematic reviews compared to narrative reviews as I see them. It may help to provide some context of how I first got to learn about systematic review methodology. In the first month of starting my PhD (no rest for the wicked!), my supervisors suggested that I consider carrying out a systematic review as a first phase in my research, which was on individual workplace performance. At the time, a good ten years ago, I had not heard about systematic review and decided to first of all familiarise myself with the methodology by consulting what I still consider one of the most useful resources on the matter (i.e., Denyer and Tranfield, 2009). Back then, systematic review methodology was still very new in the field of Business and Management and Denyer and Tranfield (2009) in particular were interested in finding a way of adapting the methodology, from its more traditional usage within the medical sciences, to our domain. Systematic review methodology immediately appealed to me when reading up on it. Why, you ask? Because it is a very structured approach to reviewing the literature, which follows a series of more or less standardised steps; this sounded good to the organised person in me. Other advantages of systematic review methodology that I perhaps came to appreciate only later on include that it is a very thorough, comprehensive way of reviewing existing literature as one aims to look at all literature – that is, different types of publications (including, ideally, grey literature; Adams, Smart and Huff, 2017)) in different subject areas – that is, relevant to one's review topic. As a result of this comprehensive approach, I always feel more confident that my findings actually represent the current body of knowledge relating to my topic. I also found systematic reviewing to be really helpful at drawing together fragmented literature that is dispersed in different subject areas – in my experience, our discipline is prone to such fragmentation, seeing that it draws from areas such as sociology, psychology, economics, anthropology ... So, for me, the structured reviewing framework underlying systematic review methodology helps deal with the issue of the dispersed body of evidence.

Further, the systematic review approach is not only comprehensive and thorough, but many systematic reviews also build a 'critical appraisal' component into their review process, through which any potentially relevant papers are reviewed in light of not just their relevance for addressing the review question(s), but also in terms of the quality of the evidence that they provide. By critical appraisal, I mean a way of judging the quality of every single piece of literature that is being considered for inclusion in the review, for example in terms of how thorough the conducted literature review was, how robust the methodology used was, how well findings were explained, discussed and linked back to relevant evidence, how logical conclusions were drawn and so forth. I found this critical appraisal process can contribute to producing a high-quality piece of review that reports on the most effective research in the area; this may positively distinguish systematic reviews from other types of reviews in which no obvious systematic critical appraisal takes place.

Moreover, I appreciated that it was possible to address quite specific review questions (in a similar way to how you would address research questions in an empirical study) rather than to just see what is out there in regards to a specific topic; for me, it made the whole process more defined and more tangible. For example, one of the questions I asked in the systematic review I did for my PhD was: 'How is individual workplace performance measured and why; what are the reasons for using certain methods of measurement and how solid are the arguments presented for different approaches?' Admittedly, this question turned out to be broader than I had imagined, leading to a large number of potentially relevant references (an aspect that I will talk more about a bit later), but it did mean that when screening papers for their relevance to my review, I could interrogate them with this question in mind. This makes it relatively easy to decide whether or not to include a paper in a systematic review on the basis of it speaking to your review question(s) – or not.

Also, oftentimes within systematic review methodology, insights gained are organised under three headings 'what we know already', 'what we do not yet know' and 'how future research can take up from here'. This is something I personally found very helpful and that I think is useful in publishing one's findings, too.

Since that initial systematic review I conducted for my PhD, and which I updated a few years later, I have returned to this methodology several times and it may even have become my 'go to' reviewing approach, which, I guess, shows how useful I find it. That is not to say that I think it is *always* the right approach for reviewing the literature nor that there are no challenges associated with using it – indeed, there can be quite a few and I will introduce you to the ones I encountered and/or that I am aware of through colleagues or methods literature shortly.

One of the advantages of being amongst the first to use a 'new' technique in your field is that you can reflect on your experiences and share these with others, whether that is informally in chatting to colleagues, or more formally at conferences or in journals. This is what I did (e.g., Rojon, McDowall and Saunders, 2011; Rojon, Okupe and McDowall, 2021) and I found that it gave me even greater insight into when and why systematic review methodology might be useful (and when it might not be), how it can be used in Business and Management research and so on.

SYSTEMATIC REVIEW: WHAT IS THE TURN OFF?

There are always two sides of the coin and that is also the case for systematic review methodology. Let me therefore fill you in on what I found to be its disadvantages or challenges.

A well thought out, comprehensive systematic review may very well draw on the guidance of an advisory panel, which researchers might consult to bounce off methodological ideas and validate own decisions for the systematic review. This panel can consist of fellow academics with similar research foci, practitioners working in relevant areas, policy-makers with a vested interest in one's topic, subject librarians, systematic review methodology experts and so forth. I tend to use such an advisory panel mostly during the scoping study of a systematic review, which is a preliminary stage concerned with determining the specific focus of the review alongside the review questions that will be used to interrogate the literature. In my experience, depending on how queries to the advisory panel members have been phrased, and also depending on the composition of the panel, you may end up with very many and potentially very different suggestions as to what they see as useful points for examination for your systematic review. Certainly this is what happened in my first systematic review, where the questions I asked my advisory panel were quite possibly too wide ranging and not focused enough and as a result I found reconciling people's different perspectives a tricky undertaking – the answers I got were rather different depending on whom I had asked ... and of course practitioners felt differently to academics; for example, one advisory panel member, a specialist in psychometrics, was very keen to learn more about specific questioning techniques for use within performance appraisal, whilst one of the practitioners on the panel was interested in querying how performance management could be made more effective, a rather broad question. Arriving at a (common) point of focus to inform my systematic review was not easy! How did I get around the issue? Well, ultimately, I reminded myself that this was *my* systematic review project and I therefore should not let myself be led down too many different paths that did not correspond to what I had in mind. Whilst I most definitely wanted to take account of my advisory panel members' suggestions, I was also keen to interpret what they said in light of other information I had gained from an initial reading of relevant literature. As I had not thought clearly enough about how to make use of my advisory panel and the information they would provide me with, I had to spend more time 'negotiating' between what people had told me and what I had learnt already from relevant literature than I would have liked. Generally speaking, I have come to realise that it is useful to consider carefully, prior to embarking on a systematic review in earnest, how to make use of the advisory panel, when and how often to consult them and how to weigh different members' suggestions at different stages of the review.

Having determined my review's focus by consulting my advisory panel as well as through initial readings of relevant literature, I needed to formulate one or more review questions. This is where my second challenge awaited: If I phrased a review question too broadly, it would be likely to yield a very large number of references in my literature research and not offer as much specific useful insight as I was hoping for. On the other hand, a very narrow review question that would only apply in very specific circumstances, to very specific populations and so forth was not going to be very helpful either. I therefore needed a good balance between too broad and too narrow for my questions. To get there, I found it useful to again consult my advisory panel members, at this stage especially those researchers that had expertise in my area of research. They were helpful in bouncing off and refining different versions of my review questions. Other individuals that could help with phrasing a 'not too broad, not too narrow' review question are researchers that have done systematic reviews themselves before and so therefore are aware of the issue and might be able to advise on how to get around it. For the systematic review I did for my PhD, however, I was not sufficiently aware of these issues and how to resolve them, so I learnt the hard way that having broad review questions can result in a lot of work ... in this particular case, the three review questions I had formulated resulted in my having to sift through more than 65,000 literature references initially and my findings being perhaps not quite as focused as would have been useful!

The subsequent literature search was less challenging, though I was really pleased I had talked my search strings through with some members of my advisory board and with colleagues who had done systematic reviews before – to ensure that my searches would capture as much as possible of the relevant evidence base. Once I had searched various literature outlets, I came to the point where, having sifted through the publications retrieved –first by title, then by abstract and finally by reading the full text – I was ready to start making sense of relevant pieces of literature. I recommend the use of a data extraction form, which should capture not only data needed to answer the review question(s), but also some descriptive statistics (e.g., publication year and country), alongside further relevant paper information, such as the publication's methodology. All of this information helps contextualise the body of evidence that one is dealing with, when explaining the findings in relation to the review's question(s).

Having collated relevant details of publications that can be considered both of sufficient relevance and of high enough quality to justify their inclusion in the systematic review, a further challenge awaits in the form of the data analysis. Unfortunately, little guidance is available on how to analyse and synthesise data within systematic reviews. Because that is so, together with a couple of colleagues, I decided to look into this particular aspect of systematic review methodology further, some years after having conducted my first systematic review. We undertook a kind of 'systematic review of systematic reviews' within the area of Business and Management and focused, amongst other things, on how researchers had analysed and synthesised literature within their systematic reviews. We found that even though many researchers did not explicitly explain what they had done and how they had analysed and synthesised literature, the approach used by most people corresponds to narrative integration (in other words, combining information from different studies and research methods to find answers to specific questions and figure out the best times for using certain interventions). Narrative integration is a useful way of synthesising literature. But it is by no means the only available approach and, as I discuss in the previously mentioned 'systematic review of systematic reviews' paper (Rojon, Okupe and McDowall, 2021), there may be more suitable and more ambitious ways of synthesising data from the literature identified. For the systematic review I did for my PhD, for instance, I was in the fortunate (or maybe not so fortunate?) position where I not only had qualitative data for analysis and synthesis (in that particular case in relation to how and why to measure performance in particular ways), but also quantitative data. This quantitative data consisted of correlation coefficients examining the relationship between personality and ability questionnaires, on the one hand, and performance assessments, on the other hand. Given I had this quantitative data, I decided to embed a (psychometric) meta-analysis, that is, a 'summary' of correlations found across all those studies that examined the relationships between personality/ability questionnaires and performance assessments, within my systematic review. Although I would not go as far as saying that I regretted having done a meta-analysis as part of my very first systematic review, I got the impression afterwards that journals in Business and Management had not quite caught up yet with the idea of using systematic review methodology for selecting studies for inclusion within a meta-analysis. Even though I feel that such an approach is slowly becoming more accepted, trying to get a paper on the meta-analysis component of my PhD's systematic review published was rather difficult at the time – it just was not how meta-analyses had previously been done and reported on! The good news is that I did get the paper published in the end (Rojon, McDowall and Saunders, 2015), so there is clearly hope, but I do think it is a matter of thinking carefully how you 'sell' a meta-analysis within the framework of systematic review methodology.

LESSONS FOR KEEPING ON TRACK

- If at first you do not succeed … do not give up. There is a misconception that reviewing the literature – prior to starting out with a study 'in earnest' – is the easy bit that just 'has to be done' … it is not!
- Think of your literature review in the context of your research more widely. How does it fit in with any other research activities you are undertaking or planning to undertake? Where can it add value and how will its findings contribute to your research and to the extant body of evidence? Having

clear ideas of this upfront will help you to stay on track and be motivated with your review.

- Time management can be an issue with literature reviews (and generally with research activities), whatever approach you choose to go for. Be aware of this from the start and give yourself enough time for each step on the way. Whilst most tasks will probably take longer than anticipated, happily, some may actually take less time than expected.

- Talk to people! Fellow researchers or methods experts can be useful both in terms of exchanging experience and advice, as well as when it comes to venting your literature review-related sorrows (the voice of experience is speaking)!

- Go for it! If you have never undertaken a systematic review, but believe that it could be suitable for your next piece of research, think no more and just do it – hopefully the lessons in this chapter will help!

REFERENCES

Adams, R.J., Smart, P. and Huff, A.S. (2017). Shades of grey: guidelines for working with the grey literature in systematic reviews for management and organizational studies. *International Journal of Management Reviews*, *19*, 432–452.

Booth, A., Sutton, A., Clowes, M. and James, M.M. (2021). *Systematic Approaches to a Successful Literature Review* (3rd edn). London: Sage.

Denyer, D. and Tranfield, D. (2009). Producing a systematic review. In Buchanan, D. and Bryman, A. (eds), *The SAGE Handbook of Organizational Research Methods*, London: Sage, pp. 671–89.

Rojon, C., McDowall, A. and Saunders, M.N.K. (2011). On the experience of conducing a systematic review in Industrial, Work and Organizational Psychology: yes, it is worthwhile. *Journal of Personnel Psychology*, *10*, 133–8.

Rojon, C., McDowall, A. and Saunders, M.N.K. (2015). The relationships between traditional selection assessments and workplace performance criteria specificity: a comparative meta-analysis. *Human Performance*, *28*, 1–25.

Rojon, C., Okupe, A. and McDowall, A. (2021). Utilization and development of systematic reviews in management research: what do we know and where do we go from here? *International Journal of Management Reviews*, *23*, 191–223.

4. The PhD supervisor–candidate relationship

Jillian Cavanagh, Hannah Meacham and Timothy Bartram

The academic relationship between the supervisor and higher degree research student can be described as a 'master and apprentice'. Here we present reflections from the authors that offer understandings of the pitfalls and challenges and strategies associated with successful PhD supervision and candidature. If we develop our understandings of the potential pitfalls in the early stages of candidature we have a better chance of supporting our students to successful completion. We provide a focused and rich context for insights into some areas of concern for students, including our reflections around the key issues and challenges of both PhD supervision and PhD candidature, the commencing point for a student, academic writing, the differences between a literature review and a theoretical framework, commencing the research and we summarise with key lessons for both students and academics.

WHAT ARE THE KEY ISSUES AND CHALLENGES IN THE SUPERVISION OF PHD STUDENTS?

Supervisors and Students Need to Do Their Homework

One of the key issues for PhD supervisors is the selection of high-quality students. Supervisors need to be very selective and do their homework on the student. The PhD process is often a long and emotional one. Supervisors need to be careful that they can work with the student and that the student has the foundational skills to be able to undertake the degree successfully. It is vital that the supervisor ensures that the student meets the basic entry requirements and has the necessary core skills and background studies in the discipline of study, has a strong work ethic and the time and resources to be successful. PhD students also need to do their homework on the supervisor. Do they have a track record of publication in your area of study? Do they have a track record of successful supervision of PhD students? Are they supportive and do they have sufficient time and energy to supervise your studies? Do you get along well with them? These are basic questions for PhD students but the answers are very important for the successful and timely completion of PhD study. In short, the supervisors and PhD students need to be selective.

Often one of the key issues is getting students to write in a scholarly way. Academics can find it difficult to write in a less formal manner; in fact, writing this chapter was challenging because we have a tendency to formalise our language. The key point of the conversation is that if the student is a management practitioner or clinician, for instance, a big challenge for them is that they often think, write and communicate like practitioners. Many of them do not have the skillset to think and write like an academic. Not only are the skills important but so is the mindset. The way around it is obviously to use journal articles as templates and look at syntax, referencing and the structure of a completed PhD. Supervisors may have to 'baby step' students through the writing process in the beginning; too much too soon will often overload the student leaving them feeling overwhelmed; think tortoise ... not hare.

Universities often have writing groups to practise academic writing or seminars on how to critique a journal article; students should go to these and practise these skills (tip: encourage the student to go more than once; it is difficult to pick up the skills in one two-hour seminar). PhD students: you need to realise that a PhD is often an apprenticeship in becoming an academic, so your writing has to conform to scholarly standards. You should have read hundreds of articles for your thesis. Reading these articles will help you to notice structures and patterns that you can use to model your future studies and articles on. When writing for journals we will often model the structure of our manuscript on published articles within the target journal. Remember you are writing for an academic audience, that is, depending on the PhD system, two or three examiners who are academics and who are judging your thesis on the basis of whether it makes a scholarly and significant contribution to knowledge.

English as a Second Language

It is increasingly common that PhD students will come from non-English-speaking backgrounds. What needs to be done in the early phase is to develop a team-based approach. Going forward, academics have an expectation that international students will need additional help. This level of competency and help required is going to differ from student to student so it is important that supervisors are clear on the levels of English proficiency of their PhD students. Setting goals to improve language skills and keeping students accountable for the quality of their writing is important. Patience from both sides is needed here; students should not expect supervisors to 'fix' their English comprehension and supervisors should not expect the same English proficiency they would find from a native speaker. Students need to be honest and upfront about their level of English proficiency; if the student is struggling, then they need to seek help as soon as possible because not seeking help is only damaging one person: the student.

Foundation Skills

In our experience it is important to learn EndNote and complete a course in how to work with a large document. Also, understand what a thesis looks like – understand the process. It is important to have a look at some theses in your area so you get an understanding of the structure and organisation of PhD theses, the major sections, standard and style of writing, how to organise the table of contents and, most importantly, how to develop a narrative between chapters. PhD students: do this before you start anything else. You may think you have good computer skills and can manage by 'clicking random buttons' but in reality some programs, such as EndNote, do require more than a basic understanding to be operated effectively, which will help you in the long run. University libraries often hold courses on various computer programs. Take advantage of these courses, even if they may not seem relevant at the time; when you are struggling to edit the contents page of your 300-page document you will wish you had gone!

Learning to Take Notes and Paraphrase

Academics often hear from students that the way in which an author writes an article is so articulate that they are not able to find a better way of expressing the message. Paraphrasing not only expresses the message in the student's own words, but at the beginning of the candidature can actually help in understanding the key concepts of the article. Get the student to create summaries of literature related to their topic; not only does this make a start on the literature review but also enables the student to understand the key theoretical frameworks and gets them into thinking about research questions. PhD students: make sure you write notes and summarise articles as these will form the basis of your literature review. Remember it is not enough to summarise articles; this is only a starting point. It is important that you read critically as you are trying to establish the gap in the literature so that your work will be able to make a scholarly and significant contribution to knowledge.

Good Study Habits

Students need to set goals in terms of what they need to do every day – developing a plan of attack. This can be done in partnership with the supervisor but at the end of the day it is the student's responsibility. It is important for the student to achieve something every day even if it is one paragraph – students: read and write every day! It is very easy at the beginning to think 'I have three plus years to finish this PhD, that's plenty of time', then all of a sudden four years have gone by and all you have is a first draft of a literature review. Supervisors and students should plan meeting times, for example, once a week/fortnight/month; this then gives the student easy landmarks for when work should be completed. If completion dates are being missed, it is important to address this as soon as possible, the reason often being that students are unsure of what they are doing or if they are doing it correctly. Supervisors and students: don't be shy if there is a problem; speak up quickly and sort the issue out. Time is the enemy of all PhD students.

Work–Life Balance

The best piece of advice is to encourage students to take time to relax, reflect and recharge. Many students experience life-changing events throughout their candidature; this can be the birth of a child, the death of a loved one or a serious illness. However, finding work–life balance is not an excuse to only do a few hours a week of work towards a thesis. It is important to come up with a plan, when to work and when to relax, that fits in with when the student is most productive. This may be late at night, early in the morning or during a Monday–Friday 9 am–5 pm working week. Full-time PhD students need to treat their studies like a full-time job. Students should give themselves regular time off, such as weekends, as this will make the process seem much more manageable. Students need to note that during the last 2–3 months of their candidature there is often little to no work–life balance; that's just the way it is. They need to put their head down and power through; it will be over soon.

WHERE DOES A PHD STUDENT START?

Finding a Topic

Students: start with what topic areas you are interested in and passionate about. Writing 80,000 words on a topic you are passionate about and enjoy is going to be easier than writing about a topic you are not interested in. What areas do you see lots of opportunity to publish? What areas does your supervisor publish in? Where do you work? What/who are your contacts? Having contacts within industry and organisations will give you an advantage when searching for research sites. It is often easier to gain access to research sites if you have a personal contact; the old adage of 'it's who you know not what you know' is good to remember here. The topic must keep your attention for three years, if not longer, so being 'bored' of the topic is only going to slow you down. Integrating two ends of the spectrum is a skill each student will need to develop. By this we mean bringing the practical and the academic together.

Making a Contribution

Every thesis must make an original and substantial contribution to knowledge. At the outset, each student must have an idea of their intended contribution. This is often difficult for students to grasp. A previous student once accounted:

> At the start of my PhD I was trying to think of my elusive 'contribution' to knowledge. During a conversation with my mum I found out a family friend, who had recently completed their PhD in Dentistry, had discovered a new enzyme in the mouth as part of her research and had had the enzyme named after her. All I kept thinking was how was my research going to make such a contribution to research?

Think about what you would like to achieve; is there a gap in theory that nobody has examined before? Are there problems in the industry that your research could begin to address or at least shed new light on potential solutions?

Principal Research Question

The questions need to be built from the gap in the literature. PhD students have to read quite a lot of quality research to understand the gap. The research questions should be developed around finding answers to the identified gap/s. Yes, reading literature is boring; yes, you will find very inventive ways of not reading literature, but at the end of the day it has to be done. So do it. Rule of thumb, if you have not found any gaps in the literature, you have not read enough literature or reviewed it critically enough. It is also important to read through journal editors' notes and future research suggestions in leading articles as academics will often discuss the current research gaps, controversies and challenges. PhD students need to read critically and for purpose.

DIFFERENT GENRES OF ACADEMIC WRITING

The starting point here is to engage in conversation about the different genres of writing that a student will encounter when writing a PhD. One of the supervisors gave an account of a thesis in crisis that was passed onto him. 'The thesis was in crisis and one of the analysis chapters was almost 50 000 words. The supervisors worked with the student to take the thesis and reduce it by 30 000 words.' The main challenge for the student was that English was not her first language and she had serious challenges with English grammar. The supervisor sought to develop a team (e.g., language expert and co-supervisor) around the student to ensure that she had effective English grammar support.

Academics take the craft of academic writing seriously and explaining the different genres to a PhD student can be quite challenging. The introduction sets the scene and at the end of this section a reader should know the context of the research project, the purpose, the contribution, key question and structure of the thesis. The literature review is used to frame the study through critical examination of literature so as to unpack the research gap and research questions. The theoretical framework is the analytical tool or lens through which your study is framed as it provides the researcher with a structured and rigorous way of answering the research question. As a PhD student, it is important to read the best journals in your discipline – speak to your supervisor about academic rankings and which journals are best. It is best to read the best journals in your discipline to get a sense of which key theoretical frameworks are out there and why and how they are used as analytical tools to solve research problems. The methodological approach is important as it provides the researcher with a systematic, valid and reliable way of empirically testing or examining the research question; students can use either qualitative or quantitative methods and often mixed methods approaches are becoming common in PhD theses. The data collection procedures are critical to a high-quality thesis and are often very challenging as the student is reliant on the goodwill of partner organisations and their staff. The results and analysis section of the thesis is a very exciting step, whether you are running regressions, doing structural equation modelling or using NVivo to analyse focus group and interview data. The discussion and concluding sections are very important to examine the extent that you were able to answer the questions and develop key discussion points that contribute to building theory, the empirical body of research and implications for organisational or management practice (depending on the topic of your thesis), as well as documenting limitations and future research and providing some nuggets in the concluding section.

Publishing from a Thesis

In our experience it is important to publish during and immediately after your PhD candidature. Writing a journal article is important in terms of skill building but also to enhance your employability within academia. Our advice is to publish from your thesis as soon as practicable by focusing largely on empirical papers that use your data. A PhD student will usually start publishing with their supervisor – so have the conversation. The big question for many students is: do I go for high-level or low-level journals? Our answer is to think strategically and develop a publishing strategy and short-, medium- and long-term publishing goals. Get some runs on the board. There is nothing wrong with publishing a paper in a B ranked journal, but also think about aiming for A and A* ranked journals. Our advice would be to start with B and A ranked journals. The job market is very competitive, so get publishing!

COMMENCING THE RESEARCH

There needs to be a systematic approach to reading literature; do not rely on an internet search to begin with. Again, this is where the university library can help. Book a time with a librarian to help you undertake an in-depth search of journal databases. Librarians know the databases better than anyone, so take advantage of their unique skills and knowledge. They are generally very helpful and approachable. Know the leading journals and authors in your field. Take notes, and it would be a good idea to produce a plan and a spreadsheet of the key articles and the name of the journal. PhD students: take your time; reading, categorising and summarising literature is not a quick process, and that's even before you start to analyse and critique it. A detailed Excel spreadsheet is a must here. Note the journal article title and journal name, its academic ranking, the key concepts and methods used and its key findings. Parts of this spreadsheet can then be transferred straight into your annotated bibliography, which will be the base for your first draft literature review.

KEY LESSONS FOR PHD STUDENTS AND SUPERVISORS

In this chapter we have discussed some of the key challenges and lessons that we have learned, both as PhD students and supervisors. In summary here are key lessons that should help supervisors and PhD students stay focused and work effectively:

1. Keep a research project simple and achievable within three years' full-time study. Try not to be overly ambitious and narrow your topic.
2. A student's research project must be marketable. By that we mean students need to be able to use their theses to build future careers in academia or within the broader private/public sectors. Try to pick a topic that can solve or identify a progression to solving an issue within industry or society. This will then not only appeal to industry leaders but also to academics wishing to continue the research.
3. A student must be able to publish from their thesis and in most cases this will be done in collaboration with their supervisors. There should be at least two to three papers in any PhD thesis. The genre of journal writing will be different, but the concepts and data will be the same. Students need to be aware that writing a PhD and writing a journal article are very

different. The processes and style of writing for a journal article can be difficult to adjust to. The 'master and apprentice' relationship does not often end at the completion of a PhD thesis. Students (with the support of their supervisor) should try to develop an article from the thesis during their candidature.

4. A PhD is only a means to an end. A PhD is a marathon and there are many highs, pitfalls and turns that will challenge both supervisors and students but the end point is really the beginning. It is not a student's life's work. A student's real academic writing starts from the point when they are writing refereed journal articles.

5. If students are struggling with any material or process during their studies it is important that these issues or challenges are dealt with quickly and effectively. Students need to work closely with their supervisors, so if there is a problem, speak up.

5.   'Finders, keepers, losers, weepers!' A doctoral candidate's reality of changing thesis advisors

Polly Black

FINDING A DIRECTOR OF STUDIES

The saga begins with my search for a good director of studies under whom to study. The topic I wanted to research for my PhD was about consumer trust and therefore spanned the trust and marketing fields. I looked at professors in both fields and decided that, since I already had considerable expertise in marketing as a practitioner who had risen through the ranks to the chief marketing officer level, I should find a director who was on the trust side. I identified a professor who was more of a generalist in trust theory, not focused on just one small dimension of trust and who had founded a centre focused on the study of trust at his university. The university in question was well set up to support part-time distance students and was near where I lived in the UK, so it seemed perfect. I rang him up.

'Well, I don't know. I'm very busy. But perhaps, perhaps. Your topic is interesting. Send me your proposal and I'll take a look.' So I sent him my proposal. He agreed to take me on, saying I was 'different' from other applicants. He never explained that, but it did not matter. What mattered was that I had a good director of studies and a place at a good university. Life was good!

Shortly thereafter my director found a second advisor for me. A second advisor who complements your director's skill sets can be a great help and a valuable asset on the team. This was not the case here. This academic was also on the business faculty with a specialty in trust, but was at a junior level having only recently completed his own PhD. When I contacted him, he told me that he had not been asked if he would take me on. He was just signed up for it by my director of studies. Therefore, he felt no particular obligation towards supporting me. He and I only had two other conversations and he never gave me any feedback on anything I wrote.

The literature review was the first challenge. During the first 18 months, I read and wrote. Periodically I sent drafts to my director. His advice and feedback, always by email or Skype not annotation, was vague but encouraging. His comments and his reports on my progress led me to believe I was on track and making good progress towards my confirmation. In the UK, a third of the way through a PhD students are required to pass an examination, which confirms their standing and allows them to continue towards completion of the PhD. Frequently referred to as confirmation, transfer or upgrade, at the university where I was studying this comprised writing the first three to four chapters of the thesis covering a review of the literature, the contribution the research was likely to make and the methodology and method to be used to collect and analyze the data. On this students are also examined in a comprehensive oral exam. Upon passing their exam, and providing their written work is satisfactory, students are allowed to proceed with their fieldwork and their thesis. Eighteen months in I had written the first full draft of my confirmation report, which my director told me was good and just needed a few adjustments to be ready. Then I got the phone call that derailed everything.

LOSING A DIRECTOR OF STUDIES

Out of the blue, my director of studies rang me up and in his usual cryptic fashion he said, 'Good afternoon. I am leaving this university and going to another. Do you want to come with me or stay here?' I was speechless. I stammered a confused response. He gave me a little more information and told me to ring him back when I had thought about it and hung up. Now what? I was not at all sure how to proceed.

The decision was not an easy one. On the plus side, the university where he was going was a much better university and equally convenient for me in terms of location. Moreover, I would get to keep the continuity of working with this director of studies who seemed to have confidence in me and who thought I was doing well. On the minus side, the new university which my director was joining specialized in a particular area that was not relevant to my research at all, and the university did not have a strong tradition in trust research. This concerned me. I decided to consult my second advisor. My second advisor told me that I had 'struck gold' in my choice of director, since he was outstanding at getting students through the PhD process and choosing good examiners. Since the new university was also a much better known and more prestigious university, he recommended that I follow. Two days later I got an email from my second advisor saying he too was leaving and would no longer be my second advisor. I had no further contact with him.

I was adrift with no oars. I felt abandoned and my emotional reaction was to cling to the one person who seemed to have faith in me. This meant changing universities in order to keep the continuity with my director of studies. My rational side, however, told me I needed to do some careful research on what both options would entail and make a more educated decision.

I initiated the process with the new university to transfer with my director. I found out that it is very complicated to transfer if you have not yet passed your confirmation. The university where I would be going had different requirements on research methods, training modules and other first year taught modules, which did not align very well with those of my current university. Therefore, I would need to take modules at the new university and these were taught modules that were only offered on site. An extra complication in my case was that the new university did not have any provisions in place for dis-tance students, though they did allow part-time study. This was a major road-block for me. However, they bent over backwards to find solutions. In the end, the head of the PhD programme there said the faculty had recently approved a pilot programme to accept distance students. This had not yet been activated, but he had got special permission from the faculty to have me as a test case. This put me in a very awkward situation because I did not feel that being a guinea pig was a good thing and yet he had gone out of his way on my behalf.

Meanwhile, I was also holding conversations with the head of the PhD programme for business students at the university where I was enrolled to see what the alternatives would be if I stayed. He had no idea. He had no clue who would take me on and no suggestions on what to do. (I later found out that this was because the university was going through a major restructuring, which included asking for expressions of interest in taking redundancy, and there were therefore many changes afoot in the faculty ranks, but I did not know this at the time.) When he asked me if I had any suggestions, I had no answer either. Because I was a distance student – and very far distant – I was rarely on campus and knew none of the other students or faculty. So I did not know anyone to talk to about this or any of the other faculty to ask to be my new director of studies. The head of the PhD programme thought since I was proposing to use a qualitative method, maybe someone in the sociology depart-ment might be good because they did a lot of qualitative research. Sociology? Really? Was there no one in the business school who could take me? He said he would look into it. I left his office feeling discouraged, frustrated and not a little annoyed.

I asked my director of studies for a meeting and we met at a pub in town. We discussed the transfer and, to his credit, he did not try to push me one way or the other, but did give me some of the pros and cons as he saw it. I then asked him for a critique of the new draft of my work that I had sent him. He said it was almost there and with a little more work it would be ready, but when I pressed him on the specifics of that, he had nothing to say. I stared at the text. In that moment I realized that he was not giving me nearly enough critical assessment and without it I was not sure how to improve my work. He had been encouraging in making general comments and in suggesting additional texts to look at, but detailed critique on what was and was not working was not his style. That moment the penny dropped and I recognized that I really had not been getting enough critical input all along, when I looked back on it. I needed more from him.

I walked back up the hill utterly disconsolate. As I saw it there was little reason to follow this director of studies and no one to be my director of studies if I stayed.

I chose to stay. I had no idea who my new director of studies might turn out to be, or even if they would be in the business school, but I turned down the offer of a place at the new university. There were several reasons. Firstly, there was the bad fit between what I was studying and that university's focus. I felt a degree from that university would not have meaning in the context of my research topic. Close to that was the fact that the university was really not set up yet to handle distance students and the university where I was enrolled was very well set up for that. But the final and most important reason, I had reluctantly come to see, was that I was not getting enough critical assessment of my work and really, if truth were told, I was floundering without much direction. I didn't even know whether my work was any good or not. I was not sure what to do next.

A short while later I got an email from the head of the PhD programme at the business school saying that he had found me someone who would act as an interim director of studies and proposed that I meet with this professor. I came into that meeting full of hope and expecting to have a positive and encouraging conversation. Instead, the first words out of the professor's mouth, after introducing himself, were 'Don't take this meeting to mean that I will agree to be your director of studies ongoing. I have a lot of students already and I am going on sabbatical. So I will give you some advice today, but don't assume that this relationship will continue.' Disconcerting, to say the least, but as I knew he was only acting in an interim role, I mentally resolved to take full advantage of all the advice I could get while it was available to me. I found I liked him. He was straightforward and specific, which suited me well and was a refreshing change from my previous director of studies. So it was a great relief to me when I subsequently received another email from the head of the PhD programme saying that this professor had (reluctantly) agreed to be my director ongoing, since there was no one else! My new director asked me for a copy of the most recent draft of my confirmation report and then promptly left for Australia for six weeks. I sent him the report.

When the report came back to me I could barely read it for the amount of black notations in the margins. As I read through his notes, I could see his frustration growing as he shredded my work. Virtually nothing was salvageable.

His comment was that the section on my research philosophy was passable and that I could write clearly. Other than that I had nothing. Devastating! Especially after having been told all along by my former director that this was good work and I was nearly ready to submit it for confirmation. However, I was heartened by the fact that he had actually read it all and commented on everything. Here was someone willing to invest his time and effort in helping me turn things around.

This is so important. I learned from what had happened that a director of studies who just encourages and does not offer much critique is not as valuable to the student as one who is more critical of the work, painful as the critiques can be at times. The encouragement is reassuring and feels good, but the critique strengthens and teaches you. Your work cannot improve without it. I clung to that consolation and started over. I rewrote just the review chapter on the trust literature taking into account his comments. Upon reading the new draft, my new director expressed that he was impressed with the difference and was now ready to help find me a second advisor. That comment I interpreted at the time to mean he had been holding back his judgement and had not been ready to commit fully until he knew if I was worth his time. Reassuring to find that I was, but disconcerting to realize he had been less than committed. He later explained to me that the real reason for not picking a second advisor right away was because he wanted to be really clear about who be a good fit in terms of skills and knowledge for my particular topic. This is a really important consideration.

My new director of studies found me a great second advisor who could bring experience both in qualitative methods (my director's natural affinity was more towards mixed methods and he had been trained in quantitative methods) and in consumer marketing (his expertise was more in trust). This balance is important. It is helpful to have a balanced team whose strengths complement each other because they can each offer advice on different aspects of your work. The only downside in this case was that my new second advisor was not experienced in supervising PhD students, though she was a good tutor and advisor.

Life was good again! A lot of work still lay ahead to get ready for confirmation, but my new supervising team was very supportive and gave good, constructive, critical feedback. I made great progress that year and caught up fast from the setback. And then it happened again!

KEEPING A DIRECTOR OF STUDIES

The next summer when I was back in the UK, my new director told me he too was leaving and going to another university! This was just before my confirmation. I couldn't imagine starting over *again!* I have to say that this time it didn't come as a surprise. He had given up his office when he went on sabbatical, and in my view professors usually don't give up their offices if they are planning on coming back. I had challenged him on it one day and he had given me an evasive answer. However, I didn't want to move. I was comfortable with the routine of this university and knew I could finish up on time within the deadline I had set myself. I didn't want to go through moving to another university. So I was cross about it when it happened. I was cross with him and I was cross that I was again faced with a choice that was unsatisfactory whichever way I jumped.

My director of studies said he would take me with him, if I wanted to transfer, and reassured me that regardless he would continue to supervise me wherever I was. This time there was a better fit with the new university and the new university was set up to handle distance students to a manageable degree, though not as well as the university I was leaving. If I wanted to stay he recommended flipping the advising team and my current second would officially become my director and he would remain on the team as second advisor, although he assured me that in practice his input would continue as before. I didn't trust that assurance. I trusted his direction and his reputation for choosing good examiners and preparing students for the final exam, and I was concerned that if the roles were reversed, he would have less influence. I had a good director of studies and I was determined to keep him and to keep him as my primary advisor.

There were actually several considerations that governed my decision to transfer. Firstly, I just did not want to start over with yet another advising team. I felt that if the advising roles were flipped, it would be like having another team because the primary director of my research would change. Since, as is common and not unhealthy, my advisors did not always see eye to eye on the direction they gave me, I feared that this would inevitably lead to reworking my approach and set me back further. Secondly, I felt my second advisor was perhaps not experienced enough to get me through. She was thoughtful and good and very smart, but I had been given to understand that she had not taken a PhD student all the way through to getting their degree before. I didn't know how good she would be at choosing examiners or preparing me for the final exam. On the other hand, I had every confidence in my current director who was very experienced, well known and well respected. I considered that his capability, and not least my confidence in that capability, counted for a lot. Lastly, as before, the new university was a much higher ranked university, though not as convenient in terms of location this time.

I applied to the new university. They said I needed to complete the confirmation first before transferring, which I did. The transfer process was slow. There were a lot of documents that needed to be produced, showing proof of my progress and that I had completed my confirmation. It dragged out and went back and forth several times. The primary concerns were making sure that the training modules I had taken were commensurate with their own, and also that I could complete this PhD part time and long distance while holding down a full-time job. In the end, they accepted my assurances and those of my director on this, but they were not happy with that. 'Distance' in their lexicon meant based somewhere else in England, not the other side of the Atlantic!

I learned two things from the experience of transferring. Firstly, requirements, expectations, procedure and even terminology can vary widely from university to university. It pays to ask for clarification and specifics. Don't assume you know! Secondly, document everything you do for your PhD as you go along. I had a hard time tracking down some of the certificates of completion after the fact to prove my progress and performance. The requirements for documentation expected of PhD students at my new university were much more rigorous than at my prior university, so I did not have nearly the level of documentation they needed. But at last all was in order. I pulled the trigger and made the transfer.

Life was good again!

LESSONS FOR KEEPING ON TRACK

- When looking for a director of studies, try to find someone who complements your strengths. Read their work and know what their specialty is as well as their preferred research method, if any.
- Balance your advising team with academics who bring different strengths and areas of expertise to the table.
- If your director of studies does not give you much critical assessment, ask for more! Or find someone who will critique your work.
- Do your homework before you make your decision on whether to transfer or not – don't make it on emotion.
- Keep calm and carry on! Even during the transition, keep working on your research. This will help to steady you and keep you on track.
- Make sure to build a network at your university so that you have resources in times of crisis – and for that matter ongoing.
- Challenge yourself to rise above the fray and clear the bar.

6. Benefits, pitfalls, ethics and realities of GenAI in research

Jerome Kiley

INTRODUCTION

Humans generally function according to the 'principle of least effort', choosing the path that requires the least energy to achieve goals. Generative Artificial Intelligence (GenAI) has become a seductive mistress as it can carry out many of our tasks quickly and efficiently. GenAI is evolving exponentially in unimaginable ways, with new tools released daily, raising debate about its potential to disrupt and revolutionise research while at the same time posing unique ethical challenges. My experience is that many academics don't fully understand how GenAI works, regarding ChatGPT (https://chat.openai.com/) as the be-all and do-all. While there are early adopters who embrace the potential of AI, others believe it corrupts academic integrity, and a third group largely ignore it, viewing it as a 'fad'. GenAI is developing rapidly, with new and complex applications (apps) emerging daily, making it difficult for most of us to keep pace while often unaware of how extensively we already use this.

Doing research in a world dominated by GenAI is complex because GenAI can do so many things, with the use thereof influenced by the aim of your study, different ethical concerns and constantly changing external realities. There are also philosophical implications that force us to rethink how we conduct research and create knowledge. The field of GenAI is complex and constantly evolving, so I will first explain what it is and why it exists before discussing its pros, cons and ethical issues.

AI, GenAI AND RELATED CONCEPTS

Artificial Intelligence (AI) is an 'umbrella' term covering an assortment of tools that aim to solve data-in-data-out pre-specified problems that previously required human intelligence encompassing technologies applied to natural language processing, forecasting, analysing, interpreting and optimising data

(Chubb, Cowling and Reed, 2022) with a common distinction made between traditional AI, GenAI and Artificial General Intelligence (AGI).

Traditional AI models have a specific focus requiring vast amounts of labelled data to train, from which they can learn, come to conclusions and make predictions. We use AI daily when searching for content on sites such as Google, Microsoft Edge, YouTube and online shopping sites. AI also influences us indirectly, driving the recommendation systems and needs-based advertising on sites we visit. Similarly, Microsoft Office, Google Workplace and other productivity apps harness AI in everything from spelling and grammar checking to generating design and layout. Statistical and thematic analysis programs employ AI to make sense of data by applying statistical techniques to identify patterns, test hypotheses and provide visualisations, while qualitative programs code and categorise non-numerical data. In a nutshell, we have adopted AI to perform many tasks and functions we previously performed while providing large corporations such as Google, Meta, OpenAI and Amazon with large amounts of data that have facilitated the development of GenAI systems.

GenAI has taken AI to the next level using probabilistic models, such as Large Language Models (LLMs), to generate human-like responses. Machine learning is employed to identify primary data patterns and fundamental structures in massive unstructured training datasets to generate neural networks. These neural networks make decisions based on statistically weighted parameters generated using programmer-formulated algorithms, while their performance is also evaluated and refined using human feedback. The number and complexity of the parameters are continuously evolving. For example, the ChatGPT-3 (Generative Pre-trained Transformer) LLM utilises 175 billion text parameters, while GPT-4 employs 100 trillion text and image parameters. While there is debate about how close this is, we are moving towards AGI that functions independently in a human-like manner, employing independent perception, learning and understanding.

GenAI IN ACADEMIA AND RESEARCH

Being able to distinguish between AI, GenAI and AGI is not as important as understanding what these technologies can do (I use GenAI going forward as an umbrella term). While computer scientists understand how LLMs and accompanying apps work, most of us have a cursory understanding of their workings. GenAI is evolving exponentially, which will continue to present new challenges and opportunities for research. While we are aware that GenAI apps are driven by foundational models (e.g. ChatGPT-3/4, Google Bard, Microsoft's Turing Bletchley v3, Tencent's Hunyuan, Baidu's ERNIE 4.0, xAI) we are often not aware of what LLM drives the APP, or how the app uses the LLM, that is, what prompts are being used. What makes this even more complex is that for-profit corporations own these foundational models that are notoriously protective of the algorithms and training data used in their development. At the same time, apps can be developed by anyone with programming or ChatGPT knowledge, with numerous videos on YouTube explaining how to do this. Hundreds of apps are available that can be used in the research and writing process, with little or no information about how these operate. The implication is that we are even further removed from understanding the tools we use than we ever were.

We can use GenAI apps to generate, format, summarise and interpret text; perform data and image analysis and pattern recognition; automate data collection; make recommendations; simulate and model reality; discover and synthesise knowledge from existing data; and provide personalised development. There is also a darker side where GenAI can serve in generating fake data and research, shape and reformat data to serve particular agendas (e.g. support a desired conclusion), access private and protected data (via the Dark Web) and manipulate discourses. While we can make efforts to identify errors and biases in outputs by externally verifying the outputs (e.g. comparing research results based on a proxy with actual sample data), this is often difficult. We are often unaware of possible biases and tend to accept outputs unquestioningly. We must adopt a critical mindset, actively reviewing the evolving literature (even blogs) that examine the inherent biases of the LLMs and gain an understanding of the functioning of the apps we use.

THE BENEFITS AND CHALLENGES OF USING GenAI IN WRITING AND RESEARCH

Why do we conduct research? The obvious answer is to advance knowledge, solve problems, develop new technologies and improve organisations and society. Postgraduate research enables our intellectual growth and development through acquiring knowledge and problem-solving, critical thinking and analytical skills. However, research also serves a pragmatic purpose in the 'academic game', enabling our academic progression and enhancing our reputation as researchers. We are also confronted by an external reality where there is increasing tension between academia and industry, with private and public organisations using GenAI to conduct independent research, threatening to make academic research irrelevant. While we are busy writing proposals, getting ethics clearance, writing up results and struggling to publish these, businesses use GenAI to conduct research quickly, efficiently and effectively.

GenGenAI can rapidly and consistently perform tasks we currently perform, allowing us to increase our productivity and the quality of our research outputs. We can use GenAI apps to quickly and accurately identify patterns in large datasets, predict potential outcomes, and perform mundane tasks such as editing and summarising information. Many academics are sceptical of GenAI, given the criticisms levelled against it. These include: a lack of creativity and originality, the inability to produce unique and engaging content, the inability to interpret context and tone, the limited ability to grasp nuances and emotions, limited fact-checking abilities, inaccuracies in gathering and analysing information, favouring misleading and biased content, inability to detect and correct writing bias and inability to generate complex or technical articles (AIContentfy, 2023). However, these limitations are being mitigated as GenAI neural networks are continually updated through machine learning, that is, GenAI is improving daily. Consider the exponential improvement between ChatGPT-3.5 and -4, released less than three months apart and the proliferation of advanced essay writing apps such as Essai.pro, HypotenuseGenAI and Cramly which write convincing, adequately referenced and, often, undetectable critical text.

While there are valid concerns about the bias of GenAI, the reality is that it generates highly accurate outputs; the rule of thumb is that the more detailed and specific the instruction, the better the output quality. Many focus on the biases of GenAI, the underlying assumption being that human researchers are less biased and traditional research methods more valid. The resistance to GenAI in academia is on par with the resistance to using Wikipedia, despite being as reliable as academically recognised resources (Jemielniak, 2019). Yes, there are biases, but these are limited and it is not clear that they are more significant than human biases, and, weighed up against the advantages, can and should not be ignored.

It is undeniable that GenAI is dumbing us down, performing the skilled tasks and making decisions we previously made. We no longer need to be able to read maps, spell, know grammatical rules, do statistics, make movie choices, shop for parts for our cars … Performing any task leads to its mastery. This also applies to conducting research, which develops in-depth knowledge and skills through the systematic location, extraction, analysis, organisation and critical evaluation of existing information and systematic investigation of related questions. Malcolm Gladwell (2008) proposed the '10,000-hour rule' required to develop expertise in a field; however, while GenAI makes the research process more efficient, there is less opportunity for skills development. We need to identify the critical skills required of academics and researchers in the GenAI age; we must acknowledge that a new skill set is required that focuses on the responsible and critical use of GenAI.

ETHICS AND GenAI IN ACADEMIC RESEARCH

The disruptive impact of GenAI has resulted in unprecedented ethical challenges resulting in the development of several ethical frameworks, such as for developing GenAI (Hagendorff, 2020), GenAI in education (e.g. Foltynek et al., 2023) and GenAI in scientific research and writing (e.g. Singh, 2022). The fact that these frameworks serve different purposes and are inconsistent is challenging. Nonetheless, Bouhouita-Guermech, Gogognon and Bélisle-Pipon (2023) note that while ethical guidelines are advancing, normative guidelines lag behind the reality of GenAI. It is helpful to consider ethical issues that arise from using GenAI in general, and secondly, relating to its use in research.

Ethics and GenAI

Using GenAI for any purpose has several unique ethical challenges that need to be kept in mind but are not necessarily within our skill set as business or social science researchers to address. We don't fully understand how these tools come to particular decisions, given that training data and algorithms and their inherent and implicit biases are hidden and that these are not always intelligible to humans. Thus, we cannot always be sure of the reliability and validity of GenAI outputs.

Significant ethical questions exist regarding how the vast data used to train LLMs is obtained. Is the dataset representative and extensive enough to train the LLM to provide valid and reliable results? Who contributed to the data? Who does this data belong to? How are the privacy and human rights of those whose data is used respected? How much agency do we have in deciding to share our personal data? To use an online app to operate our devices or access a service, we must agree to (click) the 'terms and conditions', which includes sharing personal data that can be sold. The ethics of this is dubious as a fundamental principle of a contract is a 'meeting of minds' with almost no one reading these long and complex agreements that likely require an advanced law degree to understand.

Irrespective of the ethical challenges, the genie is out of the bottle, and you cannot avoid using GenAI. GenAI permeates every aspect of society, with organisations increasingly adopting GenAI (Haan and Watts, 2023). As researchers, we must adopt GenAI responsibly to remain relevant and drive innovation in business and management research while remaining ethically accountable. We should thus adopt a healthy scepticism when selecting GenAI apps and adopting their outputs. Mittelstadt et al. (2016) outline six ethical and pragmatic concerns regarding algorithms that can assist in judging the reliability and validity of the outputs, namely:

- Is there sufficient evidence to justify the conclusions the algorithms make using inferential statistics and/or machine learning?
- Is there a clear and understandable link between the data and conclusions open to inspection and critique?
- Is the quality of their source data adequate to base the conclusions on?
- Do the outcomes of algorithms discriminate against particular social categories of people when judged based on observer-dependent fairness?
- Do the algorithms contain biases that impact how we conceptualise reality?
- Can we trace the harm caused by an algorithm, the origin thereof or those responsible?

The principle is that you should identify the LLM underlying the app you use and the limitations of the algorithms. A growing body of research examines these issues, much of which is published in Online Open Access Journals. However, given the rapid developments in GenAI, you may find non-academic resources helpful, such as online blogs and articles. Where possible, you should compare the reliability and validity of the GenAI outputs generated against external resources.

Ethics of GenAI in Research

Most of us find research ethics complex and subjective, with university Research Ethics Committees (RECs) differing widely in their focus. My experience is that many researchers, especially at the postgraduate level, view ethics as an irritation that they superficially review in their methodology. These reviews are generally based on broadly accepted ethical principles, including informed consent, voluntary participation, managing anonymity or confidentiality, avoiding harm, communicating results, avoiding conflict of interests and not falsely claiming authorship. However, just as GenAI disrupts research, it poses new and evolving ethical challenges.

GenAI can be used throughout the research process, from identifying a research problem, reviewing and writing up the literature, formulating research questions, designing research processes, collecting data, analysing data, generating predictive models and writing results. The ethics of using GenAI in research relates to the manner and extent to which GenAI is used in the research process. The extent and way in which GenAI is used impacts the academic integrity of the project, namely, the 'compliance with ethical and professional principles, standards, practices, and a consistent system of values that serves as guidance for making decisions and taking actions in education, research and scholarship' (Tauginienė et al., 2018, p. 8). However, given that GenAI is developing exponentially and ethical guidelines are lagging, measuring your research practices against this standard becomes problematic. A more useful ethical standard is the concept of Unauthorised Content Generation, 'the production of academic work, in whole or part, for academic credit, progression or award, whether or not a payment or other favour is involved, using unapproved or undeclared human or technological assistance' (Foltynek et al., 2023). A second helpful measure is that of academic misconduct: 'any action or attempted action that undermines academic integrity and may result in an unfair academic advantage or disadvantage for any member of the academic community or wider society' (Tauginienė et al., 2018, p. 9).

Journal GenAI guidelines predominantly focus on text generation, requiring the declaration of GenAI use and prohibiting ChatGPT from being used as a co-author. Nevertheless, the principle applies that you should outline your methodology and review ethical concerns. When considering using GenAI in a research project, we must consider whether this provides an unfair advantage or undermines academic integrity. However, there is no golden standard as to what these comprise. The safest approach would be to ask how others would view your use of GenAI and whether it conflicts with any policies or ethical guidelines. Provide a detailed description of the process followed, what outputs were generated and the limitations of the apps. The greater the transparency, the less likely you will encounter challenges in the future.

However, given the extensive range of functions, reviewing all the GenAI apps used in a study is unfeasible. The functions and implications of the app should be considered in deciding whether they should be declared and discussed when reporting your study.

AI TOOLS RESEARCH TOOLS, THEIR PURPOSES AND ETHICAL RISKS

ChatGPT and other LLMs can accurately and efficiently perform research tasks with suitable prompts. Research apps founded on LLMs that access search engines performing diverse evolving research functions are released almost daily. The apps are arranged in Figure 6.1 based on the complexity of their functions, accompanying skill loss and ethical risks. The LLMs can perform all these functions using the necessary prompts; however, apps tend to be more effective as their algorithms are generally more efficient.

The discussion of the apps is loosely arranged into four broad categories based on the functions they perform, namely, writing and text generation, data searching and research.

Low	Inconclusive evidence	Inscrutable evidence	Misguided evidence	**Algorithmic ethics**		Unfair outcomes	Transformative effects	Traceability	High
Project management	Graphics generation		Paraphrasing	AI detection	Paper rating	Text generation		Data interpretation	Fake research
Remote interviews	Paper formatting	Grammar checking	Data	Data analysis	**AI functions**	Article summarising	Web data collection	Synthetic data	Paper writing
Voice typing	Online surveys	Research assistant	Data management Translation	Literature mapping	Document sourcing	Data analytics	Computer vision		AI masking

Foundational Models
ChatGPT, Bard, Turing Bletchley, Hunyuan, ERNIE, xAI
Search Engines
Google Chrome, MS Bing, Consensus, Scite.Ai

Low importance		Analysing data	**Automating academic skills**		Analytical thinking	Critical reasoning	**High importance**
	Editing			Interpretation		Knowledge	

low	Language & social biases	Anonymity	Voluntary participation	**Research ethics risk**	Informed consent	Data protection	Biased data	Academic dishonesty	high
						Privacy	Confidentiality		

Figure 6.1   The GenAI landscape, ethical risks and academic skills

Writing and Text Generation Tools

GenAI is involved whenever we write anything, from comments online and messages on our phones to detailed documents in word processors. These apps vary in complexity, from the simplest that assist in the writing process to those that write on our behalf.

We unquestioningly use GenAI Apps, such as proofreaders (e.g. Grammarly, Slick Write), that provide prompts for spelling, synonyms, grammar, simplifying text and adjusting your tone; generate references (e.g. Zotero, Mendeley, Endnote) and formatting and generating graphics, tables and layout. Predictive text, text translation (e.g. Microsoft Translator, Google Translate), voice typing, text-to-speech (e.g. Google Text-to-Speech, Amazon Polly), hand-written text transcription (optical character recognition (OCR) e.g. Adobe Acrobat) and paraphrasing tools (e.g. QuillBot) are also routinely incorporated into word processing and productivity programs (e.g. Google Suite, Microsoft 365). These tools have minimal biases, as we can evaluate the outputs relatively easily, given they automate simple tasks we previously performed. There are few ethical challenges beyond the deeply philosophic ethics of linguistics and grammar, such as gender biases identified in translation apps. However, apps that identify and correct biases in machine-translated text (e.g. Fairslator) are available.

There are apps to format papers for particular journals, employing prepared manuscript templates and automatic formatting technologies to align content with journal and publisher criteria (e.g. Typeset.io). Research management apps also track activities and coordinate tasks, allowing for collaborative research (e.g. Trello) and managing notes and resources (e.g. Evernote). The tools covered up to this point perform tasks human editors, translators and research assistants would do, making research writing efficient, cost-effective and more accessible. However, we must question how our writing remains authentic and whether our 'voice' still comes through, especially when using paraphrasing and predictive text tools where the intended meaning can often be lost.

The most discussed function of GenAI is text generation with foundational models, such as ChatGPT, consistently producing high-quality, reliable outputs that are often indistinguishable from those produced by humans. With the appropriate prompts, ChatGPT-4 can generate well-written, personalised and accurately referenced content and can be trained to write in a particular style based on text examples, that is, you can train it to write like you. GenAI apps can write 'undetectable' and properly cited academic papers (e.g. Essai. pro, Hypotenuse AI, Cramly). However, the greater the extent to which GenAIs are involved in the writing process, the less the researcher's accountability, objectivity and rigour. Interestingly, while GPT-4 is more trustworthy than GPT-3.5 using standard benchmarks, it is more susceptible to jailbreaking (prompts bypass limitations or safety measures) and breaches of private training and conversation data (Wang et al., 2023).

Using undeclared AI-generated content constitutes Unauthorised Content Generation and undermines academic integrity. It is an automated 'ghost author' that violates the policies of most journals and universities. The exception is researching the GenAI model or tool, where content must be cited (tool and manufacturer), as you would reference a human respondent in an ethnographic study. However, you need to be careful here as this is not a simple and quick source for an article, as simply reporting outputs without critically analysing these against existing literature has little value. It is also unwise to use GenAI models to generate content, as you are responsible for the integrity of the content you present. While it is a quick and easy way to generate text, a literature review is not simply an overview of the literature; it is evidence that you have read and understood this and can formulate a coherent argument justifying your study.

At the same time, numerous apps have been developed to detect AI-generated content, identifying text markers such as patterns, unnatural language usage and GenAI watermarks (e.g. Turnitins GenAI detection, Copyleaks, Originality Ai, AI Detector Pro, GPTZero). However, these vary in effectiveness, making it necessary to use a combination as new apps are continuously being released to disguise GenAI-generated content (e.g. Undetectable AI, Machine Mask). It is a good idea to search YouTube for reviews of the latest tools and discussions of the latest GenAI hacks. Given that this can be disguised, as well as work and time pressures, it may be tempting to use GenAI text generation. However, what cannot be detected today will likely be detectable in the future.

Search Tools

Virtually all searches for data are conducted with AI-driven search engines such as Google Chrome, Microsoft Bing and Consensus (AI research paper driven), based on complex algorithms. Even though Google uses over 200 ranking factors, the data's validity is sometimes questionable as rankings can be manipulated, and algorithms often find the most used data (clicks) instead of the most valid information. How often have you gone past page one of a Google search? With GenAI incorporated into searches, outputs are susceptible to their algorithmic biases. Academic search engines have been around for a while, and integrated tools such as Google Scholar and Semantic Scholar are more efficient in finding relevant resources. However, challenges include confirmation bias, higher-rated scholars and journals prioritised and journals sidelining non-English articles. There is also a risk of perpetuating social biases against marginalised groups, which may either be over-represented in published studies or, conversely, largely ignored. The quality of the outputs is impacted by the implicit biases embedded in search queries, that is, the search engine gives you what you ask for. It is also noteworthy that inherent biases are more likely present in outputs generated using auto-suggested searches.

However, apps (e.g. Scite.ai) assist in evaluating research papers' credibility. A recent development is literature review mapping (e.g. Connected Papers, Litmaps, Inciteful, Research Rabbit), which identifies related papers analysing open metadata citations for themes, ratings, importance and recency. However, it is unclear to what extent these apps perpetuate biases incorporated in traditional search engines. You cannot simply assume that because a search engine or literature mapping app has provided a list of journal articles, this is a comprehensive and unbiased list of sources. For a balanced literature review, you must adopt a critical mindset to identify inherent biases in your field and your personal biases, use multiple tools, and differentiate between positive, negative and neutral citations.

Research Tools

GenAI can automate time-consuming research tasks, from reading articles and identifying and generating research questions to collecting, organising, cleaning, analysing and interpreting data. However, GenAI has made new features possible, such as data analytics, synthetic data generation, acting as a research assistant and sourcing research grants.

GenAI Article summariser apps (e.g. TLDR, Scholarcy, Grammarly) save reading time by condensing texts, journal articles, research reports and book chapters into key points. Apps such as ChatPDF take summaries to the next level, answering questions from the text of an article. These tools drive productivity; however, there are indications that they are biased towards under-represented groups and influenced by document structure and style (Brown and Shokri, 2023). While useful, you are relying on an interpretation that is not your own, while your reading and critical analysis skills are not developed, and learnings from the article's broader content are lost.

GenAI (e.g. perplexity.ai) can assist in identifying possible research questions and topics by reviewing massive amounts of current research and identifying shortcomings and gaps. While this speeds up the research process, the sources must be validated. The question should also be posed as to how this impacts our creativity and analytical skills.

GenAI is used with traditional data collection methods, such as online surveys (e.g. Survey Monkey, MS Forms, Google Forms), remote interviews and focus groups (e.g. Zoom, MS Teams) and document sourcing through search engines. Here, traditional ethical standards can be applied, including informed consent and voluntary participation; however, they are also subject to limitations, including response and sample bias and survey fatigue. However, GenAI allows access to new data sources, including web scraping, open-source datasets, social media activity, location data, user interactions, and data from dialogues, images and videos. A key advantage is that proxies, which are frequently more reliable than direct measures of variables, are often used.

When harvesting data from the web, we must consider that while people freely share information and images about themselves, they do not consider or consent to all possible uses. Ethical risks include biased data, algorithmic biases of the programs used to collect data, violating our data subjects' privacy and human rights and an absence of informed consent. On the other hand, using open-source datasets poses similar ethical challenges to the datasets used to train LLMs (see 'Ethics and GenAI' above). GenAI can also generate synthetic datasets with the same properties as real datasets, which can be used to test theoretical models and protect privacy. At the same time, a serious concern is that GenAI can be used to create fake research papers (e.g. MDClone); however, apps such SciDetect can detect simulated research.

Automated data analysis is standard practice in the business and social sciences, with qualitative data analysis programs such as SPSS (released in 1968) and MSExcel (released in 1985), while the first qualitative data analysis programs (QDAs) emerged in the 1980s (Gilbert, Jackson and di Gregorio, 2014). The outputs are valid and reliable as algorithms are transparent, and the outputs can be externally validated. However, the advent of data analytics apps (e.g. Tableau, Polymer, PowerBI) has disrupted the playing field, automating the analysis of vast datasets and interpreting these by providing insights, visualisations and predictions. Data analytics apps enhance our efficiency by analysing and interpreting data efficiency. However, these are based on complex and opaque algorithms susceptible to the same algorithmic and ethical biases as those used in LLMs (see 'Ethics and GenAI' above). We are not assured that the outputs are valid and reliable and cannot account for insights and interpretations generated. By handing over the analysis process to an algorithm, we remove ourselves from the most crucial aspect of the research process: interpreting and explaining our research findings.

Research assistant apps (e.g. Elicit.org) integrate many of the functions performed by the apps reviewed above, such as brainstorming and extracting and summarising critical information from relevant publications without perfect keyword matches. Similarly, Scite.ai answers questions by providing a complete list of the papers cited in the response, while when making a claim, Scite.ai reports the people or papers that reject or confirm this. Research Rabbit is also a helpful tool, allowing you to add academic papers to 'collections', allowing the app to learn your interests and make relevant recommendations, generating graphs of articles and co-authorship networks. Similarly, R Discovery provides free access to more than 115 million academic research papers, allowing researchers to search, organise and annotate these, providing updates on the latest developments. There are also proofreading apps directed at non-native English speakers (e.g. WhiteSmoke) that motivate editing recommendations, measure the quality of your paper against related papers (e.g. PaperRater) and evaluate its readability (e.g. ProWritingAid, Hemingway). These apps can enhance our productivity; however, they are complex, and their functions are subject to the limitations of the apps that perform the individual functions listed above.

Finally, GenAI can assist in one of the most important aspects of the research process, namely, accessing funds. Apps (e.g. Grant.io, Instrumentl. com) identify grants, connect researchers and provide grant writing tools. While ChatGPT can assist in writing proposals, apps such as Fundwriter.ai, Grant.io, Grantable and Grantboost have incorporated templates and prompts. However, first check the policy of the organisation providing the grant.

CONCLUSION

Throughout history, we have adopted more efficient technologies to automate human processes, leading to a loss of skills that have become redundant. The same is true for academic research, with computer apps playing an ever more significant role in the research process. However, the advent of GenAI, particularly the launch of LLMs such as ChatGPT, has accelerated the process dramatically. GenAI apps can perform just about any function within the research process, with their capabilities evolving exponentially. While many universities, journals and publishers treat GenAI as an illicit mistress, the reality is that social norms driven by multi-national corporations, such as Microsoft, Google and Meta, have evolved and largely normalised society's relationship with GenAI. The benefits of innovation and productivity that GenAI offers must be weighed against the ethical and pragmatic risks of using these.

In authoring this chapter, the GenAI I used included MS Word (synonyms, spell checker, layout), MS PowerPoint graphics tools, Grammarly, Quilbot, Google (augmented by MaxAI), Google Scholar, ChatPDF and Scite.ai. They all played an important role, guiding me to much of the information used and structuring the layout, but not to generate content. Quilbot and ChatPDF were used to suggest paraphrasing and a summary. However, these were rewritten to reflect my 'voice', ensuring the intended message was not lost or distorted. I can question whether all the ideas presented are adequately referenced, given that my Google searches were augmented by MaxAI, which produced ChatGPT-4-driven answers. While these outputs stimulated my thinking when using specific content, I accessed the source articles and referenced them. I am confident in the academic integrity of this chapter, with Turnitin scores of 1 per cent for similarity and 0 per cent for AI. More importantly, I am an experienced author who learned his craft through practice, trial and error. I spent more than 150 hours writing the chapter, consistently reflecting on my writing process and how this was impacted by GenAI. I grew my writing, analytical and critical skills in a world with limited GenAI and doubt these would have developed to the same extent had I been using today's GenAI.

LESSONS FOR KEEPING YOUR RESEARCH PROJECT ON TRACK

- Don't fear GenAI, use it judiciously and responsibly to enhance your productivity and efficiency.
- Weigh up the degree to which authorship, accountability and liability are reduced when deciding whether (or how) to use GenAI.
- When using paraphrasing and predictive text apps, ensure your writing remains authentic and that your 'voice' still comes through.
- Search widely for information about inherent biases of the algorithms and training data of the GenAI you are using and validate the outputs where possible.
- Stay up to date with the latest university and journal GenAI policies and guidelines.
- Report how and why you used advanced GenAI with advanced applications.

- Don't just rely on GenAI guidelines and policies. Apply your mind to identify ethical issues that could be challenged now or in the future.
- When searching for literature, adopt a critical mindset, identify both personal biases and inherent biases in your field, use multiple tools, and differentiate between positive, negative and neutral citations.

REFERENCES

AIContentfy. (2023). Unveiling the drawbacks: exploring the disadvantages of AI in article writing, 6 November. https://aicontentfy.com/en/blog/unveiling-drawbacks-exploring-disadvantages-of-ai-in-article-writing#: ~: text = While %20AI %20can %20generate%20text,potential%20for%20plagiarism%20and%20unoriginality.

Bouhouita-Guermech, S, Gogognon, P. and Bélisle-Pipon J-C. (2023). Specific challenges posed by artificial intelligence in research ethics. *Frontiers in Artificial Intelligence* 6:1149082. doi: 10.3389/frai.2023.1149082.

Brown, H. and Shokri, R. (2023). How (un)fair is text summarization? https://openreview.net/forum?id=-UsbRlXzMG.

Chubb, J., Cowling, P. and Reed, D. (2022). Speeding up to keep up: exploring the use of GenAI in the research process. *GenAI & Society* 37, 1439–57. https://doi.org/10.1007/s00146-021-01259-0

Foltynek, T., Bjelobaba, S., Glendinning, I., Khan, Z.R., Santos, R. Pevletic, P. and Kravjar, J. (2023). ENAI Recommendations on the ethical use of Artificial Intelligence in education. *International Journal for Educational Integrity* 19, 12. https://doi.org/10.1007/s40979-023-00133-4

Gilbert, L.S., Jackson, K. and di Gregorio, S. (2014). Tools for Analysing qualitative data: the history and relevance of qualitative data analysis software. In Spector, J., Merrill, M., Elen, J. and Bishop, M. (eds), *Handbook of Research on Educational Communications and Technology.* New York: Springer. https://doi.org/10.1007/978-1-4614-3185-5_18.

Gladwell, M. (2008). *Outliers.* New York: Little, Brown and Company.

Haan, K. and Watts, R. (2023). How businesses are using artificial intelligence in 2023. https://www.forbes.com/advisor/business/software/ai-in-business/.

Hagendorff, T. (2020). The ethics of GenAI ethics: an evaluation of guidelines. *Minds & Machines* 30, 99–120. https://doi.org/10.1007/s11023-020-09517-8.

Jemielniak D. (2019). Wikipedia: why is the common knowledge resource still neglected by academics? *Gigascience*, 8(12), giz139. doi:10.1093/gigascience/giz139. https://www.ncbi.nlm.nih.gov/pmc/articles/PMC6889752/.

Mittelstadt, B.D., Allo, P., Taddeo, M., Wachter, S. and Floridi, L. (2016). The ethics of algorithms: mapping the debate. *Big Data & Society*, 3(2). https://doi.org/10.1177/2053951716679679.

Singh, S. (2022). The ethics of using GenAI in research and scientific writing. https://paperpal.com/blog/news-updates/industry-insights/the-ethics-of-using-ai-in-research-and-scientific-writing.

Tauginienė, L, Gaižauskaitė, I., Glendinning, I., Kravjar, J., Ojstersek, M., Robeiro, L., Odineca, T., Marino, F., Cosentino, M., Sivasubramaniam, S. and Foltynek, T. (2018). Glossary for academic integrity. ENAI report (revised version), October. https://www.academicintegrity.eu/wp/wp-content/uploads/2023/02/EN-Glossary_revised_final_24.02.23.pdf.

Wang, B., Chen, W., Pei, H., Xie, C., Kang, M., Zhang, C., Xu, C., Xiong, Z., Dutta, R., Schaeffer, R., Truong, S., Arora, S., Mazeika, M., Hendrycks, D., Lin, Z., Cheng, Y., Koyejo, S., Song, D.X. and Li, B. (2023). Decoding trust: a comprehensive assessment of trustworthiness in GPT models. Conference proceding: 37th Conference on Neural Information Processing Systems. https://doi.org/10.48550/arXiv.2306.11698

7.   Awful #14: putting on my novice researcher's shoes and developing my research question

Deisi Yunga-Godoy

Do you recall the moment when you slipped into your first pair of shoes? I, unfortunately, don't. How I wish I did, as it would mean I had the awareness of taking my initial steps. In observations of countless children in my life I see their hesitation and conquering of fear to take that pivotal first step. Simultaneously, I've witnessed how this hesitation is eclipsed by curiosity, endowing them with an unknown bravery that propels them forward.

This may seem like an extensive introduction, perhaps delving too far into the past, but I assure you it's a journey worth taking, as it was for me. As a young, ambitious student, my desire was to become a university professor. Yet, the path ahead was beyond my imagination. My naivety led me to believe that writing a research question was the simplest activity in the world. After all, I had been writing since my teenage years, so why would it be any different now? Everything appeared to align perfectly, until I confronted the initial hurdle on the path to realizing my dream: writing the research question.

As that naive young researcher, I thought that developing and justifying my research question would come as easily as walking. Well, reality proved to be more challenging than I had anticipated. I had to timidly take baby steps which were small, awkward, and certainly graceless. The first advice I received was simple yet profound: one must 'read to write.' However, my initial predicament arose when deciding what to read. Should I delve into papers from the last year, the past decade, or perhaps trace back to the dawn of recorded time and the first written papyrus?

This is where the initial challenge surfaced– how to select the material to read? I yearned to absorb every piece of information within my research field, but this approach led me astray in the vast landscape of literature. I found myself at a crossroads, unsure of which path to follow. With each article I perused, a new idea or question surfaced, a potential Eureka! moment. Yet, with each revelation, I realized each, while individually commendable, steered me toward alternate directions. Consequently, I found myself with numerous different versions of my thesis research question – some focusing on historical processes, others on recent research, and some on exploratory studies. Others were candid attempts to unearth something entirely new that weren't new by any means, they were just new for me.

I spent countless hours in coffee shops, libraries, and serene havens, carefully chosen to provide me with the tranquility and focus necessary to dig into the realm of research within my chosen topic. This activity proved to be an enriching and fruitful one, not only deepening my understanding of the subject I hold dear, but also cultivating an acute discernment as a coffee connoisseur. I now see this as a time of discovery. Like a child that holds in to walls and constantly falls while learning how to trust, I was trusting my ever-growing research intuition.

Several months passed in reading and it helped me to clarify my ideas, when I believed my ideas were crystallizing, I presented nervously my initial research question to some colleagues. Their feedback, although predominantly valuable, echoed a recurring theme – 'it's too broad; narrow it down.' Each colleague, with a genuine willingness to help, offered suggestions on how to refine my question and proposed diverse literature to peruse. The spectrum of recommendations spanned from the ancient wisdom of Aristotle to the latest publications in my field, constituting a staggering 2,000 years' worth of material to review! I found myself back at square one, grappling with the overwhelming task ahead.

What escaped me then was the realization that I held the power to choose to decide the trajectory of my research. Subsequently, I've come to understand that while it's essential to heed the advice of experts, colleagues, and mentors, the ultimate decision rests solely with me. Whether I opt to focus on the latest developments in my field from the past year or delve into a historical literature review spanning the genesis of research in my domain is my choice. The essence lies in the versatility of being a researcher – I can write about whatever intrigues me and need not feel constrained by singular choices. The beauty of academia lies in the fact that I can work to answer a variety of questions, each project complementing the others, creating a rich tapestry of knowledge. Yet, in my earlier years, this understanding eluded me. I harbored the misconception that my thesis had to be flawless, a paragon of perfection. Little did I grasp the true essence of it – perfection lies in completion. This realization dawned with my second revelation: 'it is better done than perfect.' A dear friend and invaluable mentor in my career once told me, 'Write something bad, write something awful, but write.' This advice showed me the importance of taking action over obsessing about an unattainable perfection. Hence, this vignette is aptly titled 'Awful #14,' a testament of my journey. I call this putting on my shoes and taking my first step, and in my mind, taking that first step is testament of the bravery needed to start.

Going back to my journey, my initial naivety translated into months of getting lost and found again in literature. At this point I knew what to do … it came to me as this sudden realization that it was time to panic. Although I had a pretty good handle on my own limitations, I realized that attempting to juggle an assortment of articles and my colleagues' well-intentioned opinions was an exercise in futility. I was bound to end up expanding my research question once again. So, lesson number one: *Just don't go there.*

Whenever someone offered advice on my research, it usually stemmed from their personal research interests and experiences. While their input was valuable, I learned not to get swept away by the initial allure of a shiny new paper or book that seemed relevant. Now, I take the time to scrutinize the methodology, findings, and theories before deciding if they should be integrated into the fabric of my research.

Lesson number two concerns learning how to go through recommended literature efficiently. Much to my surprise, I discovered the *time spent reading gave me the discernment to select the papers that truly piqued my interest and seemed relevant, while discarding the ones that didn't.* Now, I was on the right path, defining the characteristics of the papers that would become part of my study. Or so I thought, I got lost a couple of extra times, but nothing to panic about.

The influx of information after all those months also heightened my awareness of the broader world beyond my supervisory team – a world teeming with experts who could potentially lend me a helping hand. I decided to take a more proactive approach, reaching out to researchers at conferences and through email. The worst-case scenario was a simple response: 'I have no time for you,' assuming they bothered at all.

In my quest for expertise within my academic field, I anticipated encountering venerable scholars, adorned in the elegance of 'bow tie wearing martinets,' individuals of formidable stature, often distinguished by an h-index of 40 or more. Contrary to this notion, however, I met a vibrant consortium of wonderful individuals that responded or sent a paper or two. Their collective wisdom not only guided me in matters pertaining to my research question but also extended to methodological design, anticipated outcomes, and contingency planning in the face of unforeseen challenges. Not all responses were positive, with some suggesting we deferred contact to a more advanced stage in my research. Others remained unresponsive; the overarching outcome exceeded my initial expectations substantially. It is with this short preamble that I give you my third lesson: *Don't be concerned about initiating contact with seemingly unapproachable experts in the field; many do respond and are happy to do so.*

To expand my research network, I wrote a myriad of emails, joined specialized research networks, and had an active participation in academic conferences, thus expanding it considerably. Consequently, I am certain in my belief that such endeavors helped both my present research undertakings and subsequent scholarly pursuits. One truth remains: the individual responding to one's call may evolve into an invaluable mentor, collaborator, or even an enduring confidant – in my case, it's all the above. These researchers, these friends that became my family and are the friends that, at the beginning, were kind strangers that decided to guide me and hold my hand in this path while attempting to learn how to walk.

Now, a few years later, I have learned not just to walk the research path by myself but to put my researcher shoes on not being afraid of letting people hold my hand when I need it. And here it comes my last lesson: *It's ok to be vulnerable, to let others know that you certainly don't know everything. Let yourself be helped and guided time and again.* Becoming an expert in a field while a true beginner in another is a fantastic characteristic of our profession.

8. Reply all, tweets and social media: technological friends for developing a professional identity that need to be treated with care

Hugh T.J. Bainbridge

If is often stated that the most important asset an academic possesses is their reputation.

A reputation can be sullied in many ways, sometimes by bad luck or unfortunate circumstances beyond one's control. And, I suppose, sometimes by others. But most often, the damage that is done is self-inflicted.

For me, a formative experience in thinking about this occurred early. Flushed with the excitement of an acceptance letter for my first prestigious conference I had speed read through the letter to find that the paper had been scheduled as 'Poster session'.

I had already been informed of the status of this session format by other PhD students. I remembered the pearls of wisdom they had passed on. Poster sessions are 'the worst', they said. 'No one comes to them. You will go all the way to the conference for nothing.' And, devastatingly, 'They only give them to students. The real sessions are reserved for the important research.'

Aghhh! I thought and promptly fired off an email to my more experienced co-authors. 'Why did we get a POSTER SESSION?'

But in my haste, I had overlooked one important detail. My indignant email to my co-authors was a 'Reply all' and was now also flying across the globe to the Conference Stream Chair ...

***

Seeing my future career pass in an instant before my eyes, I did the only logical thing. I sought professional, expert, assistance. Not the medical kind. Real, expert, IT assistance.

A few minutes later a representative from the university IT group looked at me with bored indifference. I rapidly explained the seriousness of the situation with accompanying hand movements that helpfully indicated the direction taken by outbound and inbound emails. Finally, he tired of my explanation. 'No', the IT expert said. 'I can't delete your email before the recipient reads it.'

So, resigned to whatever fate awaited me, I trudged back to my desk to await a scolding email from the big name in the field, which I thought would probably foreshadow a cascading set of consequences that would forever blight my career.

And true to my fears, there at the top of my inbox sat an email from the Stream Chair …

***

It turns out that the Conference Stream Chair had the tact and presence of mind (as opposed to me) to write a generous reply that outlined the merits of the session format.

I've often reflected on this 30-minute period. In an age where social media facilitates instant responses to a broad audience, and technology makes bad decisions forever accessible, it helps me often to think about this formative experience and to consider the merits of a 'pause' before pressing the button 'SEND'.

PART II

Getting data

9. Epistemological odyssey: a journey of self-discovery

Neve Abgeller

THE CALL TO ADVENTURE

My doctoral journey, marked by its intensity and challenges, demanded exceptional motivation, determination, and dedication. This pursuit, seemingly a solitary endeavour, was in fact underpinned by a vital network of collaboration and support. I am profoundly grateful for the pivotal role played by my family, friends, and supervisors. Their support was not just encouraging but fundamental, providing a solid foundation for every stage of this academic journey. The obstacles I faced were significantly lightened by their constant support and guidance. The achievement of my doctoral degree is as much a testament to their invaluable contributions as it is to my own efforts. Their indispensable support was crucial in overcoming doubts and shaping my academic success.

At the commencement of my doctoral studies, I embarked on this academic journey with an extraordinary level of enthusiasm, armed with readiness, dedication, and a resolute commitment to excel in academia. Within my programme, I engaged in several research methodology modules, notably 'Foundations of Management Research', which emerged as a pivotal point in my academic trajectory. This module marked the initial instance where my confidence was profoundly challenged, introducing me to a surplus of unfamiliar terminologies such as 'ontology', 'epistemology', and 'axiology'. I swiftly recognized that mere superficial understanding of these concepts was inadequate; a deeper, more nuanced comprehension was crucial.

Despite repeated attempts to internalize these terms, their abstract nature rendered retention elusive, challenging my intellectual grasp. However, over time, through persistent study and engagement, I have attained a profound understanding of these complex topics. I now find myself not only confident but also passionate about engaging in discussions surrounding these fundamental concepts of research philosophy. This transition from initial confusion to comprehension and enjoyment marks a significant milestone in my academic development.

As my confidence in academic discourse has grown, so has my eagerness to share my narrative and explore a topic that captivates me: epistemology. Epistemology is fundamentally concerned with the nature of knowledge, encompassing beliefs and assumptions about what constitutes acceptable, valid, and legitimate knowledge (Burrell and Morgan, 1979). This concept, along with ontology and axiology, forms the cornerstone of research philosophy. The chosen philosophical stance of a researcher significantly influences the entire research design and, consequently, the knowledge contributed to their field (Burrell and Morgan, 1979; Tsoukas and Chia, 2011). It was a profound journey to fully comprehend these concepts' depths.

Discovering my own epistemological stance was a formidable challenge, akin to a roller coaster with its highs and lows. I fluctuated between regretting my awareness of epistemology and celebrating it as a pivotal realization for any researcher. Years later, I have evolved into an ardent proponent of researchers actively engaging in reflection on their epistemologies. I argue that such introspection, coupled with an openness to alternative viewpoints, fosters enhanced awareness of the contributions made to knowledge. My early recognition of the importance of epistemological reflection spurred me on a quest to identify and understand my own epistemological beliefs. This narrative recounts my journey towards that discovery.

THE EPISTEMOLOGICAL QUEST

The initial encounter with research philosophies often evokes a profound sense of confusion, a sentiment I vividly recall from my early academic experiences. This confusion, a natural response to the complex and abstract nature of these philosophies, mirrors the reactions I observe in my current students. As they grapple with understanding and reflecting on their own research philosophies, I find a deep resonance with their journey. My own path from initial unfamiliarity to now considering research philosophy as one of my favoured topics in academia highlights a crucial aspect of our academic growth.

In assisting students, I draw upon my experiences, highlighting that confusion is not just commonplace but an integral part of the learning process. It serves as a catalyst for deeper inquiry and understanding. The journey towards comprehending one's epistemology often begins with a phase of disorientation, a necessary prelude to intellectual clarity. This process involves challenging preconceived notions and entrenched beliefs, fostering a transformative re-evaluation of one's academic direction. Such a state of confusion, far from being a hindrance, is a vital step towards achieving a nuanced understanding of research philosophy. It was a relief to realize that this confusion was not indicative of a flaw in my comprehension, but rather a natural and essential phase of academic exploration and growth.

My journey into the realm of epistemologies marked a gradual improvement in my understanding, beginning with the realization that my implicit adherence was to positivism. This revelation led me to introspect about my prior ignorance on the subject. My training in research methods had not prompted me to question the underlying philosophical assumptions, leading me to an inadvertent alignment with positivist principles. However, it became evident that my research practices and beliefs did not completely align with a positivist epistemology.

This dissonance with positivism sparked a period of confusion and self-reflection. I recognized that in the context of social sciences, the notion of absolute objectivity, a cornerstone of positivism was, for me, not tenable. I firmly believed that research cannot be entirely separated from the researcher's personal ideas, beliefs, and assumptions. This stance is particularly relevant in social sciences, where the researcher's involvement enriches the research process, unlike the natural sciences where objectivity might be more feasible.

Confronted with this realization, I found myself questioning the very foundation of my epistemological stance. While I was certain of not being a positivist, identifying my true epistemological alignment remained elusive. Each new epistemological perspective I encountered resonated with me in parts but never wholly encapsulated my views. This lack of a definitive epistemological identity left me hesitant to label myself, driven by a belief that my current understanding was insufficient to make a well-informed choice.

I understood that every researcher, knowingly or unknowingly, operates under certain epistemological assumptions influencing their research design and contributions to knowledge. Acknowledging this, I recognized the need for extensive reading and reflection to synthesize these perspectives and align them with my beliefs and assumptions. This commitment to deeper exploration and understanding was essential for me to confidently identify and embrace an epistemological stance that truly reflected my academic philosophy.

As part of my doctoral training, I was given the task of articulating my epistemology while simultaneously reflecting on epistemological approaches within my doctoral field. This posed a significant challenge due to my ongoing quest to define my own epistemological stance. The complexity was further compounded by the difficulty in establishing the implicit epistemologies of others, especially when their research methodologies did not explicitly reveal their philosophical underpinnings. For instance, the use of quantitative methods, such as questionnaires, might suggest a positivist approach, yet it could equally align with critical realism or pragmatism, depending on the researchers' objectives and beliefs. Additionally, external factors such as editorial directives or journal requirements, requiring researchers to write as

'I' or 'we' rather than using the passive voice, could skew the apparent episte-mology, leading to potential misinterpretations.

This dilemma made me hesitant to critically analyse the work of others in my field, fearing that any inference I made might be an unjust representation of their philosophical positions. This led to an epiphany: the most reliable source of understanding these researchers' epistemology would be the researchers themselves. Consequently, I embarked on an empirical study that extended beyond the scope of my initial assignment. I reached out to 35 leading trust researchers, inquiring about their epistemological perspectives.

The response was overwhelmingly positive, far exceeding my expectations. The willingness of these academics to engage in this discourse not only facil-itated my research but also instilled a sense of belonging within the academic community. Of the 35 scholars contacted, 27 responded, many providing detailed insights beyond the requested brief answers. This enthusiastic par-ticipation invigorated my own research endeavours, fuelling late-night corre-spondences and significantly boosting my motivation for my doctoral journey. The profound gratitude I felt for their contributions was evident in my interac-tions, reinforcing my commitment to my PhD and enriching my understanding of the complex landscape of epistemological diversity in my field.

As I continued my quest to identify my own epistemological stance, I found myself invigorated and closer to a resolution, shedding the desperation that once clouded my journey. Engaging with eminent trust researchers, akin to a teenager meeting their rock music idols, was enlightening. This interaction highlighted that a researcher's epistemology is a reflection of their cognitive framework, offering a gateway into the nuanced realms of their scholarly endeavours. This understanding enhanced my ability to appreciate their con-tributions to knowledge, armed with insight into the foundational assumptions guiding their research.

Yet, this exhilarating exploration was contrasted against the pressing reali-ties of my PhD timeline. While I had successfully outlined the epistemological positions of leading trust researchers and identified predominant epistemol-ogies in trust literature, my own epistemological identity remained obscure. Driven by an almost obsessive determination, I delved deeper into academic literature, often sacrificing sleep for nocturnal study sessions, in pursuit of clarity. Despite engaging with various academics to understand their epistemo-logical choices, a definitive alignment for myself was yet to be found, leaving me feeling under-informed and hesitant.

Confronted with the necessity to articulate an epistemological stance for an assignment, I experienced a sense of reluctance, feeling compelled to adopt a position that did not entirely resonate with my views. Nevertheless, I chose to align with an epistemology that approximated my beliefs, promising myself future exploration for a more congruent fit. Employing a process of elimination, I excluded positivism, postmodernism, poststructuralism, and interpretivism, recognizing that these did not align with my established perspectives. This deductive approach left me contemplating between critical realism and pragmatism as plausible options, both resonating with potential alignment to my evolving academic philosophy.

As my exploration of various epistemologies progressed, I increasingly identified with pragmatism, particularly attracted to its emphasis on methodological pluralism. Pragmatism prioritized addressing the research question through the most suitable methods, aligning with my belief in the complementary strengths of both quantitative and qualitative approaches. Despite this inclination, I remained somewhat hesitant to fully embrace pragmatism due to its frequent association with producing practice-oriented knowledge, this often being narrowly interpreted within the practitioner community.

With the deadline looming, I opted to describe pragmatism as my epistemological view in my assignment, though with reservations. My commitment to authenticity in academic writing meant I focused only on the aspects of pragmatism I resonated with, resulting in a less comprehensive treatment of the topic. However, the assignment's segment reflecting on trust researchers and their underlying epistemologies was more fulfilling, as it incorporated an empirical study extending beyond the assignment's requirements. This approach provided valuable insights, revealing shared beliefs and uncertainties among leading researchers.

THE RETURN WITH THE EPISTEMOLOGICAL ELIXIR

The completion of this assignment, despite many struggles and sleepless nights, was a significant milestone. Following my supervisor's advice, the research was expanded, leading to a publication in the *Journal of Trust Research* (Isaeva et al., 2015). This process, including interactions with co-authors, reviewers, and conference participants, facilitated a deeper understanding of my epistemological stance.

Ultimately, I firmly embraced pragmatism as my guiding epistemology, carefully distinguishing it from mere pragmatic research decisions and broadening the understanding of 'practice' beyond its conventional interpretation. This journey from uncertainty to clarity not only solidified my epistemological identity but also reinforced the importance of explicit epistemological reflection in shaping research design and methodology. My experience has transformed me into an advocate for researchers to be conscious of their epistemological assumptions and their impact on scholarly contributions. I conclude with my lessons, in relation to finding your own epistemology and keeping your research on track.

LESSONS FOR KEEPING YOUR RESEARCH ON TRACK

1. Recognize that all researchers, consciously or not, operate under episte-mological assumptions.
2. Understand that these beliefs inform research design and methodology.
3. Embrace initial confusion as a part of the learning process.
4. Seek guidance from experienced researchers when needed.
5. Clearly define your epistemological stance to contribute meaningfully to scholarly discourse and assist future researchers.

REFERENCES

Burrell, G. and Morgan, G. (1979). *Sociological Paradigms and Organizational Analysis: Elements of the Sociology of Corporate Life*, Burlington, VT: Ashgate.
Isaeva, N., Bachmann, R., Bristow, A. and Saunders, M.N.K. (2015). 'Why the epis-temologies of trust researchers matter', *Journal of Trust Research*, 5(2), 153–69.
Tsoukas, H. and Chia, R. (2011). 'Introduction: why philosophy matters to organization theory', in H. Tsoukas and R. Chia (eds), *Philosophy and Organization Theory*, Research in the Sociology of Organizations, vol. 32, Bradford: Emerald, pp. 1–21.

10. A tale of two surveys: reaching respondents using Web questionnaires

Mark N.K. Saunders

INTRODUCTION

When thinking about this chapter, Charles Dickens's (2011, p. 5) opening line from his 1859 novel *A Tale of Two Cities* came to mind: 'It was the best of times, it was the worst of times …' This, for me, sums up my feelings when trying to reach small and medium-sized enterprise (SME) owner-managers as potential respondents for two Internet questionnaires as part of a series of applied research projects on SME success with my co-researcher David Gray.[1]

Over the years David and I have undertaken a fair number of research projects where data were collected using questionnaires. Through these projects we gained some understanding of the realities of distributing questionnaires by hand, by mail and online. Respondents to our questionnaires have included employees in a single organisation, customers of different organisations and people with specific roles, such as owner-managers or directors of services, working for a wide range of organisations. Based on our experiences, we would like to think we are reasonably experienced in undertaking survey research using self-completion questionnaires.

Rather than recounting the entire process of survey research, in this chapter I focus upon a crucial aspect of David's and my learning from these projects: the gaining of access to potential questionnaire respondents. Although access is often considered in the research methods literature, the focus is usually on gaining cognitive access and, in particular, how to enhance response rates once potential respondents have been reached. In contrast, where difficulties associated with gaining physical access to collect data are acknowledged, the focus is usually within the context of gaining permission via a gatekeeper in one organisation.

In this chapter I consider two contrasting realities associated with gaining physical access to respondents from a large number of organisations who hold a particular role. In doing this I have drawn particularly on a paper David and I co-authored in *Human Resource Development Quarterly* and our co-authored chapter for the first edition of this book (Saunders et al., 2017; Saunders and Gray, 2018). In particular, I consider the issues and implications associated with gaining access when we undertook two surveys using Web question-naires. The first was to distribute using a compiled list (database) of potential respondents purchased from an external company, and the second a volunteer panel hosted by an external company. I present this as a tale of two surveys, the first being what often felt 'the worst of times', and the experience of the second being, by contrast, 'the best of times'. I conclude by outlining our learning from these experiences.

THE TALES' CONTEXT

Over a period of years David and I worked with a large United Kingdom (UK) firm, undertaking a series of fully funded research projects focusing on a range of aspects relating to SMEs' success. These studies were commissioned to identify factors that contributed to SMEs' longevity and robustness focusing on those SMEs that had survived the financial downturn following the 2008 worldwide financial crisis. Two of these studies, 'Triggers for Success' and 'Winning New Business', involved survey research using Web questionnaires. For both, our funder wanted to be able to generalise about UK SMEs' success from the data collected. This we knew would entail having a representative sample and a sufficiently large number of returns.

For both these studies we committed to attaining at least 1000 complete responses to the associated survey questionnaires. We knew that there were dif-ficulties in accessing SMEs and that there were wide variations in Web-based survey response rates (Shih and Fan, 2008; Mellahi and Harris, 2016) and so we planned carefully. Both projects were high profile, the associated reports being publicised widely and launched at major London venues with audiences comprising the government minister for Business and Enterprise at that time, main quality UK newspapers' business reporters, and over a hundred inter-ested business leaders.

THE WORST OF TIMES: USING A COMPILED LIST OF POTENTIAL RESPONDENTS

For the Triggers for Success study's survey, we planned to email our Web-based questionnaire to a compiled list of potential respondents, which we would purchase. Being what we considered to be cautious, we assumed a likely response rate of 10 per cent, the lowest percentage suggested by Baruch and Haltom's (2008) analysis of published research. This meant we needed to deliver our questionnaire to at least 10,000 SMEs to achieve the 1000 responses. Using publicly available UK Government's Department of

Business, Innovation and Skills data we devised a quota sample of SMEs comprising six separate size bandings (based on number of employees) for each of the UK's 12 economic regions, a total of 72 different groupings. Through this we hoped to represent the variability in size and number of the population of private sector SMEs.

Contact details and demographic data for 10,000 private sector SMEs matching our quota specifications were purchase from a reputable database company. Alongside demographic data for each SME, details included an email address, telephone number and named contact allowing us to personalise each email accompanying the Web questionnaire. Acknowledging that some email addresses were likely to no longer be valid (termed 'hard bounce back') the database company provided details for a further 1789 SMEs, giving a sample of 11,789 SMEs. Within each of the regional quotas, each SME was checked by us to ensure it met the SME size criteria of less than 250 employees (as defined by European Union recommendation L124/36) and was in the private sector. This resulted in 913 SMEs being removed from the sample provided because they were large enterprises (for example, a major snack food manufacturer and a national health care chain of retail outlets), in the public sector (for example, a National Health Service pharmacy) or in the not-for-profit sector (for example, a registered charity). Using the contact details our questionnaire was then emailed to the remaining 10,876 SMEs.

Within a week of distributing our Web questionnaire we knew we had a problem with gaining physical access. Some 4892 emails containing the link to our questionnaire had been bounced back having not reached the intended recipient. This meant our 4892 number of intended respondents were non-contactable. We spoke to the Information Technology (IT) services experts at our university who informed us it was impossible to work out the precise reason for bounce back and advised us to contact the database company. We did this, providing them with a sample of 91 of the email addresses that had 'bounced'. Following their checking, the company responded that, of these 91, only nine were invalid and that bounce back of 10 per cent of this was 'well within the expected bounce back rate for emails that are invalid'. They considered the problem of bounce back was beyond their control and that our emails were being blocked for one or more of a number of reasons. These included the content of the email such as the hyperlink or particular words such as 'survey' or 'questionnaire', the recipient's email server settings, SPAM filters and/or anti-virus software, or some other reason triggered by our email and hyperlink to the Web questionnaire we had designed. In summary, it was not the database company's problem to solve but ours.

We were left with a sample of 6084 potential respondents, not only far fewer than we were anticipating, but also insufficient if our cautious response rate of 10 per cent was realised. One month after the launch of the survey, despite two follow-up emails to these potential respondents, it was clear we had a problem. Although 578 questionnaires had been returned, only 508 were complete and useable, a response rate after excluding non-contacts of 8.5 per cent. This was insufficient for our analysis purposes as we were hoping to disaggregate the data by sector and region, and unacceptable given the commitment to a minimum of 1000 returns we had made to the client funding the research.

The compiled list (database) we had purchased contained telephone contact details for the majority of SMEs. We therefore recruited four recent graduates to telephone these enterprises and invite them to complete the questionnaire by telephone. Unfortunately by the end of their first day, our newly appointed research assistants were dispirited; potential respondents were, with a few exceptions, refusing to take part in our research. By the end of that week all our research assistants had resigned, and we had only an additional 70 completed questionnaires. We decided to send one final follow-up email to the sample, thanking SME owner managers who had already responded and inviting those who had not yet responded to take part.

But then a crisis arose. Our university's IT services team received a very irate email from the director of an SME regarding our repeated emails to his company requesting they complete the questionnaire. Within this email he threatened legal action, stating: 'the matter has now been escalated to a formal legal issue against the university'. I immediately telephoned the company's director and discovered the email address provided by the database company was incorrect. Rather than it being the address for general communications, it was the company's 24-hour emergency email address, only to be used by the company's clients if there was a business-operations threatening problem requiring immediate attention. Inadvertently our email request to participate in our research had called staff away from other work three times. Fortunately, my sincere telephone apology to the SME's director and follow-up email to the correct address later that day was accepted. Not surprisingly we deleted the 24-hour emergency email address from our database. The database company also apologised to the company director and admitted liability.

We needed an alternative plan to gain physical access quickly. We decided to try using our networks and contacts. We knew that Chambers of Commerce and other employer groups nationally had large numbers of SMEs as members. David had collaborated with our local Chamber of Commerce on a previous research project, so contacted their chief executive asking for help with contacting her network of members. Here, our own research and knowledge came to the fore. As commercial organisations, Chambers of Commerce rely on membership fees and other sources of income to continue to provide their services. Hence, we offered a financial incentive to persuade them to directly email the survey to their members.

The chief executive of our local Chamber of Commerce agreed to email all their SME members using an introductory letter we drafted which included the hyperlink to our questionnaire. However, one Chamber of Commerce was neither likely to be sufficient in terms of number of responses or geographical coverage. Using contact details for other chief executives, we adopted snowball sampling to involve other Chambers of Commerce chief executives and their equivalent networks. Three further Chambers of Commerce supported the Web questionnaire delivery significantly. In addition, we gained support from a range of employer groups with whom we already had links. These, in combination with the Chambers of Commerce eventually provided 589 responses. As before, we made comprehensive efforts to explain the purpose of the survey to each Chamber of Commerce and employer group and how the data provided by their members would be handled with rigorous attention to confidentiality. Fortunately, the emails sent on our behalf by the Chambers of Commerce and employer groups received negligible bounce back. A week after these first emails had been sent one follow-up reminder was sent. This thanked those who had responded, and encouraged those who had not to do so.

David was keeping a daily running total of the number of respondents completing our questionnaire on his office whiteboard. Although numbers were increasing, it did not look as if our back-up plan would provide sufficient complete responses. We therefore decided to incentivise direct mailings using selected directories of small businesses resulting in 349 additional responses. A further 84 responses were generated by emailing our existing SME contacts and asking if they would also be willing to help.

Six weeks later, having followed the daily tantalising rise in the total number of respondents, we had received 1600 useable responses that met our research funder's criteria of being private sector SMEs. Of these 1004 we deemed complete, using the American Association for Public Opinion Research (2023) criterion of 80 per cent or more of the essential questions being answered. We had met the number required by our funder, although when compared with our initial quota we had over-representation of SMEs from certain UK regions (notably London and the Southeast). In our subsequent analyses we established the extent to which these differences between our sample and the population impacted significantly on our findings, reporting this where significant.

THE BEST OF TIMES: USING A VOLUNTEER PANEL

The contract for the 'Winning New Business' funded research also included a Web questionnaire with at least 1000 returns. Acknowledging the unsatisfactory nature of our previous experience when using a compiled list (database), we decided to use a volunteer panel of SME owner managers. Access to this was purchased through an online panel company. Potential respondents for our volunteer panel had already self-recruited to the panel company by signing up to participate regularly in their online surveys; and would decide, upon receipt of an email, whether to participate in our specific survey. The panel company would incentivise panel members to become respondents and complete our survey and, although their specific mechanisms of self-selection and incentivisation remained unknown, they were certified as meeting industry guidelines.

We paid the panel company for each fully complete questionnaire we received, providing the respondent met six criteria. In deciding on our criteria we had tried to ensure these would screen out inappropriate respondents while remaining sufficiently large to account for low response rates. At the same time, as the panel company charged extra for each criterion we included, we had to assess the benefits to sample accuracy of adding each criterion. Our first four criteria comprised (1) the size of the organisation (being between 5 and 249 employees, thereby excluding the smallest micro businesses), (2) being located in the UK, (3) being in the private sector and (4) having been operating for at least three years. These combined with data from the demographic questions such as UK region and sector would allow us to assess the representativeness of our sample. The contract with the online panel company meant we had no control over who received the questionnaire and were unable to request contact details from responding SMEs. We therefore added two further criteria: (5) the respondent was the owner, owner-manager, manager or senior person in the SME; and (6) where the respondent was a senior person, they had worked for at least one year with the SME. These last two criteria meant those responding should be likely to have a good understanding of their SME and its operations.

The questionnaire was delivered in waves by the online panel company using a hyperlink in an email written by the company to SME owners, managers or other senior people who were members of their volunteer panel. Our explanation of the research was included at the start of the questionnaire followed by six screening questions to ensure that our inclusion criteria were met. Responses to the screening questions were tracked by the online panel company in real time through the survey software to ensure those potential respondents who were screened out were not re-sent the questionnaire. The panel company also tracked how many respondents finished the questionnaire, allowing them to keep a tally of the total number of completed questionnaires.

Overall, 2373 respondents consented to participate in 'Winning New Business' research and undertake our questionnaire. Of these, 1128 met the six prespecified inclusion criteria and 1015 completed the questionnaire, it taking one month from launch to exceed the target of 1000 responses. Of these, all had 80 per cent or more of the crucial questions answered, these being considered complete returns. Once again, demographic data, when compared with Department for Business Innovation and Skills estimates indicated over-representation from certain UK regions (notably London and the Southeast) and certain sectors (notably manufacturing and finance and insurance activities). These differences, while significant, were overall not as marked as those using data obtained using the compiled list; data collected rarely differed significantly between early and late respondents. As with the data collected using a compiled list, subsequent analyses took account of these differences.

LESSONS FOR KEEPING YOUR PROJECT ON TRACK

In reading this account, I hope you will have thought of a number of learning points that may be applicable to your own research. Despite this, I feel it may be helpful to list those David and I feel comprise our key lessons when gaining physical access for large-scale online survey research:

1. Always have a contingency plan that can be put into operation if response rates are lower than expected.
2. Check externally sourced databases and compiled lists for accuracy carefully, whatever the reputation of the source from which they are obtained.
3. Establish the likely response rate and representativeness of respondents either by examining findings of similar research or a pilot study.
4. Recognise the importance of contacts and networks in gaining physical access and, where appropriate, incorporate this in the research design.
5. Ensure the compiled list or volunteer panel is sufficiently large to accommodate very low response rates and support reliable statistical analysis.
6. Think carefully about incentivising completion of questionnaires and, if possible, allocate funds to do this.
7. Monitor questionnaire returns on a daily basis so that potential problems such as lack of representativeness are ascertained as early as possible, and the contingency plan can be activated.
8. Be persistent and follow up non-respondents and organisations that help in distributing the questionnaire with polite but regular reminders to maximise returns.
9. Have a contingency plan to activate if response rates are lower than expected.
10. Ensure that reporting of method outlines the process of gaining access, incorporating explicit recognition where samples are not representative of the target population and, if necessary, an explanation of the contingencies used to mitigate such problems.

NOTE

1.   Professor David Gray died in 2019. This chapter draws heavily on our work together and is dedicated to him.

REFERENCES

American Association for Public Opinion Research. (2023). *Standard Definitions: Final Dispositions of Case Codes and Outcome Rates for Surveys* (10th edition). Lenexa, KA: AAPOR.

Baruch, Y. and Haltom, B.C. (2008). 'Survey response rate levels and trends in organizational research'. *Human Relations*, *61*, 1139–60.

Dickens, C. (2011). *A Tale of Two Cities*. London: Penguin Books (originally published by All the Year Round in 1859).

Mellahi, K. and Harris, L.C. (2016). 'Response rates in business and management research: an overview of current practice and suggestions for future direction'. *British Journal of Management*, *27*(2), 426–37.

Saunders, M.N.K. and Gray, D.E. (2018). 'Bounce back, firewalls and legal threats: reaching respondents using Internet Questionnaires', in K. Townsend and M.N.K. Saunders (eds), *How to Keep Your Research Project on Track: Insights from When Things Go Wrong*. Cheltenham, UK and Northampton, MA, USA: Edward Elgar, pp. 59–66

Saunders M.N.K., Gray D.E. and Bristow, A. (2017). 'Beyond the single organization: insider insights from gaining access for large multiorganization survey HRD research'. *Human Resource Development Quarterly*, *28*(3), 401–25.

Shih, T.H. and X. Fan. (2008). 'Comparing response rates from web and mail surveys: a meta-analysis'. *Field Methods*, *20*(3), 249–71.

11. Finding the truth amongst conflicting evidence

Heather Short

INTRODUCTION

As a researcher, I frequently worry about whether my research is unearthing the truth – but what is truth? As my research perspective is subjectivist, I believe that meaning is created through social interaction, changing according to context and so leading to new realities. Consequently, I believe that there is more than one reality, each of which is constructed from how people perceive things and how they act: everyone sees the world differently and has her/his own interpretations of how she/he and others act. This can really complicate finding the truth in research – but does make it very interesting! An obvious problem is whose truth am I looking for? Mine – or the research participants'? Bearing in mind that each person is likely to have a different view of the truth not only from me, but also from each other, this becomes very complicated. I could get completely stuck in 'analysis-paralysis' regarding this and so I accept that people are 'truthful' if they seem to be reflecting reality as they see it – so, on a very simple level, if what they say aligns with what I see them doing.

At the start of my research career, the more academic literature I read, the more convinced I became that some researchers were paranoid; while some were content to believe everything that their research subjects told them, others seemed reluctant to believe anything and went to extraordinary lengths to prove the wisdom of this approach. On reflection, I realised that these extremes aren't confined to academia as such views are common in all aspects of life. The more I thought about it, the more I recognised that, although my own inclination to believe others varies between these two extremes depending on the circumstances, I needed to use a more sceptical approach in my research if it was to be credible and widely accepted. Also, as I read more and more academic research literature, I appreciated that I should consider whether I was always willing – or able – to hear the truth; to quote George Bernard Shaw, admittedly out of context, might I and my research participants be 'separated by a common language'?

Therefore, in this chapter, I will first look at possible reasons for research participants appearing to be less than truthful, including my own shortcomings. I'll then explore specific instances of this in my research, which will lead to my Lessons for Keeping on Track in the search for finding the truth amongst conflicting evidence.

WHY DON'T PARTICIPANTS TELL ME THE TRUTH?

My early research was predicated on the premise that everyone who took part in it wanted to tell me 'the truth, the whole truth and nothing but the truth'. However, the more research I have done, the more I have discovered that this is seldom the case. That is not to infer that I am unlucky enough always to choose research participants who are outright liars, more that they are a mixture of normal people who may not appear to be wholly truthful for various reasons.

Some people are just too nice and give me answers that they think I want to hear, even if they know these don't reflect reality (Yin, 2014). Once, I asked participants in a group interview (who knew I was researching the importance of trust in workplace settings): 'Do you think that trust is important at work?' They answered 'Yes' which I accepted unquestioningly, not realising that they had automatically given me the response they thought I wanted. I am still blushing at the naivety of my questioning. Now I would ask several more probing, open-ended questions which would be more likely to build up a picture of the role of trust in the workplace.

Other research subjects appear to hope that their answers will make them look more impressive than they actually are by exaggerating their role in situations or their position in their organisation's hierarchy. The latter is exacerbated if people see themselves as representatives of their organisation and so give corporate answers (Watson, 2011). Participants literally appear to be 'puffing themselves up'; they seem to grow in size, their chest is often thrust out and their gestures become more expansive. Now I always emphasise that I am interested in the individual's opinion, rather than the official company line – which I can obtain from its annual report. I also use my first name – certainly not my title (Doctor)! – and try to put her/him at ease and to make the situation uncompetitive and non-threatening. I adopt a relaxed approach with straightforward language and welcoming gestures, such as smiling and nodding while the participant is speaking.

Sometimes research subjects seem to want to finish an interview as quickly as possible and so give monosyllabic responses which do not invite further exploration of the topic. They also look at the clock and may even be reluctant to take their coat off or to sit comfortably. I was surprised the first time this happened because I try to conduct interviews at a time of the interviewee's choosing and I make it clear how long the interview will last – and ensure that the time isn't exceeded. However, when I looked at this objectively, I realised that the interview had been arranged several weeks beforehand and that it was taking place in what was now a very busy time for the interviewee. Consequently, however interesting I thought my questions were, all this person could think about was how soon he could get back to his day job. I now rarely arrange interviews more than a couple of weeks ahead and always check before the interview begins that the time is still convenient – potentially this saves both of us time and effort.

WHY DON'T I HEAR THE TRUTH?

With experience (and maturity) I have realised that research subjects aren't always responsible for (apparent) lack of truth in their responses; *I* may be at fault …

Although I try very hard to be a neutral researcher, I am aware that my personal biases, preconceived ideas, experiences and relationship to the research and with participants will inevitably colour my memory and interpretation of our conversations. Therefore, provided interviewees agree, I always record interviews to avoid poor recall and inaccurate/biased memories.

Sometimes, I realise – typically when transcribing a recorded interview so it is too late to do anything – that I have not grasped what an interviewee is trying to tell me and so I have not explored a potentially important area. This may be because the participant used technical language and/or acronyms/abbreviations that I didn't understand, perhaps deliberately to try and impress me with her/his expertise. Again, the tape has helped me recall 'puffed up' body language with the interviewee probably speaking quickly, to deter interruptions. I used to be too frightened to interrupt when this happened – I didn't want to look silly – so I didn't seek clarification and consequently my data was of less use than it could have been.

Occasionally – again as interview recordings show – some interviewees appear to have perceived my non-understanding, even if I haven't, and consequently they have dumbed down their answers so that the interviews have been less useful than they might have been.

Nowadays I try to admit how little I know and ask for explanations. Although this usually gives me more useful information, a couple of interviewees have become impatient at, for example, my inability to grasp what they see as simple concepts and the interview has effectively ended. In both instances, I appreciate that I should have been sensitive to the interviewee's mood, but I'm uncertain of how I could have gained value from an interview where I understood very little of what was being said (even when I listened to the recording several times).

Just as demands on interviewees' time can change between planning the interview and it taking place, sometimes I have been pressed for time or pre-occupied by other matters when conducting interviews and so have failed to take opportunities to clarify what interviewees are trying to tell me. This has been painfully obvious when listening to the recording of such interviews. Now I would ask the interviewee whether we could rearrange the interview at a mutually acceptable time.

However, these were not the only problems encountered during my PhD research ...

WHAT HAPPENED IN MY PHD RESEARCH

By the time I started my PhD research I knew, at least in principle, much of what I have already discussed concerning potential lack of truth in research participants' responses and so I decided to undertake ethnographic research which would include observations, interviews, both semi-structured and infor-mal ones, and photographs. I felt that this would give me a better opportunity to find out about e-learning in small and medium enterprises (SMEs) than visiting organisations occasionally to conduct interviews or sending question-naires to participants.

In exchange for researching within an organisation, I offered to work there unpaid. As an SME owner-manager with considerable business experience in areas such as project management, general management, IT and finance, I thought this would be an attractive proposition. It would also be very advantageous for me – I felt that by working in an organisation alongside its employees, I would be able to see and hear what was actually happening, as opposed to what people chose to tell me, so that I could then explore specific issues further through interviews. I thought that this would help me discover the truth – even possibly revealing instinctive behaviours of which the partici-pants themselves were unaware!

I was confident that I knew many of the problems I was likely to encounter and how to deal with them. However, I was not prepared for the extent to which research participants, potential and actual, would give me misleading and exaggerated or understated responses. Although these distortions of the truth were seldom deliberate, they led me down many blind alleys and ulti-mately changed my intended research substantially.

DESPERATELY SEEKING RESEARCH SITES

I wanted to undertake my ethnographic research in three SMEs which employed at least ten people who undertook some e-learning. I expected to work in each place for about three months which I hoped would be long enough for the research participants and I to get to know each other so that they would be more likely to be honest with me than they might have been with an interviewer they met only fleetingly.

Although I expected that finding suitable research organisations would need time, hard work, much planning and some luck, I was surprised that it took more than 18 months. Initially, I allowed self-selection by making friends, colleagues and acquaintances aware of my quest, interrogating an online business directory and undertaking extensive networking, both online (LinkedIn and Twitter) and face-to-face, including business networking breakfasts/meetings and exhibitions. Some organisations appeared suspicious of my offer to work unpaid or were reluctant to give a stranger access to their inner workings. Apart from these few exceptions, there was much enthusiasm for my unpaid labour.

Some responses ignored my requisite organisational size; one-(wo)man-bands blithely glossed over having no employees which I only discovered after concentrated probing. People from other – larger – concerns, seemingly keen to benefit from my unpaid work, actually lied about the size of their organisation – later justifying this by saying something like 'We function like an SME.' In retrospect, I remember that few of them would meet my eye, some fiddled nervously with their teacup/pen and most of them spoke very quickly, talking over my questions.

However, the biggest 'untruths' concerned the use of e-learning, perhaps through genuine ignorance/confusion about what I meant by e-learning. Although I read my e-learning definition to participants, my assumption that we were 'singing from the same hymn sheet' was misplaced. Contrary to what I thought, we weren't; as I eventually realised, we each had a different understanding of the term. This was more difficult to detect than other 'untruths', perhaps because these were genuinely held opinions; participants were using their own understanding of e-learning, with both of us unaware of the chasm between our definitions.

I realised – in retrospect – that many people thought that e-learning referred to formal learning methods, typically online courses, which few of them had experienced or indeed their organisations could afford. They ignored my definition's inclusion of informal methods such as use of social media and forums.

Consequently, in my initial discussions with gatekeepers, many SMEs who were using informal e-learning excluded themselves from my study and I missed the opportunity to research in some potentially relevant organisations.

Longer, more probing conversations might have rectified this, although discussions at networking meetings are, through necessity, constrained by time
and fairly superficial. Although it took me a while to realise the gulf between
our definitions, it was better late than never; had I continued with this fundamental misunderstanding, it may have invalidated my research. From then on,
I discussed the term e-learning more fully with my research participants; I no
longer assumed any common understanding of it and it became the crux of our
conversations and interviews.

IS IT TRUE …?

More worrying were the people who seemed deliberately to mislead me
regarding their organisation's suitability in the hope that, by investigating
e-learning within it, I would actually introduce and implement such learning.
This level of deception was very difficult to ascertain in initial conversations
as some people spoke very plausibly about the e-learning which occurred in
their SME; indeed, I nearly selected one such organisation as a research site!

The CEO convinced me that the organisation was an ideal research site,
speaking with authority, giving me little opportunity to ask questions and
when I did, sweeping on, ignoring my question. Needless to say, I wanted
to see how this 'ideal organisation' functioned. My visit started badly when
I discovered that the address they used was for mail only; the work happened, not at the impressive historic building where I arrived, but in a tatty,
temporary-looking 'hut' around the corner. My suspicions increased as I saw
piles of paper on every desk and available surface (even the floor!), but little
computer equipment. Seemingly oblivious to the incongruity of this, the CEO
ushered me into a meeting room, introduced me to the managing director and
proceeded to talk enthusiastically and assertively about their huge e-learning
opportunities, which included selling it to organisations and running courses
for a local college. He brushed aside all my questions – he was a very large
man and literally waved his arms as if to push my questions away; he acted as
if my questions were not worthy of his time – I would see how it worked when
I joined them for my research.

It was so surreal that when I emerged into the fresh air – I had felt stifled
throughout the meeting – I could hardly believe it had happened. Had they
really expected me to introduce e-learning to their organisation and to spear-
head its move into selling e-learning, with complete disregard for the fact
that this would afford me no opportunities to undertake my planned research
activities? Apparently so; I moved on …

Whenever a suitable organisation was suggested, I telephoned the gatekeeper, typically the managing director or a senior manager. During this conversation I checked the organisation's suitability by ascertaining its size and

turnover/balance sheet total, and questioning the amount of e-learning under-taken. This removed several businesses from my rapidly diminishing shortlist.

Next I arranged face-to-face meetings at seemingly suitable organisations which allowed me to ask more probing questions to give me a more holistic view of the company, particularly regarding e-learning. I also tried to meet as many employees as I could and to see them working (Savin-Baden and Major, 2013). This left me with three seemingly suitable SMEs so my research could begin. However, more 'untruths' emerged during the research itself ...

'THEY TOLD YOU WHAT?!'

Management at my first research site (MakingCo) had said that staff undertook some e-learning and that this should grow so I was surprised when initial con-versations with employees suggested that little, if any, occurred. This became more confusing when I saw them using lots of informal e-learning, such as watching YouTube videos and using online help facilities.

Further discussions with managers clarified that *their* concept of e-learning only considered formal online courses. However, informal conversations and semi-structured interviews with workers revealed that none of *them* undertook any online courses and were surprised that management thought they did. Furthermore, many of them hadn't considered that e-learning could include some of the very informal methods they used, which they thought didn't seem like 'real learning', and so they had told me that they did very little e-learning. They were too busy to read the two-page explanation of my research and it became obvious that they hadn't listened to my brief explanation of the research, much less my definition of e-learning.

MakingCo's employees were so busy that they could pay limited attention to me; they all seemed totally consumed by their jobs. When they could spare me time, I needed to use terms they could relate to, while trying to check their understanding of the term e-learning.

However, on reflection – and listening to interview recordings – it is clear that, although participants and I were confident that we were talking the same language, we definitely were not. Despite me having several conversations with MakingCo management before starting there, assertions about e-learning usage were based on misunderstandings and miscommunications between management and workers. Although I had chosen MakingCo as a research site because of inaccurate information, my research there was useful as it alerted me to potential gulfs of understanding about e-learning both between me and the research participants and between management and workers.

Armed with everything I had learned at MakingCo, I was confident that my time at the next SME, LearningCo, would be even more useful. I had been particularly impressed by its managing director's claim that all employees had access to extensive e-learning; LearningCo seemed to use lots of e-learning.

LearningCo's online learning system appeared to be very comprehensive so I was surprised to see few employees using it. One claimed that it took too long to find information so she used Google instead while another appeared to have no idea how to use the system. The managing director assured me that she regularly accessed it to brush up on particular subjects before visiting clients and also said that several clients had chosen LearningCo specifically because of its e-learning system.

Part of my work involved ascertaining how many people in each client company used the e-learning system so I was astonished to discover that not only did few customers use it, but that no one at LearningCo had accessed it for at least six months. Again my choice of research organisation seemed to be based on an untruth or, at best, a misconception. However, discovering why LearningCo employees didn't use their own e-learning system ('too time-consuming'; 'too complicated'; 'not user-friendly') added an interesting dimension to my research. Also observing them using simple, free, informal e-learning methods/media instead was invaluable. Nevertheless I continued to question whether I could have chosen my research sites more carefully.

Having learned so much about how to deal with 'untruths' at MakingCo and LearningCo, I was confident all would go smoothly at HelpingCo, my third SME. I had already met the CEO and the manager for whom I would be working and it appeared to be an ideal research site. Employees' use of LearningCo's e-learning system was apparently so successful that it was being sold across its industry and I was promised access to not only employees who used it, but also customers.

I put into practice everything I had learned at MakingCo and LearningCo. For example, I discussed the concept of e-learning I was using for my research at length with all research participants. Again I found disparities between the e-learning which management told me employees undertook and what employees did. It was immediately evident that HelpingCo employees did not like using the in-house e-learning system; they appeared to use it only to the extent necessary to successfully 'pass' their annual performance review. The rest of the time they used a wide array of e-learning ranging from Wikipedia to technical forums.

It was becoming increasingly obvious that I should change the title of my PhD. Originally I had planned to explore the role of trust in e-learning in SMEs, but it had become more and more evident during my research that, although this was an interesting area which had not yet been explored, there was a more fundamental yawning gap in research, namely, how is e-learning understood and undertaken in SMEs? This new thesis title sat more comfortably with the realisation that most people were not deliberately lying to me; we each had a different understanding of e-learning.

HelpingCo was the only research site where I felt I had been deliberately misled. It became apparent during my time there that the manager who had assured me that I would be able to discuss usage of HelpingCo's e-learning system with customers was deliberately obstructing any possibilities for this. For example, dates and times of visits to clients were changed at short notice to occasions when I had other commitments. I am still uncertain whether this was to ensure that I was not distracted from the substantial amount of work allocated to me or for some other reason.

WHAT DID IT ALL MEAN?

Looking back at this research experience, I wonder whether I was unlucky or gullible. On balance, I think it may have been a mixture of both, but I am certain that such situations are not uncommon in research. I learned so much during my ethnographic research; I gathered huge amounts of useful data, but I also picked up valuable experience in how to deal with seemingly less-than-truthful research participants. I now observe body language much more carefully to try and gauge how truthful someone is being, for example, people who avoid my eye, mumble, fidget, play with jewellery/gadgets or talk over my questions, are seldom telling the truth, or at least not answering everything I'm asking about. I have also learned that it is not the end of the world if I have believed an 'untruth', provided I recognise it at some point; indeed, it can add interesting additional dimensions to my research findings, perhaps even changing the focus of my research.

Below I have summarised some lessons I've learned about keeping my research on track in the face of misunderstandings, exaggerations, understatements, omissions, 'untruths' and downright lies.

LESSONS FOR KEEPING ON TRACK

1. Spend time understanding potential research sites before committing to collecting data there, recognising that they may not be what they seem.
2. Look for hidden agendas in both gatekeepers and participants.
3. Ensure common understandings of the research focus and terms – and of each side's expectations, for example, ask for the same information in different ways and compare results.
4. Observe body language carefully.

5. Expect the unexpected – keep calm, remain positive and you will probably still obtain useful data (even if it is not what you were originally looking for).
6. Reflect on and review interviews/observations carefully immediately after they have taken place.

REFERENCES

Savin-Baden, M. and C.H. Major (2013), *Qualitative Research: The Essential Guide to Theory and Practice*, London: Routledge.
Watson, TtJ. (2011), 'Ethnography, reality and truth: The vital need for students of "how things work" in organisations and management', *Journal of Management Studies*, *48*(1), 202–17.
Yin, R.K. (2014), *Case Study Research: Design and methods* (5th edn), London: Sage.

12. Dealing with the practical difficulties of case studies

Kenneth Cafferkey and Hetal Doshi

While it is easy to acknowledge that researchers are infinitely more interested in and excited by empirical work than the research subjects themselves, this usually masks a sense of being stuck between a rock and hard place on behalf of the researcher. Unfortunately, there has always been an empirical gulf between what researchers would like to do and what they are permitted to do in terms of access. Having a well-crafted research question is simply not enough; having the right access for the right question has become equally important.

Research access is a complicated part of our business. Just ask any PhD or Masters' student what they are researching and you might get the name of a company/sector rather than a research question. The 'who' of research is increasingly becoming as important as the 'what' of research. Anyone who has endeavoured to gather original data understands that access to case organisations or subjects to research is a game of trade-offs, compromises and sacrifices (Leonard-Barton, 1990). Getting in, staying in and getting out with something valuable is akin to walking a tightrope. No longer can academic research be seen as a novelty from an organisational perspective, it would potentially be more realistic to view it as a hindrance due to the deluge of research requests contemporary organisations receive.

With ever-increasing numbers taking up Masters' and PhD programmes, alongside the changing pressure within the academic landscape to produce, it is easy to see why organisations are under heavy bombardment in terms of access requests (Flyvbjerg, 2006). The tide has well and truly turned and a power shift is clearly evident, while a generic, almost sterile report on the overall findings was once considered the acceptable acknowledgement for access, this is no longer the case. Organisations are increasingly aware of the costs (their costs) to allow research participation and are increasingly looking for something more tangible and useable from the research. To illustrate this point, we draw on a conversation with an HR director of a multinational company. The plan was an entire workplace survey of almost 1000 people. We arrived at our meeting armed with the research instrument, pleasantries were exchanged and the HR director asked, 'How much will this all cost?' We replied, 'Nothing, we will incur all the costs.' We were then asked how long the research would take per person to fill in the survey to which we responded, 'Circa 15 minutes.' The HR director then proceeded to explain that it cost on average around $40 per hour per employee and that if we wanted to survey approximately 1000 employees that would cost the organisation $10,000 in wages alone, not to mention the lost revenue due to loss of production. We were speechless and left that meeting under no illusion that access is not only a complicated part of our business, but it is 'big business'. What is more, the HR director politely and generously informed us that sponsoring the local tiddlywinks team for $10,000 would generate more goodwill in public relations terms and was infinitely less risky than allowing the research.

While access can be viewed almost as the Holy Grail in the research process, the reality is it is not as simplistic as first assumed. Organisations increasingly want something tangible for the time, effort and costs associated with granting research access. This is where academic credibility and organisational reality face off in what can be a very uncomfortable series of exchanges for the prospective researcher. Organisations don't really care for academic integrity, methodological requirements and absolute independence on the part of the researcher and, to a certain extent, nor should they. Previously validated scales mean little or nothing to an organisation, psychological properties even less. From an organisational perspective if you want to know if someone is happy: 'Are you happy?' Yes/No is probably the most legitimate way of answering such a question. For researchers, however, it's understandably a little more complicated. Organisations care about ensuring a semblance of reality as opposed to worrying about desirability bias or leading questions and in all honesty you really can't blame them for that; where academics answer to anonymous reviewers, organisations answer to shareholders and stakeholders. It is a classic chalk and cheese relationship and here the story begins. While the case method is possibly the most exciting and rewarding form of research in the social sciences, it is nonetheless a very fine balancing act whereby multiple considerations have to be taken into account simultaneously (Stake, 1995).

In this chapter we explore access, involvement and interference to relate our experiences with research projects.

ISSUES OF FINDING SUITABLE RESEARCH SITE/ LOCATION TO ANSWER PROBLEMS/RESEARCH QUESTIONS POSED

As previously stated research access is possibly the top concern of any prospective case researcher as let's face it, sending out a largely anonymous postal survey to a few hundred managerial respondents is infinitely easier and less time consuming. However, finding the right research site to study a specific question is altogether a more difficult, if not daunting matter (Baxter and Jack, 2008). There almost always seems to be a divide over the right access versus the right opportunity (i.e. any access). While acknowledging the purposeful-ness of the trajectory from research question to method/instruments to securing the right research subjects or case, in reality it is not as simple as that (Saunders et al., 2016). In an ideal world we would all study innovation at Apple, human resource management at Google and marketing at Facebook. Unfortunately, we don't live in such an ideal world and therefore academics essentially study what they can. Take, for example, an area of interest the author has in High Performance Work Systems (HPWS). One would assume that a prerequisite to research HPWS would be that any participant organisation would be 'high performing' on some easily recognisable dimension; where in actual fact nothing could be further from the truth. It appears that academics essentially study whoever will grant them access, be that in terms of a cross-sectional multiorganisation survey or an in-depth case study, irrespective of suitability. As a case researcher one has to become accustomed to hear the word 'No' or worse still being completely ignored, so much so that any semblance of hope in access can be viewed as Nirvana.

The process of locating and cold calling suitable case participants can be an arduous task, it's hard not to feel like you are posting out something similar to the dreaded stationary catalogue we all receive every month in the mail. After repeated failure from the cold-calling method one cannot simply give up and abandon the case method, which would be the easy option. Some years ago I used a survey to find prospective case study participants. A cross-sectional, multi-industry study was used to find participants for case studies. The survey research consisted of creating an index of the 'best of the best' so to speak and contacting the companies in question informing them of their exempla-rily managerial success while simultaneously pitching the possibility of an in-depth follow-up to extol the virtues of their accomplishments. Surely this would work? Reporting high instances of relative success over competitors, hailing unparalleled levels of innovativeness, and acknowledging excellent strategy configurations would undoubtedly awaken the deepest sense of desire for acknowledgement from even the stiffest upper-lipped management? Well … kind of.

While flattery is always a useful starting point, in any event most of the organisations declined the opportunity. Flattery was naively viewed as the trump card whereby the managing director would run to the board with the acknowledgement of greatness and further avenues for the researcher to eulogise the inspirational company would undoubtedly be forthcoming? How wrong could we have been, after contacting the top ten companies, seven never even acknowledged receipt of the request, one respectfully declined, one agreed to meet and then declined, and one company after a mammoth series of negotiations finally agreed to participate. On reflection those negotiations were possibly the most interesting aspect of the entire research – perhaps we should have kept a detailed research diary and tried to publish that experience in a methods journal! In any event, a suitable case organisation for the research was sourced; in fact, it was a perfect organisation on every parameter to study, however, the process of finding and securing access in that instance could have made for interesting research in and of itself. While extremely time consuming the process did have a few advantages. The survey gave a level of validity to the case selection, which in turn enhanced the credibility. While ultimately time consuming in the extreme, however, without going to such extremes a suitable company would have never been sourced. Would we recommend this approach? We would if you have the time and resources available after exhausting all other avenues.

Lessons Learned

On reflection, possibly finding more common ground between the research question and the objectives of potential case organisations to research would have proved more fruitful instead of merely looking for a host case organisation to conduct the research in. Again, this was possibly naiveté on our part. From experiencing a series of failed research funding attempts this is now better understood, no matter how much the researcher believes they have an extremely interesting and well thought out proposal it must serve some higher purpose. Unfortunately, interesting to the researcher may not be interesting enough! Alignment of interests is the best ploy whether it is securing access to a case or acquiring research funding. This does not necessarily mean any compromise in the research or any bias of the results, it simply suggests a mutual gains approach whereby the researcher has to do extra or supplementary work that is outside the remit of the actual study for the organisations' or funding providers' benefit. Again, it's a balancing act.

NEGOTIATING ACCESS

As previously stated, negotiating access is an extremely delicate process (McDonald et al., 2009). There are two main approaches to finding a case organisation. The first is what we term the 'mass marketing' method whereby the prospective researcher sends out many requests for access and hopes to evoke a sense of interest from a prospective organisation. It's a one shot only method, the researcher has a single-page letter/phone call to stir enough interest or all is lost. The problem with this method is there are multiple researchers and a limited number of case organisations and how does one make a lasting impression. What do you talk about? What do you leave out? What commitment are you looking for? All the while trying not to come across as desperate. Unfortunately, the success rate can be as negligible as it has been with my experiences of speed dating.

The second approach is the 'personalised marketing' method. Where you gain personal information about the person of interest, ask a witty question, engage with them on their social media platforms, talk about common connections and and hope to stir some level of interest. In research terms, this approach is more strategic and can yield more success. The emphasis is on building rapport over a longer timeframe, establishing a sense of trust between the parties whereby mutual gains can result. As opposed to the mass marketing method the personalised approach allows the researcher preparation time and is also spanned out over a longer timeframe that allows the opportunity to build relationships. Within this method there is the opportunity to use multiple means to increase the credibility of both the research and the researcher. This leads to an interesting example of a previous case study.

Rapport with this company was already established as a small project had been conducted there years before; however, a number of the core people had since moved on or retired. Nonetheless, a letter of introduction was sent to the managing director and the human resources director from which a sterile and almost instant generic response declining participation emerged. Completely dismayed with such a response there was a feeling that all was lost. Reminiscing about the excellent relationship that was established with the previous managers and team leaders; surely that was worth something? Something drastic needed to be done so the research team proceeded to contact previous managers, some retired, some working for competitors, and asked if they would be prepared to give a 'nudge' to the present management to consider the research. Low and behold the previous managers agreed to assist and a letter was received from the company asking for a meeting to discuss access. A flat refusal was turned into an opportunity, and that was all that was needed.

The access negotiations began in earnest. Compromise, sacrifice and U-turns categorised the proceedings. Access negotiations are such a delicate process, the organisation can literally pull the plug at any time and the researcher is left with nothing; both parties are all too aware of this power imbalance. The issue becomes one of preservation whereby maintaining at least some semblance of integrity over the initial research question becomes paramount while also making accommodations in the organisation's favour. This is an often overlooked aspect that few researchers tend to talk about; unfortunately, in the 'real world' the integrity and credibility of the research in and of itself may not be enough to evoke the required interest from a case organisation. Balance becomes paramount, all too often an inexperienced researcher or research student goes into a negotiation meeting with a research question and comes out with a completely different one such is the dominance the organisation has on proceedings. Again, this is a topic that many are not too willing to talk about as perhaps they view it as a slight on their credibility. Knowing the line between efficacy and futility is a key consideration in this respect. In this instance, after an exhaustive process, a balance was finally reached which consisted of addressing all of the initial research goals while also conducting supplementary research on behalf of the organisation. In reality it was about a 70–30 split, time consuming: yes, but the research goals would be achieved.

Lessons Learned

There are a number of ways and means to gain research access; using personal contacts can assist greatly. Such is the problem with the flood of access requests that contemporary research takes on a 'needs must' approach. The caveat to remember is that it is not access at all costs as sometimes those costs can be too great and the research suffers and, unbeknownst to the researcher, they have suddenly morphed into some sort of organisation consultant at the behest of management. Overall, the key thing to remember is that flexibility is critical to ensure the negotiations are a success.

GAINING RESPONDENT PARTICIPATION AND INVOLVEMENT

Building a connection and getting interviewees and survey respondents to open up to organisational reality can be extremely difficult. We have all encountered a reluctant or the downright disinterested interviewee and despite cajoling or encouragement they simply refuse to open up (Dundon and Ryan, 2010; see also Townsend, Chapter 15, this volume). The disinterested interviewee is perhaps a bridge that can never be crossed, nor can any common ground be found, and it's important not to dwell on it. The reluctant interviewee is an altogether different issue, they toe the company line and never venture off script in almost a 'big brother is watching sense'. Thankfully, most interviewees fall somewhere in between these two extremes. The same can be said for quantitative research in a case study, where some employees are all too aware that the employee attitude survey has a code number (overtly or covertly) and may answer with that in mind. Similarly, reluctance can compromise research whereby a respondent almost uses a single continuous line to answer multiple Likert-style questions simultaneously which leaves the researcher with an awkward moral dilemma.

Dilemmas can turn into absolute hazards when participation and involvement take a sinister twist, whereby the organisation or a particular manager 'plants' particular individuals in the research to ensure a particular predetermined outcome. Having encountered such incidents on a small number of occasions this can really make the research futile in the extreme. In one instance, a stratified sample of employees was requested for particular focus groups, which was to be determined by production requirements (a normal occurrence in case research in a manufacturing environment) (Kitzinger, 1994). What actually transpired was that a particular manager filled the focus group with his golfing buddies who were obviously prepped to portray the organisation, and the manager, in an overly positive light. It was only later that an employee exposed the situation and stated, 'they done you up like a kipper'. Another incident in a different organisation, a focus group on employee engagement from supposedly shop floor employees, turned out to be a group on a graduate programme (a graduate programme that was effectively a year-long job interview) who spoke like their lives depended on projecting a positive light on the organisation. In this instance, the research simply had to be aborted as it was futile because the organisation in question was merely using the research as some kind of public relations exercise. What this exposes is a situation whereby participation perhaps needs to be better thought through as in this instance research access was requested and negotiated with senior management. The vast majority of those involved as participants in the research did not have any say in these negotiations and, with that in mind, could one actively say that their participation was voluntary? This is a very muddy area in research; for example, take a hypothetical situation whereby a middle manager meets the researcher and agrees to an interview in comparison to the same manager who receives an email from the HR director/CEO directing them to participate. In both instances, the starting point for participation is entirely different and therefore the potential for bias raises its head.

Lesson Learned

It is always best to check and double-check participants before and during interviews, ask for background information from HR etc. and confirm this in the interview and/or ask a third party to confirm who the participants are. It must be stated that suspicions were raised when at a managerial meeting it almost felt as if the answer was a starting point and the role of the researcher was to cheerlead all the way to the predetermined answer. Essentially the thing to understand is that people have different motives that can have a massive influence on what happens. The old adage applies: if it looks or sounds too good to be true, then it probably is.

WHEN INVOLVEMENT BECOMES INTERFERENCE

Projecting a positive slant can be a priority for an organisation; sometimes, in extreme cases, the level of involvement can actually constitute interference.

Similarly, certain topics can be off limits and the elephant may be in the room but we are not permitted to acknowledge its presence. This is extremely difficult as a researcher's natural instinct is not only to acknowledge the elephant, but to question the elephant. Items such as industrial action, redundancies or scandals can be viewed as portraying an organisation in a less than favourable light and in a public relations sense organisations may not want it highlighted. However, sometimes what is off limits can extend beyond what is normally classified as front page news. There was one incident a number of years ago, where despite agreeing to a human resources study, the HR manager wanted questions on work–life balance to be removed as the manager did not want to give the employees 'notions'. Maintaining the integrity of the research can be problematic in such instances. Interference can also take the form of the over-eager (or possibly sinister) manager who shadows the researcher. One's sense of awareness is always raised when a manager will not let the researcher out of their sight. Another occasion was when the researcher was briefed and debriefed before and after focus groups that clearly showed a sense of paranoia of the manager in question who was literally anxious as to what the employees were saying in a confidential interview. The same manager actually walked us into the office of each interviewee and then set about basically watering plants as an attempt to stay in the room to the point whereby it was bordering on comical. In such instances, there was a sense of wearing a cow bell whereby everyone knows you are coming and potentially act accordingly. It actually turned out that the manager in question was paranoid and was of the opinion that the researcher was there to spy on *his* work. In the same organisation, the simple act of requesting to sit in the staff room for no particular reason, bar to interact with employees, caused absolute consternation for the same manager.

Lessons Learned

What was learned in such instances is that the merits of what one is researching may not be the same as why someone participates in the research. The researcher should always be cognisant of this fact. People naturally have their own agenda and generally will not do anything to compromise their own situation or reputation. It is when reservation turns to smoke and mirrors that issues can arise and the research can then become compromised.

READJUSTING RESEARCH INSTRUMENTS WHILE ALSO KEEPING RESEARCH CRITERIA ON TRACK

As previously stated, organisations usually have little regard for previously validated scales and possibly even less for reverse or negatively worded questions. This can become extremely problematic whereby management refuse to allow a reverse worded question in a survey, for example: 'I do not receive the necessary support to do my job properly.' In certain contexts, positivity takes priority over reality in terms of survey design and organisation, or at least some managers are more concerned with a sterile '85 per cent of our staff are happy' rather than actually delving deeper into reasoning and reality. This is not only confined to quantitative research, it also happens in qualitative research. In qualitative research, management too can veto certain questions; one instance highlights this point whereby a manager said, 'Don't ask that, we are not great at that, ask this … instead.' This bending approach happens frequently when signing off on qualitative research schedules. It becomes more serious in relation to tampering with previously validated survey questions.

Readjusting takes on a whole new meaning in certain contexts or high-power distance cultures where everything is sanitised by the organisation and above all else management and leadership is required to be seen in a positive light, that is, 'our beloved leader'-type research. In some senses, it's almost like everything ought to be seen through an organisational filter/lens where academic research credibility is irrelevant and the researcher is almost viewed as a journalist with the sole purpose of 'happy clapping' or projecting the organisation or certain people in a positive light. In a qualitative sense, in certain cultures interviews can become futile and projecting oneself in a positive light in the hope that such information is then passed on to superiors can become commonplace. Regardless of the adjustments required in some situations, it is always best to use multiple sources to answer a specific research questions as this can sometimes provide interesting insights into what is actually happening. Drawing on one particular example, using a qualitative focus group to interpret results of a survey led to a realisation that the demarcations in the survey were seriously flawed and did not reflect organisational reality. Therefore, what the survey addressed and what the participants interpreted were completely different. This meant having to change tack on the spot and return to the research questions to find if there was any qualitative support for what the research was trying to achieve. In terms of keeping the research on track, such an approach led to completely different but more interesting findings. The actual findings and resultant conclusion to that particular research would have been completely different had only the quantitative approach being employed.

Lessons Learned

Readjusting instruments to reflect organisational reality or organisational pressure is problematic on a number of levels. Firstly, the integrity of the research can be compromised, and, secondly the possibility of publishing the finished work can run into all sorts of difficulties. While organisations may care little for validation, journal editors certainly do. It is well worth the fight to retain as much previously validated work as possible as it is too easy to compromise in the heat of the moment in the quest for access. Sound reasoning at the start can alleviate many problems later on; unfortunately, most of us learn this the hard way. Overall in case research one has to balance a degree of rigidity with fluidity as situations change; too much of either can seriously compromise the research.

REFERENCES

Baxter, P. and Jack, S. (2008). 'Qualitative case study methodology: study design and implementation for novice researchers'. *The Qualitative Report*, *13*(4), 544–59.

Dundon, T. and Ryan, P. (2010). 'Interviewing reluctant respondents: strikes, henchmen, and Gaelic games'. *Organizational Research Methods*, *13*(3), 562–81.

Flyvbjerg, B. (2006). 'Five misunderstandings about case-study research'. *Qualitative Inquiry*, *12*(2), 219–45.

Kitzinger, J. (1994). 'The methodology of focus groups: the importance of interaction between research participants'. *Sociology of Health & Illness*, *16*(1), 103–21.

Leonard-Barton, D. (1990). 'A dual methodology for case studies: synergistic use of a longitudinal single site with replicated multiple sites'. *Organization science*, *1*(3), 248–66.

McDonald, P., Townsend, K. and Waterhouse, J. (2009). 'Gaining agreement does not mean gaining access: the complexities of supported research', in K. Townsend and J. Burgess (eds). *Method in the Madness: Research Stories You Won't Find in a Textbook*. Oxford: Chandos Publishing, pp. 119–33.

Saunders, M., Lewis, P. and Thornhill, A. (2016). *Research Methods for Business Students* (7th edn). Harlow: Pearson.

Stake, R.E. (1995). *The Art of Case Study Research*. Thousand Oaks, CA: Sage.

13. Is a pilot necessary?

Polly Black

Pilots are essential – that is the valuable lesson I learned. Why? Because there is always something you have not foreseen that will derail or weaken your research if you don't test the approach ahead of time. It is OK to have a derailed pilot – indeed it can be advantageous. It is not OK to have your main study derailed!

In my case, I was thinking of using qualitative interviews. I learned three big lessons from doing the pilot study.

First, remain in listening mode; resist the temptation to engage in the conversation. I thought I knew how to conduct interviews, having done a number of them and having watched others doing them behind a one-way mirror more times than I could count. However, listening to the pilot interview transcripts, I saw that often the key phrases were in my words as I checked for understanding. Thus, what I had on the tape was the participant agreeing with me on the summary, not the key data summarized in the participant's own words. I addressed this in future interviews by asking the participants instead to summarize their thoughts to capture their main point(s) for me.

Second, use the findings and material from your pilot to strengthen your main study. I was doing exploratory interviews and therefore was using a relatively unstructured approach. However, I found that several of the participants had difficulty articulating their thoughts in such an unstructured format. This meant I needed to think of an alternative way to get to the information I needed. I therefore used some of the data collected in the pilot to develop plausible examples as vignettes for participants to react to. This was very helpful in opening up the conversation. Participants said the vignettes were very realistic. This meant that the participants could easily relate and this allowed the conversation to flow naturally while ensuring discussion of the specific areas of interest to me.

Third, use the pilot to test for weaknesses in your overall research design. In my case, I had too narrow a target population. From the literature, I had decided on a target population that I thought would be an intense sample, but the pilot data made me realize that this target population was too narrow and I was not getting the full story. Without the pilot I would not have seen this weakness in the research until later, and that would have added both time and cost to the research.

I am converted! I now know first hand that pilots are invaluable. I will never undertake a piece of research without doing a pilot first.

14. Access confirmed?

Wojciech Marek Kwiatkowski

My PhD research project, which examined the delivery of knowledge-intensive business services highlighting the subjective and social qualities of knowledge, utilised an interpretivist case study research strategy. Concerned with depth of understanding rather than theory-building, I sought to collect all data from a single organisation. I was fortunate to get in touch with an operations manager of a suitable organisation months before I was ready for fieldwork. Although my newly acquainted gatekeeper lacked the authority to grant access himself, he seemed convinced he should be able to persuade the managing director to let me in.

Intending to begin data collection in July 2016, I contacted the operations manager in June and was provided with the email address of the managing director. I reminded my gatekeeper I was waiting for a reply every fortnight. In August he told me he did not think there was anything he could do. I had no reason to question his intentions. It seemed that he had simply overestimated his influence. Perhaps I was somewhat naive in thinking I had access before actually getting my foot in the door of the organisation, before obtaining formal, virtually irrevocable approval and conducting the first interview.

Finding a replacement organisation was a laborious and debilitating process defined by repeating a script over the phone, generic mailboxes and false assurances that someone would get back to me. As time passed and pressure mounted, I was increasingly frequently slipping in and out of a defeatist attitude. I do not think I would have persevered if it was not for the support and advice of my most-trusted colleagues. I finally secured access in December 2016, meaning I had my first interview and not simply assurances of future interviews.

My experience serves as a warning about the precarious nature of access. It is a caution that although it might easily appear as having been secured, it might eventually slip through the fingers of the qualitative researcher, putting his or her world in turmoil. Restoring balance can be difficult. Therefore, I would advise against locking other people out and making it a personal failure.

15. So, I guess we're probably finished then

Keith Townsend

The old adage that one should 'never give up' was clearly not thrust in to the popular lexicon by a qualitative researcher. Sometimes you have to know when it's time to give up.

This is relevant not only for the number of interviews you might complete, but also when you know you are just not going to get quality data from an interviewee.

Throughout 2011 I was involved in a research project that looked at a range of HRM topics in multiple workplaces. I had completed more than a hundred interviews across five different organisations when the next interviewee (let's name her Jenny) entered the room to meet with me.

I was as charming and welcoming as possible and I tried all the tricks of engendering rapport that I'd learnt through my life and research career.

For 11 minutes the conversation was one-sided. My side. Jenny's responses were mostly monosyllabic, occasionally grunts, and all delivered by a person whose body language made it very clear that she would rather be anywhere but in that room with me.

If this were in the first 10–20 interviews of the project then I probably would have persevered, worked harder to find middle ground and to develop rapport further, but Jenny was the most active 'non-participant' I'd met in over ten years and hundreds of interviews. So after 11 minutes I gave up and said, 'So I guess we're probably finished then.' To which Jenny replied, 'I guess so.' Please note that it was a statement, not a question!

Our project had reached the point of data saturation long ago, and we were looking at more organisations for some level of generalisation. But Jenny wasn't willing to contribute and I wasn't willing to waste any more time trying. It's only with experience though that one can recognise the point where different tacks or different strategies are better than giving up. Sometimes you just have to give up.

Thank you Jenny; you may have contributed little to our project, but you have contributed much more to my understanding of qualitative research methods.

16. Your incentives are too lucrative: caution in rewarding interview participants

Catheryn Khoo

As a new researcher, I had heard many stories in the lunch room and at research seminars about the difficulties of gaining access to participants. The stories included those of doctoral students whose theses could not be completed on time because they could not find people to interview, and stories like these worried me at a time when I was dependent on a time-bound scholarship. I was determined that I was not going to be held back by my participants, or lack thereof.

I started planning months prior to data collection. I had needed to follow homebuyers from when they first begin to look for a house to the point when they sign the final Sale and Purchase Agreement, so I knew I could be following some people for months or even, possibly, years. Debates on whether or not the promises of incentives will motivate research participants to be involved remain unresolved (see for example: Frick et al., 1999; Perez et al., 2013), hence my plan was to make it very attractive for people to want to participate in my project. Rapport development strategies discussed in qualitative research methods literature were put into practice as I attempted to convince local businesses to help with my access to participants. I persuaded a mortgage broker and a few real estate agents to help me recruit potential homebuyers. I convinced businesses to throw in vouchers for free carpet underlay for the participants' new home, a free colour consultation for any interior decorating work they might want to undertake, and access to two hours of electrical or plumbing work. I also had a law firm donate a $600 home transfer package as a prize draw that my participants would be eligible to win after their interviews with me. As it turned out, I had gone overboard.

My research project, as one can imagine, sailed through without any trouble with participant access. To make a long story short, I completed my PhD ahead of time, and was called into my viva. I was somewhat confident, until one of the examiners asked me about the impact of the participants' incentives on the trustworthiness of my data. 'Excuse me?' I had said, as a strategy to buy me two more seconds of thinking time, to which he replied, 'Did it ever cross your mind that your data might be biased because your respondents only participated in your research because of the incentives?' Of course it had not. And neither had it occurred to any of my three supervisors. In my reply, however, I explained to the panel that the winner of the home transfer package did not even claim her prize despite my repeated reminders through emails and phone messages. This implied that the respondents were genuinely motivated to share their stories for my research. The panel was appeased by my response.

I have learned since then not to give my respondents anything more than $20 worth of vouchers – one of those things you will never pick up from a research methods book, except for this one of course.

REFERENCES

Frick, A., Bächtiger, M.T. and Reips, U.D. (1999). 'Financial incentives, personal information and drop-out rate in online studies', *Dimensions of Internet Science*, Lengerich: Pabst Science, pp. 209–19.

Perez, D.F., Nie, J.X., Ardern, C.I., Radhu, N. and Ritvo, P. (2013). 'Impact of participant incentives and direct and snowball sampling on survey response rate in an ethnically diverse community: results from a pilot study of physical activity and the built environment', *Journal of Immigrant and Minority Health*, 15(1), 207–14.

17. Sales skills for researchers

Colin Hughes

A number of years ago I set out to gain access to several ICT multinational firms to collect data using semi-structured interviews. I had good contacts in a lot of organisations so I assumed that access wouldn't be an issue. How wrong I was! I learned five key lessons which, with my background in sales, I should already have known. These could be viewed as lessons relating to the sales skills that researchers need to gain access (to interviewees) – in other words: developing an effective sales process, selling the benefits of the research and addressing any concerns or perceived risk that might be present.

LESSON 1: THE IMPORTANCE OF QUALIFYING YOUR PROSPECTS/RESEARCH PARTICIPANTS

As I was hoping to finalise participant organisations I hit a major stumbling block. I was looking to conduct research into virtual sales teams, which have managers and employees based in different locations; this is what sales professionals would refer to as my 'sweet spot'. I had first-hand knowledge of many organisations who were utilising virtual sales teams and I assumed, incorrectly, that most global organisations were operating the same model. However, I soon realised that some organisations had recently decided to co-locate all of their sales managers and employees. While they were willing to participate, they couldn't offer me the right kind of access. I had not 'qualified' the leads, as one would do in an effective sales process. Once I was aware of this issue, I saved a lot of time in subsequent dealings with organisations. Instead of arranging meetings, I scheduled phone calls and asked a small number of qualifying questions up-front. This way, I could ensure that the fit was right for me as well as for the organisation.

LESSON 2: SEEK PERMISSION FOR ACCESS FROM THE 'REAL' DECISION MAKERS

In another organisation I was assured that access would not be an issue. The person, who was quite senior, had no idea that their colleagues in other parts of the business would object so strongly. In this instance, others in the organisation were afraid that the findings would not reflect positively on them. Maybe if I had spoken to the 'real' decision makers earlier in the process, I could have built relationships and gained access. It is always worth asking one or both of the following questions: 'What is the decision-making process in your company to get this approved?' or 'Is there anyone else in the organisation that needs to approve this research and if so can we engage them as soon as possible?'

LESSON 3: COMMUNICATE THE VALUE OF YOUR RESEARCH FOR THE ORGANISATION

Customer Value Proposition (CVP) (Anderson, Narus and Van Rossum, 2006) is a common term used by sales professionals. Researchers too must communicate the value of their research and link this to the organisations' challenges or needs. At first, I was finding it a little difficult to connect the two so I developed a one-page explanation outlining the common issues faced by virtual teams (which were likely common to the organisations I spoke with) and highlighting how my research could help to resolve such issues.

LESSON 4: BUILD TRUST WITH DECISION MAKERS

As there are certain risks associated with granting access, organisations need to be able to trust researchers. Their decision to trust is based largely on perceptions of trustworthiness related to the researcher's ability, benevolence and integrity (Mayer et al., 1995). I needed to ensure I was coming across as trustworthy by highlighting my track record as a researcher and scholar and the fact that the research would be of a high standard (ability), by assuring the organisation that I would protect the organisation and participants throughout the research, for example, confidentiality or anonymity (benevolence) and lastly, by convincing the organisation of my honesty and character (integrity). As such, I had to ensure that any information I provided to the organisation or which was discoverable online (e.g. LinkedIn) communicated my trustworthiness. I also decided to record a short video which explained my research in a very accessible manner. This proved to be very effective as a number of participants later told me that I came across as someone who was professional and trustworthy in the video and that this motivated them to participate.

LESSON 5: ALWAYS AGREE THE NEXT STEPS AT THE END OF EACH MEETING

My first request for access was made to an organisation with whom I had significant work dealings. While there was an open door and people were interested in the research, they were also very busy. I didn't set any firm dates for follow-up as I was busy at work and wasn't quite ready to conduct the research. However, after three months had elapsed my contact left the organisation before agreeing my access with colleagues, which meant I had to start again from the beginning. I learned that, similar to an effective sales process, it is essential to confirm the next steps (with agreed dates) at the end of each meeting. At least that way the contact person has a deadline to work towards and you can keep the research on track or find out early if there are problems with access.

CONCLUDING THOUGHTS

The parallels between agreeing research access and making a sale are quite strong. Researchers can benefit from adopting the characteristics of effective sales people, who are process driven, good communicators and able to reflect on their experience (especially setbacks) to enhance their future effectiveness.

REFERENCES

Anderson, J.C., Narus, J.A and Van Rossum, W. (2006). Customer Value Propositions in business markets. *Harvard Business Review*, *84*(3), 90–9.
Mayer, R.C., Davis, J.H. and Schoorman, F.D. (1995). An integrative model of organizational trust. *Academy of Management Review*, *20*(3), 709–34.

18. Being flexible in interviews: make sure that you account for power imbalance

Qian Yi Lee

Like all PhD candidates going through the adventure of qualitative interviews, I struggled with a multitude of issues (yes, the consent forms need to be signed; yes, all information will be de-identified and anonymous). I was lucky enough to have been prepared by my supervisors and peers on almost everything that could go wrong but there was still one hiccup that might have turned out differently had I been ready to handle it.

I undertook a total of 56 interviews across two organisations; in the 56th and last interview with the most senior manager of the second organisation, a unique opportunity was presented to me. Before this, I had faced occasions where interviews with this manager had to be postponed due to work issues that had cropped up at the last minute. On one of those occasions, she offered me her deputy to be interviewed instead of her, and like all good PhD candidates I would never say no to extra interviewees, so I told her I would like to be able to speak to them both on separate occasions if possible. The manager said she would get back to me. A few days later, I was able to secure a slot for her interview but no word on her deputy so I thought that was an opportunity missed although I was confident with the volume and quality of data I had already collected.

On the day of the interview, I was ushered into the room with the manager inviting me to take a seat, when she said, 'Oh! If you don't mind, my deputy would be joining us.' I had a split second to make a decision and at that point in time I felt that saying yes was the only way to go. This was because I needed some data from the deputy and if I said no, I might have been unable to arrange another time to speak to the deputy, or worse, I might have even lost both participants. I was leaving the country in a couple days so it wasn't as if I could make another convenient time.

Throughout the interview process I tried to tweak the questions that I had prepared for one-to-one interviews to include both participants but it only took the first question for me to realise that the power was skewed towards the more senior participant. The deputy was extremely reserved and seemed to spend most of her time there taking notes or nodding silently. Thankfully, she did make contributions at certain junctures, even though the bulk of her responses were mainly backing up her boss's statements or filling in the gaps that her boss may have missed. I don't believe that she was scared of her boss per se, but it seemed that she was unlikely to contradict what her superior had to say. So the deputy would allow the manager to speak first and if she had anything to add she would do it after.

Had I been notified beforehand, I might have insisted on conducting the interviews separately or, alternatively, I would have prepared other questions that would allow participation from both parties. Alas, not everything in research can be planned for. You think you have it all planned out, but there is always something that happens that you are not fully equipped to handle. So, when collecting data in the workplace, be prepared and ready for whatever could be thrown at you to make the best out of what you have. And remember, in unusual situations it would be beneficial to make additional field notes to help you during the analysis stage.

PART III

Getting it together

19. What precisely do you mean? Interpreting qualitative data

Rebecca Loudoun and Keith Townsend

INTRODUCTION

There is an old joke about a man who despairs about a tarnished reputation after 'just one' indiscretion with a goat – I'm sure each country has its own version of the joke and if you are unfamiliar and wish to acquaint yourself with such humour then a quick Google search will allay your curiosities. Without going too far into the premise of the joke, it is an anecdote that demonstrates that people can interpret the same activity in different ways. Transformed into the qualitative data setting, this story is an important one about how one individual's perspective can be substantially different from others in the interpretation of interview questions and how this might impact data analysis. While qualitative research is valuable for answering the 'how, rather than how many' questions and for understanding the perspective of those people being studied, deliberate strategies need to be used to evaluate the interpretation of meaning from the swathes of qualitative data that can be collected in a research project.

According to Miles, some four decades ago 'qualitative data tend to overload the research badly at almost every point: the sheer range of phenomena to be observed, the recorded volume of notes; the time required for write up, coding, and analysis can all be overwhelming' (1979, p. 590). Computer-based technology and data analysis software can be of great assistance; however, the qualitative researcher still has to be able to establish the validity and credibility of the data collected and interpretations and findings arising from these data. Researchers must also be cognisant of the reality that interviewees might have differing interpretations of the interviewer's, or interviewers' research protocol. Interpretation is ok, but understanding precisely what interview participants mean by their words is important.

This chapter reports on the experience of a baseline data collection designed to establish an 'anchor' to compare qualitative data over three time periods. We were well aware prior to any data collection that this project would face challenges eliciting information as the organisation was beset by low morale and low levels of trust in management. As a means to overcome these difficulties, we implemented a method of inquiry that is rarely used in workplace research. The interview schedule involved 'word association'; a technique that has been used in psychology for a century and in market research for decades. This research method, however, while providing the authors with a means of placing a measurement on the 'time one' experience of the employees, was not without its problems. For example, participant interpretation of the questions and instructions were varied, and furthermore, when it came time for the researchers to code the data, many responses proved complex and ambiguous. Aligning with the theme of this volume, this chapter does not have a research question as such, rather, it tells a story of an experiment in data collection that became more complicated than we had anticipated. We also describe and consider how successful our strategies were to get the project back on track.

The value of qualitative research has been questioned in some circles recently, however, the value of this research over time is undeniable (Cassell and Symon, 2007). Linking events and meanings during the construction of a social reality is a key goal of qualitative research (Van Maanen, 2011, p. xxi). Just as there are a variety of research analysis techniques, researchers must also be aware that there is the danger related to the various possible 'interpretations' of their data. Alvesson (2011) argues that the complexity and uncertainty of the research practice and meaning taken from interviews is contestable. It is unreasonable to expect then that all interviewees will interpret questions the same way.

The Word Association Technique

Psychologists have used word association tests for more than 100 years; it is considered one type of 'projective technique' where participants are given a stimulus and asked for an immediate response (Lykke Nielsen and Ingwersen, 1999). The method emphasises immediacy and limits the participants' capacity to formulate what might be deemed an 'appropriate' response in their context. Although the technique can be quite time consuming, it can hold benefits as well depending on the research questions under investigation. Industrial relations researchers tend to be less interested in the personalities of research participants, instead focusing more on their *experiences*. Hence, it seemed like this approach might pay dividends when investigating matters in an organisation that were known to have problems with employee morale, trust and culture.

DATA COLLECTION APPROACH

The research project for which these data were collected is an ongoing project designed to measure change in one division of an Australian public sector organisation with approximately 2000 employees. Six executive-level, head-office managers were interviewed and 52 additional interviews with staff at all levels of the organisation were conducted across five of the 15 worksites. This number of interviews fits within the upper end of the zone presented by Saunders and Townsend (2016) as appropriate for single sector research projects. At each worksite a vertical and horizontal representation of the workforce were interviewed. While the employees were randomly selected from the roster and invited to participate in the interviews, the site managers of each workplace were not randomly invited as there was only one at each site.

Longitudinal qualitative studies are somewhat rare in Human Resource Management (HRM) research, so the researchers turned to different disciplines for ideas on data collection methods. This seemed a reasonable course of action as researchers regularly draw from different disciplines for theory – why not methodology?

The interviews began with a series of introductory questions aimed at rapport building where the interviewers would ask about the interviewees' background and share overlapping experiences. Given the low levels of trust in this organisation, the rapport-building stage was particularly important and was often longer than would typically be the case. Once this stage was completed an explanation of the remaining interview process was provided along the following lines: *There will be a handful of questions and I will ask you for many of them to give the first three words that spring in to your mind. Kind of like a word association thing, for example, if I was to say 'sky' you might say 'blue', 'cloud' and 'grey'. There's no right or wrong answers here, just throw out the first three words that come in to your head.*

It was following this outline that the interview generally began. Three examples of interview questions within the protocol are as follows:

1. When you think about the relationship between the union and management at this workplace, what are the first three words that come to mind?
2. When you think about the future of your organisation, what do you think are the three key issues facing your organisation?
3. When you think about the person who is your immediate line manager, what are the first three words that spring to mind?

After documenting these responses on a worksheet, the researchers then progressed to delve into the individuals' answers to gain a deeper understanding of the respondent's views on the matter. This initial stage of data analysis involved the researchers discussing their findings between interviews, and then again at the completion of the interviews each day. This process allowed developing themes to be further investigated at the next data collection point, which in this case was within a day or two.

Following the interviews keywords provided were transferred to an Excel spreadsheet and coded using a colour. For example, positive descriptive words were highlighted green; negative descriptors were highlighted red; neutral words were highlighted yellow; and words that did not seem to fit this initial allocation were highlighted grey.

As we had six word association questions with three response words to each and 52 participants (6 x 3 x 52) = almost 1000 data points needed coding for each of the three time periods. We naively thought we would eventually transform our words to colour coding, and then to numerical data for quantitative analysis, which seemed to make a great deal of sense to us until we started the second stage of the data analysis.

DISCUSSION

One of the first identifiable problems with this approach was the diverse literacy skills of the workforce. Simply put, some employees could not generate three separate words to explain what they wanted to say. This meant that our optimistic expectation of having three responses from each participant was not met.

Other interviewees provided statements or monologues instead of three words as requested. They found it difficult, and sometimes impossible, to narrow this down to only these separate words. We drew on a number of plan Bs to deal with this problem. One strategy was to select keywords for the participant and check with them if they were a fair representation of what they were saying. This was successful most of the time but there was still the risk of the researcher adding their interpretation of the meaning of the interviewees' thoughts rather than the participant still having their own spontaneous voice.

An example of this potential for misinterpretation occurred when one participant was asked about the *relationship* between the union and the management at their workplace. We naively expected the employee to use words that described 'the relationship'. However the participant responded: 'well, I reckon that staff representatives are too cosy with the union here, but I'm not sure of a word that you could use for that.'

In this instance, determining one word to represent this view was beyond the comprehension skills of the individual; we felt the word 'cosy' did not adequately represent the views of the employee and would lead to misinterpretation during the analysis phase. 'Cosy' can be interpreted as warm, gentle and positive, but just like the individuals in movies and jokes who faced different views over their various one-off indiscretions, there are multiple ways to interpret 'cosy' under these contextual circumstances. If we were to return to the dataset at time two and just see the word 'cosy' without the context around it, that might conjure warm, positive thoughts, not the negative connotations that the employee was trying to convey.

Another strategy used was to record a short phrase rather than keywords. This was the approach taken in the example of 'cosy' above. The downside of using this approach was that as researchers we would lose (to some extent) the single thing that the word association method was most revered for – the immediacy of thought as opposed to the formulation of a response that seemed appropriate in the context.

Interpretation of events and words is essential for those of us who perform qualitative research. We do not measure volume as such, nor do we measure numerical associations, we interpret meaning. Context is often an important part of understanding research – the context of a particular team working in an organisation, the context of a particular industry sector, the context of a particular organisation operating within multiple national regulatory regimes for example. However, the context of individual quotes becomes important for researchers and the end users of our research as well. This means that researchers should aim to avoid 'cherry picking' the quotes that best illuminate their research agenda, but use those quotes that illuminate their research agenda within the context of the quote provided. This reminds us of a research project where an inexperienced researcher came to our team meeting with enthusiasm about an idea for an article. The research team enquired and thought yes, indeed this was a good idea. So how much data did we have to support this? Well, our inexperienced enthusiast told us it was just really from one interview. Okay, but it was a key theme from this interview? Not really explained the inexperienced enthusiast; it was one quote, in one interview. Running the risk of mixing metaphors, that 'cherry picking' was veering into the 'just one goat' territory.

Another example of this interpretation problem is a respondent who answered the same question about relationships between union and management with the word, 'rabble'. The respondent was very quick with this word and said it with great enthusiasm; we presumed it was meant as a description of a poor relationship. 'Rabble' after all means disorderly, easily interpreted as negative. When pressed on what he meant by rabble, the respondent went on to explain that in his view, the union was such a 'rabble' and he thought it was wonderful to see. He liked the fact that his union appeared slightly disorganised, but excitable on issues. For this employee, 'rabble' should not be coded red as a negative word, but green as something positive.

The question about management–union relationships illustrates the third problem we found with interpretation. Some participants did not focus on the 'relationship' between union and management at all. Where we were expecting words to describe the relationship along the lines of 'mistrustful', 'positive', 'adversarial' – all of which are easy to code – instead we were given words to describe one party in the relationship such as 'good union reps'.

We initially considered these responses unhelpful for the research and put our heads together to try and think of a way to better phrase the question to ensure participants focused on the relationship rather than the parties. However, after some discussion we decided that this type of comment was useful after all. Although it was beyond the dichotomous 'positive/negative' coding, ultimately phrases like this were worthwhile because they could be coded as 'positive towards union' and hence, comparable with data collected at time two and time three.

In combination, the strategies used to address these problems of interpretation resulted in us having multiple categories for each question; rather than the expected three (positive, negative, neutral) we ended up with seven categories. In the example of the relationship question discussed here our coding ended up as follows:

- Generally positive
- Generally negative
- Neutral
- Positive towards union
- Negative towards union
- Positive towards management
- Negative towards management

REFLECTIONS

It is not unusual when using a new research method for the first time to face developmental problems. This was certainly the case for us with the word association technique. It was clear that we were unable to use our word association data as we had originally hoped. Virtually all of the problems encountered with the approach centred around interpretation: participants interpreting the questions differently to how they were intended; participants providing answers that didn't fit the format requested and thus required the researchers to convert their response to the one-word format; researchers trying to ensure ambiguous words provided by participants were coded in such a way they didn't lead to misinterpretation in the future.

However, there were many positive aspects of this data collection approach as well. For example, the method resulted in a large bank of data from 52 interviews for each of the three time points coded in a relatively user-friendly format. This helped with the often time-consuming task with qualitative data of theme identification. We were able to identify a high level of consistency in themes quite quickly. Words could be transformed into numerical data and along with this came the corresponding strength of numerical values. The quotes garnered through interviews were more than enough to flesh out the data and provide the 'lived' example to the themes. Our capacity to provide the organisation a report with some measureable level of satisfaction or dissatisfaction was difficult, but we were able to provide the organisation with some tangible point to compare their results following forthcoming interventions.

Despite these benefits we have not been able to use these data in any scholarly management journal articles, primarily because we have not been able to come up with a way to fit our 'three words' data with appropriate theories. Perhaps that's just our failing, but it may also suggest the approach is in need of further development before it can be useful to both an academic audience and an industry audience. By adapting our analysis to be more inclusive of context, we provided a more nuanced understanding of how employees feel about various aspects of their working experience. There is no doubt this was attractive for the partnering organisation as it allowed us to provide a more interesting and detailed report of the intervention under investigation. The strategies employed to overcome problems with interpretation mean that the possibility of developing this approach further for future studies could yield rewards for researchers and their partnering organisations. We came to the end of the project, looked at each other and said, 'just one word association technique' but we do not hold out hope that this will become an often-used phrase of despair!

LESSONS

- By all means experiment with data collection techniques on projects that allow experimentation – on your PhD, you need to either stick to tried and true approaches or back up your methods with a very convincing argument about why you've taken your particular approach and the specific benefits of that approach.
- Maintain the importance of context in qualitative research, but do not let context overtake your key role – understanding the phenomena under investigation.
- Trying to quantify the qualitative can lead to the worst of both worlds, but sometimes it can be quite useful. Practitioners often want different things to academics, so don't be afraid to offer practitioners something that might not get past the conservative review process of top journals, but might offer the practitioners some interesting insights.

REFERENCES

Alvesson, M. (2011) *Interpreting Interviews*. London: Sage.
Cassell, C. and Symon, G. (2007) *Essential Guide to Qualitative Methods in Organisational Research*. London: Sage.
Lykke Nielsen, M. and Ingwersen, P. (1999) 'The Word Association Methodology: a gateway to work-task based retrieval', MIRA '99 Conference, Glasgow. http://bcs .org/upload/pdf/ewic_mi99_paper6.pdf.
Miles, M. (1979) 'Qualitative data as an attractive nuisance: the problem of analysis', *Administrative Science Quarterly*, 24, 590–601.
Saunders, M.N.K. and Townsend, K. (2016) 'How many participants are sufficient? An analysis of research articles using qualitative interviews in highly regarded organization and workplace journals', *British Journal of Management*, 27, 836–52.
Van Maanen, J. (2011). *Tales of the Field: On Writing Ethnography* (2nd Edition). Chicago, IL: University of Chicago Press.

20. Analysing quantitative data

Sameer Qaiyum and Catherine L. Wang

Catherine: Quantitative research has numbers, statistics, but also some element of art to it. People and organisations that we study are not just objects; they have feelings, emotions, and characters. A good quantitative research design must capture the intricacies of people and organisations, in choosing samples, developing research instruments, putting in place measures to ensure robustness, and executing the research. A too simplistic research model (say simply testing 'one variable just influences one other variable') cannot reveal true relationships between variables in a complex world or business system, as such relationships are often confounded by other intervening variables. I like to think that quantitative research is a balance between science and art, in order to seek truth as close to the reality as possible. In this chapter, Sameer (who was my doctoral student) and I discuss his experience of designing his doctoral research, screening data, and analysing data.

Sameer: I agree with you, Catherine. When I designed my research, I followed your advice and included the most important mediating and moderating variables that may influence the relationships based on the literature review. My research focused on how firms can implement strategy processes to develop organisational capabilities that subsequently improve firm performance. I developed three research models to examine: (1) the influence of strategy processes on firm performance: (2) the mediating effects of different organisational capabilities in the relationships between strategy processes and firm performance; and (3) the moderating effects of environmental dynamism and other factors on the above relationships. I then used questionnaires to collect data from 260 Indian high-tech firms, plus another 26 second questionnaires from 10 per cent of these sample firms. The 26 second questionnaires were collected to test common method bias, as you advised. I took the issue of common method bias very seriously, and really benefited from thinking about it at the research design stage.

Catherine: That is right, Sameer. As I tell my students, a strong quantitative study requires a great deal of insights into theory, methods, and reality. A robust quantitative study starts from the research design. To achieve this, when I design a study, I use certain techniques (what we call procedural methods) to optimise the validity, reliability, and generalisability of the study. For example, I have often been asked by journal reviewers about the common method bias in my data (and indeed, as a reviewer, I have also asked many authors about it!). If a common method variance is high, the strength of a significant relationship (between two variables) could have been inflated by using a single method or a single respondent. This is why common method bias can be a concern. There are several ways to deal with this, for example, by gathering objective data (such as financial data) that have been audited and published in the public domain, and/or by collecting data from more than one respondent about the same issue or the same organisation, in order to corroborate data. In your case, Sameer, we discussed the different options. You mentioned that reliable objective data from Indian high-tech firms were rarely available, so you decided to collect the second responses. Now, let's talk about how you use statistical methods to screen data to ensure their validity and reliability.

Sameer: I have a mathematical background (as part of my first degree in engineering). I never felt intimidated by quantitative methods, but again I never thought that I would encounter so many challenges when I started data analysis. Although simple tests like non-response bias using ANOVA and common method bias using Harman's one-factor test (Podsakoff and Organ, 1986) were easy to grasp by just reading the SPSS Manual, the first hurdle arose when you suggested that I use Structural Equation Modeling (SEM), a more stringent test of common method bias (Podsakoff et al., 2003). This was a challenge to me, as there were only a few very technical articles that described the test, and no textbooks or Internet resources available at the time. Having gone through these articles, I reverse engineered how to do it by painstakingly dissecting the diagrams that described the test. After much trial and error, I was able to conduct the test. This boosted my confidence, and momentarily I thought I had conquered data analysis. Little did I know my roller coaster journey of data analysis had just started.

Catherine: I believe that using SEM to test common method bias was your first brush with SEM. You taught yourself and used it correctly. Regarding common method bias, there was a second issue that you faced: how to analyse whether the second respondent from each of the 26 firms (10 per cent of the sample) statistically corresponded in the same fashion as the first respondent in the same firm. Any statistical difference between the two respondents responding to the same question for the same firm can spell trouble, as it may raise concern about common method bias. What tests did you use?

Sameer: Once again, I was in the dark, as there were no textbooks on how to analyse the extent to which two respondents on the same issue within the same organisation converge, and even papers published in top journals only reported that they had conducted the analysis with no elaboration! After much learning and reverse engineering, I worked out how to use Microsoft Excel to calculate the inter-rater agreement between the two respondents (LeBreton and Senter, 2008) and the intraclass correlations to confirm that the two responses converged. To do this, I had to understand the mathematics behind those techniques, something which most of us doing quantitative analysis are surprisingly not used to.

Catherine: That sounds great, Sameer. I always think that, once data are screened, the most exciting phase of data analysis happens. This is when I test research hypotheses, and I do this with anticipation and trepidation. It's all comforting if my hypotheses, or at least some of them, are supported, and I can move on to write up my findings, and of course, research papers. But, there is always a but, what if many or even all of my hypotheses (in the worst case scenario) are not supported? What if I need to use some unfamiliar analytical techniques to try and resolve some of the problems? What if new software packages have to be used? Such surprises can throw us into complete darkness – hopefully momentarily. My experience is that these surprises often lead to new ventures that often take me to new discovery and learning. Sometimes the rejected hypotheses tell us fascinating stories, if we can find out why. Sameer, you have these sorts of experiences in the ups and downs in your data analysis, don't you?

Sameer: Yes, I do. After data screening, I felt that half of the data analysis task had been done. However, I was wrong! Several impediments were waiting to reveal themselves as I moved to test the hypotheses in my first research model. The first of these impediments, or roadblocks as I like to call them, was how to test a mediation model (where an intervening variable acts as a mediator between two other variables). If I had followed Baron and Kenny's (1986) traditional approach to test mediating effects, I could have calculated regression coefficients using SPSS. However, Catherine, you suggested a more stringent test using covariance-based SEM (Preacher and Hayes, 2008). There were a number of software packages for performing SEM which could do this, and I decided to use AMOS for two reasons. First, my university had a licence for AMOS, as I did not want to pay for software from my limited funds. Second, there were plenty of textbooks and Internet resources on how to use AMOS. I taught myself AMOS and the theoretical underpinning of the covariance-based SEM. Learning the former was much easier than learning the latter. To learn AMOS, I read textbooks and articles, and also watched some great videos available on YouTube that succinctly described how to do analysis in AMOS. However, learning AMOS's theoretical underpinning, the maths behind it, was easier said than done. AMOS is like Windows, and its user-friendliness means that you do not necessarily need to learn the mathematics behind it. However, I wanted to. For me, it was important that I had at least a working knowledge of what I was doing and not just producing results by pushing a few buttons. I did learn some of the mathematics behind it, but by no means all of it. I did not have that much time during

	my doctoral study to indulge in such luxury as to master the mathematics of covariance-based SEM.
Catherine:	I remember very well how impressed I was at how quickly and accurately you grasped the covariance-based SEM. That also boosted my confidence in your ability to learn and use advanced statistical techniques, though your challenge did not stop there. Usually, mediation models have only one mediator variable, but your first research model had more than one mediators. How did you solve the problem?
Sameer:	Yes, mine was a multiple mediator mediation model that required even more advanced techniques. I kept on searching for an article that could put my misery to rest. In the end, I managed to find one (Siegfried and Ledermann, 2011), and after at least 30 readings of this article, I managed to decode this unique technique that is, for some strange reason, called phantom model technique. No wonder; I did feel like a phantom after learning the technique! To perform the technique, my working knowledge of the mathematics behind covariance-based SEM became very handy. I never realised that a stand I had taken earlier to learn some of the mathematics of covariance-based SEM out of principle would come to help me later on in such a fashion. However, it did.
Catherine:	Excellent, Sameer. You completed the analysis for your first research model. Let's talk about your two other research models that required the construction of a second-order construct. A second-order construct is a latent construct that is statistically created out of the first-order variables that are directly measured using questionnaires. Thus, second-order constructs are measured indirectly through a statistical construction done at the data analysis stage. Moreover, your second-order constructs were formative constructs (as opposed to reflective constructs). Formative second-order constructs cannot be analysed by covariance-based SEM. How did you go about the analysis?
Sameer:	This again sent me on a wild goose chase to find a suitable analytical technique. I then came to know about an alternative technique called PLS-SEM which can handle second-order formative constructs. PLS-SEM and covariance-based SEM shared some of the theoretical underpinnings. That meant that I could learn PLS-SEM quickly. To perform PLS-SEM, I also learned two rival software applications, SmartPLS and WrapPLS, making use of their trial versions as the licences were not available at my university. However, these trial versions came with either severe restrictions or expiry dates. By this time, I did not have funds to buy an individual licence, but I noticed that SmartPLS offered a free licence of the previous version of the software to individual researchers. Smart marketing technique I would say to get researchers hooked onto the software! I immediately jumped on this opportunity and secured a three-month licence. Even better, they still automatically send me a three-month licence after three months, even now. I again followed the trusted path of reading and re-reading seminal articles to understand SmartPLS and its underpinnings, and

watching YouTube videos to fine-tune my understanding of it. By this time, I had begun to use social media platforms as a learning tool. This proved very helpful to me as I started posting on forums such as those managed by academics and software developers and created valuable contacts online. I continue to use these contacts if I struggle with a particular analysis. Now that I have completed my PhD, as a guesture of giving something back and developing the academic community, I help budding researchers resolve their underlying issues online on these platforms.

Catherine: I knew that your eagerness and ability to learn is unbounded, and at that point I was also impressed how resourceful you are, Sameer! Now, let's talk more about your third research model. The research model and the ensuing hypotheses demanded that you demonstrate that the effect of one independent variable A on the dependent variable B (let's call it Path X) is greater than the influence of another independent variable D on the same dependent variable B (let's call it Path Y). Traditionally, researchers simply look at the regression coefficients of Paths X and Y, and whichever is greater is declared more powerful. You wanted to provide statistical evidence of the comparative strengths of the regression coefficients. What did you do?

Sameer: The problem I faced was again new with little details about it widely available. Although a new consensus is building among experts that simply looking at the regression coefficients is not enough, little knowledge exists on how to statistically prove one regression coefficient is stronger than the other. Solving this problem took me on a similar journey of discovery: reading and re-reading articles (e.g. Paternoster et al., 1998). Similar to the other challenges I had, there was a dearth of quality publications on the solution. Even when I found a solution, I realised that none of the software incorporated it. Thus, I was left with little option but to do all the complex calculations using Excel again. For the umpteenth time, I was finding how useful my decision was to learn the basic maths of what I was doing, rather than being satisfied with some software manuals. This made the learning of the complicated maths of statistically demonstrating Path X is greater than Path Y much easier. Ironically, I started with Excel and, after a detour of AMOS and SmartPLS, I am back to Excel.

Catherine: It was a few months' intensive learning and thorough data analysis, Sameer. Looking back at your experience, what lessons have you learned?

Sameer: Data analysis can be a messy business, and the only thing that kept me on track was perseverance and a knack for continuous learning. I have three key lessons from my learning journey:

1. *Never assume that you have learned all you need.* Every time I thought that I had learned what was needed to do the analysis, a new problem emerged from nowhere. After a while, I replaced the pretension of 'I know everything' with 'I know nothing.' This change in stand had a very positive effect on

keeping my research on track. I approached every analysis, small or big, with an attitude that I might need to learn something new.

2. *Think outside the box when it comes to new-to-the-world problems.* When I encountered new issues for which solutions are not widely available in my areas of research, I made contacts with experts on social media platforms. This proved extremely useful. These experts not only helped me with ideas on how to tackle the problem but also pointed out newly published articles in journals beyond my core areas of research, which might be otherwise very hard to find or take up a lot of time and energy to find.

3. *Learn some of the mathematical underpinnings of user-friendly software.* The user-friendliness of the statistical software might lead us to believe that we hardly need to comprehend the mathematical foundations of these techniques. However, my experience is that learning the theoretical underpinnings behind the techniques has proved extremely helpful. At times, we may need to do analysis that no software incorporates. At this stage, much time can be lost if we do not have a working knowledge of the mathematical underpinnings. Thus, the time we initially spend on understanding these mathematical underpinnings is worth it, and that can help us immensely to keep research on track at a later stage.

Catherine: Sameer, you did brilliantly in learning new analytical techniques and software packages along the way. You used them effectively to test your complex research models. However, I want to emphasise that every research project is different. As researchers we don't have to use very advanced analytical tools and software packages such as AMOS and SmartPLS. SPSS alone is sufficient to produce robust results that, together with a solid theory behind them and a sound research design, can push knowledge boundaries. Certainly, we shouldn't be put off by these advanced techniques, thinking that we cannot take on quantitative research. Even qualitative researchers can benefit from basic quantitative skills to enable the understanding of quantitative results in publications.

Like you Sameer, I was a doctoral student and went through a sharp learning curve. I also taught myself statistical techniques and software packages, with the guidance of my supervisor. A few books were life savers to me as a doctoral student, and I often recommend them to my students and researchers new to quantitative methods. Below, I list them as recommended reading.

REFERENCES

Baron, R.M. and Kenny, D.A. (1986). 'The moderator-mediator variable distinction in social psychological research: conceptual, strategic, and statistical considerations'. *Journal of Personality and Social Psychology*, *51*(6), 1173–82.

LeBreton, J.M. and Senter, J.L. (2008). 'Answers to 20 questions about interrater reliability and interrater agreement'. *Organizational Research Methods*, *11*, 815–54.

Siegfried, M. and Ledermann, T. (2011). 'Estimating, testing, and comparing specific effects in structural equation models: the phantom model approach'. *Psychological Methods*, *16*(1), 34–43.

Paternoster, R., Brame, R., Mazerolle, P. and Piquero, A. (1998). 'Using the correct statistical test for the equality of regression coefficients'. *Criminology*, *36*(4), 859–66.

Podsakoff, P.M. and Organ, D.W. (1986). 'Self-reports in organizational research: problems and prospects'. *Journal of Management*, *12*(4), 531–44.

Podsakoff, P.M., MacKenzie, S.B., Lee, J. and Podsakoff, N. (2003). 'Common method biases in behavioral research: a critical review of the literature and recommended remedies'. *Journal of Applied Psychology*, *88*, 879–903.

Preacher, K.J. and Hayes, A.F. (2008). 'Asymptotic and resampling strategies for assessing and comparing indirect effects in multiple mediator models'. *Behavior Research Methods*, *40*, 879–91.

RECOMMENDED READING

Byrne, B.M. (2009). *Structural Equation Modeling with AMOS: Basic Concepts, Applications, and Programming*, 2nd edn. New York: Routledge.

Dancey, C. and Reidy, J. (2014). *Statistics without Maths for Psychology*, 6th edn. Harlow: Pearson.

Field, A. (2009). *Discovering Statistics Using SPSS*, 3rd edn. Thousand Oaks, CA and London: Sage.

Hair, J.F. Jr, Black, W.C., Babin, B.J. and Anderson, R.E. (2009). *Multivariate Data Analysis*, 7th edn. Harlow: Prentice Hall.

Tabachnick, B.G. and Fidell, L.S. (2006). *Using Multivariate Statistics*, international edition, 5th edn. Harlow: Pearson.

21. When the words just won't come

Dawn C. Duke

I was invited to write this chapter not because of my research background in Neuroscience, but because for the past decade I have been working in Researcher Development, providing skills support for early stage researchers. In this role, I have delivered workshops, writing retreats and coached many young writers through tough spots. The truth is that writing is hard. It is hard for everyone. The lovely newer researchers I work with often imagine that those of us that have been around awhile just sit down and magically write wonderfully flowing sentences that come together to create iron-clad arguments with amazingly interwoven ideas. The most important thing for you to know is this is just not true. We all struggle with writing from time to time, and none of us write perfect drafts the first time around, not even my emeritus professor friends. In this chapter, I will share with you stories of researchers struggling with writer's block and what helped them overcome this. For a bit of extra inspiration, I will sprinkle this chapter with quotes from famous writers, who have battled with their own blocks and lived to tell the tale.

> If I waited for perfection, I would never write a word. (Margaret Atwood)

> The easiest thing to do on earth is not write. (William Goldman)

THE BLANK PAGE

There it is, perfect and white. Whatever goes there has to be just right. One word, two words … no that isn't it. Delete, delete. More words. No. Delete, delete, delete. Every word down, taken away again to leave the lovely pure page. The words aren't worthy, they can't stay. I remember watching a young researcher, I'll call him Dan, do this over and over again at a writing retreat. It was painful to see, minutes went by, an hour, and everything put on the page, taken away again.

I sat down next to him and ask what was wrong. 'I just can't find the words', Dan said. 'I think of something, but it just not right.' So I had him talk to me about what he wanted to write, about his wonderfully interesting research. His eyes lit up and out came words, not on the paper, but it was obvious he had a story to tell. His research journey was there ready to come out and fill the pages of this chapter that was currently just a blank page.

So I asked Dan if he had written anything about this part of his research before. He had written an abstract for a conference ... but that isn't the same as a chapter. I asked him to humour me and to copy the abstract onto that pretty white page of his, which he did, sceptically. After that I asked him to start writing underneath the abstract ... but not to write the chapter. Instead, I asked him to write about what he would like to write about today. And then I gave him some very specific rules: (1) no backspace or delete buttons, (2) keep writing for ten whole minutes, no stopping, (3) sentence structure doesn't matter, neither does grammar or word choice. In fact, it doesn't have to be in complete sentences even (4) suspend all judgement.

With an unsure look on his face, he agreed and started typing while I timed him and policed the delete button. After ten minutes he had almost filled two whole pages. I asked him to read through and highlight parts that he thought were most interesting. From this, I asked him to pick a topic from what he had written that is important to this chapter and to start writing about that for another ten minutes. At the end of this ten minutes, there was a big smile. 'I think I have it!' he said. I told him to keep writing and then later he can go back and delete the bit at the top he didn't need any more. By the end of the day, when I went to check on Dan's progress he had a really good start to his chapter and was excited about what he was going to write the next day. There are two big take-home messages from Dan's story. The first is not to have a perfect white page in front of you when you try to start writing, and the second is to keep writing!

The first words on a page can be terribly intimidating. A really easy trick is to spoil the blank page from the start. Put something else on it, anything will work, but previous writing that is vaguely close to what you want to address is particularly beneficial. You can always take it away later, but psychologically, seeing words on the page already can help, especially for those with perfectionist traits.

> I love writing but hate starting. The page is awfully white and it says, 'You may have fooled some of the people some of the time but those days are over, giftless. I'm not your agent and I'm not your mommy. I'm a white piece of paper, you wanna dance with me?' And I really, really don't. (Aaron Sorkin)
>
> It is perfectly okay to write garbage – as long as you edit brilliantly. (C.J. Cherryh)

The other 'trick' I used with Dan was called 'free writing'. I love free writing and use it frequently in workshops and in my own writing. The idea is let go of that inner critic and allow yourself permission to write poorly. I have seen it work time and time again, getting words down on paper works wonders. It even can lead to surprises. At times you can start freely writing and end up in a totally different place than you expected, sometimes with interesting new ideas. And even if you don't, you can always edit it later. Writing is like a hot tap, you have to let the cold water run before you get to the hot. Turning it off and then on again doesn't work. Writing and then deleting prevents you warming up. Sometimes you have to work through those poorly constructed sentences and unclear themes to get to the innovative ideas and eloquent arguments.

> What I try to do is write. I may write for two weeks 'the cat sat on the mat, that is that, not a rat.' And it might be just the most boring and awful stuff. But I try. When I'm writing, I write. And then it's as if the muse is convinced that I'm serious and says, 'Okay. Okay. I'll come.' (Maya Angelou)

NOT ENOUGH TIME

About a year ago, I was working with an amazing group of part-time PhD students, they were all professionals and teaching academics at the same time they were working on doctorates. This was a group of very busy people! I had them all together for a session about developing the argument for their methodology. I used the start of the session to explore what they most needed from this session and the one theme that came out over and over was that they didn't have enough time to write. It wasn't that they didn't know what they wanted to write, it was that they had such busy days that carving out hours to sit down and write significant amounts of work was just impossible. They all felt the time slipping passed and with it an increasing sense of urgency that something must be produced, but there was no time to do it in.

Once people start feeling behind, the mountain they need to climb can look evermore daunting and the time needed can seem increasingly impossible to find. Therefore, what I did was introduce them to a time management technique, called the Pomodoro technique, founded by Francesco Cirillo (http://cirillocompany.de/pages/pomodoro-technique). Pomodoro is Italian for 'tomato' and is named after tomato-shaped cooking timers, because it is a task/ time management technique that relies on strict timing of specific tasks. This technique is not something I made up, and if I am honest I don't always follow all the 'rules' either when teaching it or using it myself. However, the overall concept is extremely helpful for very busy people that have to get a lot done, and it can be used strictly as described on the above website, or more flexibly.

When using the Pomodoro technique to help you write, you decide on a specific writing task for that day and you identify at least one 30-minute time slot within that day that you can work on your writing. With your task in mind, you sit down and set a 25-minute timer and then you must focus solely on that writing task at hand. You do not look at emails, go on the Internet, or answer the phone or door. You do nothing but the writing task for the full 25 minutes. When the timer goes off, you stand up, stretch and have a five-minute break. If you are lucky enough to have another 30-minute slot, you can repeat the Pomodoro again and write for another 25 minutes. A 25-minute session is referred to as one Pomodoro, and after each one, you should have a five-minute break. If you complete four Pomodoros in a row, it is suggested that you take a 15- to 20-minute break. The idea is to work in a focused way for short periods of time. Perfect for those of us who find we don't have big blocks of time to dedicate to writing.

I introduced this technique to these part-time PhD students during this half-day training session, by actually having them use the technique. In this case, I started the first Pomodoro in combination with free writing to help them get a lot of words on the page quickly. Then the next Pomodoro we used to edit and pull out ideas from the free writing, showing them that these periods can be used for different aspects of writing. The key is to identify what you are going to focus on and do just that during the Pomodoro.

Weeks later I ran into one of the ladies who was at this session and she said they had formed a Pomodoro group. They had signs up on their door or hanging on their computer when they were in the middle of a Pomodoro, so others would know not to disturb them. She and several of the students would try to plan their Pomodoros at the same time so they could have their breaks together. The most important thing was she now felt like the task was now doable. This technique is great for breaking up a huge task, like writing a proposal or thesis, into smaller chunks. This helps you feel the progress you are making, and makes you realise you can achieve something, even if you only have short periods of time throughout the day to work on it.

> The secret of getting ahead is getting started. The secret of getting started is breaking your complex overwhelming tasks into small manageable tasks, and then starting on the first one. (Mark Twain)

FINDING FOCUS

Although for the last decade I have worked supporting other researchers with their doctorates, the first thing that came to my mind when asked to write this chapter was my own doctoral experience of authoring my first publication. It was very early on in my PhD, only six months or so, however, my supervisor was convinced that my first data set merited publication and he suggested I work on getting a draft together. I remember staring at the data, and then determinedly sitting at the computer and putting words down, only to find myself waffling and winding and getting lost down in the literature. Again and again, I would try, but there was no direction.

I felt my data was rubbish, it didn't mean anything. How was I supposed to write? Weeks went by. I started to avoid my supervisor for fear he would ask for the draft. Then one day, I was just sitting there playing with the data, moving it around … not writing, when something clicked. An idea was forming, I could feel it. The patterns in the data were coming together. A story was emerging.

Knowing I needed to catch the idea before it vanished into the depth of my mind, I started scribbling down words, trying to bring the idea into focus, trying to crystallise the story. It was painful and took perhaps hours, but by the end of that day I had a sentence. Only one sentence, but a beautiful sentence that would guide that first publication. It was the paper's thesis statement, the heart of its story.

A thesis statement is a sentence (or a couple of sentences) that encapsulates the central 'argument' of your work. In academic writing this argument is your story. A good thesis statement lays out before you what you need to prove and how you are going to do it. It is your anchor that can bring you back when your get lost in the detail or pulled astray by interesting but peripheral literature. A strong thesis statement should be an assertion that expresses a point of view that a reasonable person should be able to disagree with. In other words, no politician speak. Politicians often say things like, 'I believe all children should have access to a good education' or 'People should be able to afford to heat their homes.' These are statements that have an opinion, but they are so broad and idealistic that it would be hard for a reasonable person to argue the opposite. Politicians do this on purpose, of course. They don't want anyone to be able to argue against their ideas. However, this is not academic.

In order to move our academic fields forward and develop academic thoughts, we must develop arguments that can be debated and push researchers on both sides to develop the body of evidence to further inform thought. Therefore, the thesis statement: 'Grammar schools provide increased school choice and expand upward mobility for children from low income backgrounds.' Or 'While expanding grammar schools may give the perception of increased school choice and diversity, they actually lead to less children having access to high quality education because they drain resources from local state schools.' People arguing either of these points care about high-quality education, as do most people. The clear debate here how to achieve this end. This is an area that can be debated and which can be informed by research. In fact, you can see the research question within those statements, but they go beyond the question to include the direction of the argument you build within the piece of writing. With a statement like this you can outline a whole thesis.

The beauty of a good thesis statement is it grounds you, it is your focus. Once I found that sentence, it remained my light throughout the journey of that first paper. When I got lost in the detail of the data or in the vast amount of literature, I could look back and remember where it is I wanted to go with this paper. Side paths are for another day, perhaps another paper. This sentence lit the way so that I was able to figure out what I needed to write next.

> I always worked until I had something done and I always stopped when I knew what was going to happen next. That way I could be sure of going on the next day. (Ernest Hemingway)

WRITING COMMUNITIES

There are times when a doctorate can feel quite lonely, none more so than when you are in the final stages of writing your thesis. You are so close, but you are tired, your mind is weary and the worst part is you have entirely forgotten why your research is important anyway. I had a researcher who was in this state at the most recent writing retreat I delivered, we'll call her Maria. Maria had finished with all the analysis and had written the majority of her thesis, she just needed to write the final chapter to bring it all together, but she had lost the spark. She came into the writing retreat feeling that perhaps nothing she had done was worth a PhD, and therefore, was demotivated and almost physically unable to write.

In our writing retreats, we have writing groups and writing mentors. The writing mentors bring their groups together and everyone introduces themselves and their research and they say what they hope to get done over the course of the retreat. This builds a mini writing community and allows group members to support each other to achieve their goals. The mentor, in this case me, then goes around and talks to the participants in a bit more detail to see how we can best support them over the retreat. When I first talked to Maria, she seemed quite down and admitted to not having written anything for a while. She was concerned that she hadn't even read any of her earlier chapters for almost a year and feared they were not strong enough. Therefore, we decided she would take a bit of time to go through her different chapters and then come back to me to talk about what she saw as her major contributions to knowledge.

Just before our first break I sat with her and she told me all about her research (which was fantastically interesting!). However, she was still sceptical about the worth of the work. I suggested she chat about her work with some of her group members over coffee and biscuits. Throughout break I watched her having a quite animated conversation with a couple of her group members. I had to pull them away from each other to get them all back to writing at the end of the break. I suggested to Maria that she sit down and just start writing the different things she was explaining to her group members during their conversation. At this point, it was not important to worry too much about the idea of a 'contribution to knowledge' but to focus on what her group members found interesting about her research and write that down. At lunch, I noted again she was very engaged with her group members again and that there was definitely a true smile on her face, which hadn't been there when she first came in.

Over the weekend, Maria became more and more positive about her work. One of her group members was very interested in her methodology, commenting on how innovative it was, which really made her feel good. By the morning of the second day, she started really writing. She had seen her research through her writing group members' fresh eyes and that helped her recognise what was special in her work. At the end of the retreat, the group exchanged emails and vowed to keep in touch to motivate each other to finish this final year. I sure hope they do.

Over my years of working with researchers, I have come to appreciate the need for community more and more. Workshops and especially writing retreats that gather people in one place to write together in a supportive, encouraging community can be a catalyst for creativity and a spark to reignite lost enthusiasm. With the wonders of modern technology, this can even be done virtually, through different forums or groups. We use Skype to deliver virtual writing retreats for our researchers who are off working across the world. This type of support can be a real lifeline when people are feeling stuck. There is no reason anyone couldn't make their own writing communities, either face to face or virtual. The most important ingredient is participants dedicated to writing and supporting each other, as well as biscuits … I do find those essential for writing, but that may just be me.

> If you have other things in your life – family, friends, good productive day work – these can interact with your writing and the sum will be all the richer. (David Brin)

MAKING WRITING A HABIT

My final word of advice to all newer researchers out there is to make writing a habit. A researcher always has something to write. There are proposals, publications, conference papers and of course your thesis, but there is also writing for yourself. For your ideas to truly form, they need to become real, writing gives ideas shape. This allows you to clarify your ideas and to work with them, to mould them, to challenge them. Putting these thoughts on paper allows you to go back over them and see how they have developed over time. Just a bit of writing every day adds up significantly over time. If you do this, you will be amazed at the amount of material you have for your thesis or for publications. No writing is wasted. Always remember the best cure for writer's block is writing.

Writing about a writers' block is better than not writing at all. (Charles Bukowski)

LESSONS FOR KEEPING ON TRACK

- Know that writing is hard for everyone, you are not alone.
- Allow yourself to write badly. You can always edit later.
- Don't start writing with a pure blank page, put something … anything on it.
- Learn to break down your writing task and use short periods of time productively to help move your writing forward even when life is too busy.
- Craft a clear statement encapsulating your main position and argument to give your writing structure and prevent you losing your focus.
- Develop a writing community to maintain motivation and make the writing process more enjoyable.
- Make writing a habit. This is the best way to prevent writer's block in the first place.

REFERENCES

Angelou, Maya. (n.d.). GoodReads.com Retrieved 19 December 2016: https://www .goodreads.com/quotes/154213-what-i-try-to-do-is-write-i-may-write.

Atwood, Margaret. (n.d.). BrainyQuote.com. Retrieved 19 December 2016: https:// www.brainyquote.com/quotes/quotes/m/margaretat457937.html.

Brin, David. (n.d.). Freelancewritinggigs.com Retrieved 19 December 2016: http:// www.freelancewritinggigs.com/2015/04/15-encouraging-writing-quotes-for-when -you-feel-like-a-failure/.

Bukowski, Charles. (n.d.). GoodReads.com Retrieved 19 December 2016: https:// www.goodreads.com/quotes/372045-writing-about-a-writer-s-block-is-better-than -not-writing.

Cherryh, C.J. (n.d.). GoodReads.com Retrieved 19 December 2016: https:// www .goodreads.com/author/quotes/989968.C_J_Cherryh.

Goldman, William. (n.d.). BrainyQuote.com. Retrieved 19 December 2016: https:// www.brainyquote.com/quotes/quotes/w/williamgol378655.html.

Heminway, Ernest. (n.d.). GoodReads.com Retrieved 19 December 2016: https://www
    .goodreads.com/quotes/805766-when-we-came-back-to-paris-it-was-clear-and.
Sorkin, Aaron. (n.d.). BrainyQuote.com. Retrieved 19 December 2016: https://www
    .brainyquote.com/quotes/quotes/a/aaronsorki750752.html.
Twain, Mark. (n.d.). Quotes.lifehack.org. Retrieved 19 December 2016: http://quotes
    .lifehack.org/quote/mark-twain/the-secret-of-getting-ahead-is-getting/.

22. Conducting research 'with' and not just 'on' organisations

Carol Woodhams

In the winter of 2016, I sat in a freezing cold office at a shared desk working on confidential data in a National Health Service (NHS) trust in East Anglia in the East Midlands of England. I'd spent the night in a cold hotel room, I'd walked to the trust in the rain, met my HR contact, and was now to spend three days analysing payroll data with only a cold sandwich and another night in a cold hotel to look forward to. This was a particularly difficult assignment because I was not allowed to remove or copy data to analyse it in more comfortable circumstances. The temporary HR department at the trust was tiny, and the warmth of the reception I experienced didn't compensate for the desk under the stairs and the draft from the window. I will admit that I questioned my motivation, my sanity and the reason for me being there. What did I expect to get out of it? As I finished my analysis, I presented the outcomes in report format to the senior HR director with a promise of follow-up and jumped into a nice warm car to complete the five-hour drive home to Devon in the south-west of England. This was my eighth and final pay gap analysis conducted under these circumstances for NHS trusts all around England.

I wouldn't blame you if you did wonder what I was doing. On the face of it, I was pursuing research 'impact'; in line with the higher education sector's preoccupation with interacting with organisations to produce knowledge that offers solutions to real-world problems (known as Mode 2 knowledge production by Gibbons et al., 1994). One of my research specialities is pay gaps on the basis of gender, ethnicity and disability. In East Anglia I was analysing the data of one in a series of NHS trusts with the aim of recommending solutions to their pay gaps. The university I was working for covered my out-of-pocket expenses, but I was not directly paid. I was, however, developing insight and experience of reward and salary structures in the NHS. In the end, I left that university before I could reflect on and write up the 'impact', that is, ways that my report influenced positive change to narrow pay gaps in these trusts. Maybe my bespoke reports made a difference to HR practice on promotion, retention and reward. Maybe the reports were filed and forgotten about. Because I left my post, I didn't undertake the necessary follow-up to find out. However, the effort wasn't in vain. It took another two years for me to see that that it made sense in career terms, and a further five years until I really saw the benefits. But more on that later.

Years down the line from that chilly experience, in this chapter, I have the opportunity to reflect on my experience of studying organisations and people in organisations.

RESEARCH *WITH* ORGANISATIONS OR RESEARCH *ON* ORGANISATIONS?

As researchers, we carve out our own manner of engaging with organisations to suit our research agendas. Kayrooz and Trevitt (2005) explore via case studies of research with organisations how context, research purpose, design and method need to be intertwined to create an effective approach. My way has always been to approach organisations in collaborator mode. By this, I mean actively working *with* organisations to solve specific problems and implement changes by undertaking applied research that creates the framework for recommendations and their practical application. It's a hands-on, interventionist (Lukka and Wouters, 2022), problem-solving approach, engaging with existing data and processes within HR departments to create outcomes that are not only helpful to me, but also helpful to my collaborator organisations. I leave collaborator organisations with a bespoke report that benchmarks their HR outcomes in relation to other similar organisations. I suggest follow-up discussions, months or even years later, once changes have taken effect. This approach has been well received and I have frequently found my 'services' have been recommended across organisations in the same sector. And, after working alongside and building trust with these organisations, I usually come away with data for publications. Although not from the NHS trust in East Anglia.

Researchers working *on* or *in* organisations approach the organisation as a site to collect data for analysis and publication. Using a variety of research designs that range from the objectivist experimental to fully immersive case study, researchers pursue 'basic/fundamental knowledge production (Bentley, Gulbrandsen and Kyvik, 2015) to advance academic theory as top priory and organisation development as secondary. This was the approach I took to collect data for my doctorate. Later on, reflecting on that experience, I realised there were easier ways to gain access to organisations, especially where sensitive pay data is involved, and adopting the role of unpaid consultant is one way.

On that note, I have in the past resisted being costed to undertake research at official university consultant rates. Sometimes when I have been approached by organisations to undertake, for example, an analysis of patterns and trends of factors underlying their own pay gaps, with the objective of paying for my time, an approach to the university research funding team has resulted in costs that are so high, they're not feasible for public sector organisations. Typically, the resolution has involved a compromise agreement; that the organisation gets the benefit of my services, and I get the benefit of the suitably anonymised and General Data Protection Regulations (GDPR)-sanitised employee data that I can use in publications. That kind of agreement has formed the basis of many of my research papers.

Sometimes, however, my approach might be overly obliging! Earlier this month I spent a couple of hours redrawing an infographic that had already taken up many hours of my time to produce. I am no graphic designer! One of the senior civil servants at the Department of Health and Social Care wanted the line graph on the infographic to be given exactly to scale which meant I had to go back and plot it accurately. Creating infographics wasn't something I learnt during my PhD training and hasn't evolved as part of my skill set but every day is a learning day when you work with organisations! And to my benefit, the infographic might now form part of a briefing package to the Secretary of State for Health and Social Care. Which is lovely, impactful payback.

UPFRONT CONSIDERATIONS: NEGOTIATING THE PROJECT STRUCTURE, THE BRIEF AND THE TIMEFRAME

Negotiating the brief and the timeline when working with organisations is a critical but delicate task. You need to consider balancing the expectations of both parties, yourself and the organisation, with resources available, the feasibility of the project and potential outcomes. It's well worth spending time on this stage. Based on my experience, here's a few things to consider upfront.

Stakeholders

Stakeholders are really important to the shape and conduct of a research project. I have found that forming a stakeholder group will assist you in understanding stakeholder standpoints, ensuring that your research aligns with their goals as much as possible. Finding a skilled and neutral chair of this group can deflect some of the heat generated by diverging stakeholder goals from you, if needed. A steering group can also be helpful in providing skills and experience to advise on, or even co-design, your research agenda. The sponsoring organisation is the most important party to include on a steering group.

Stakeholders can be unpredictable and having an inside view of your research isn't always beneficial to you. One of my research projects took place in a turbulent political context of strikes and pay negotiations. Most of the stakeholder group, which included both organisation management and union representatives, were much more interested in arguing with each other on that issue than discussing the research agenda and outputs. Once again, a skilled chair can shut down irrelevant conversations in a way that doesn't alienate either group. Take advice from the organisation on the representation of groups on the stakeholder panel ensuring, as far as possible, an even balance of power between groups. Keep numbers manageable. I would advise no more than a dozen stakeholders. In another project, one of the stakeholders saw an early draft of findings and objected to it strongly. So strongly, in fact, that she raised complaints direct to my colleague's boss – the dean of an elite Russell Group university – and the two of us were summoned to appear in front of him with only 24 hours' notice. In the end, it was all caused by a misunderstanding, but I was very junior, and it certainly caused distress for me at the time.

To a large extent, distractions caused by conflicting stakeholder perspectives and misunderstandings can be limited by anchoring the research in a specific brief.

The Brief

The brief provides a touchpoint for discussions about your research project. The brief should include information about the research objectives, scope and deliverables. Include a Gantt chart. Ensure your stakeholder group have a clear understanding of inclusions and more importantly exclusions, what the research will achieve and what they can expect as outcomes. Don't be overly ambitious about what can be achieved within a specific timeline and resource allocation. If the proposed scope seems unattainable, present alternatives and negotiate. Have confidence in your position. It is likely they want to work with you, as much as the other way around. Negotiations may require compromise, so be flexible and adaptable.

MORE UPFRONT CONSIDERATIONS: INSURANCE, LEGAL AND ETHICAL REQUIREMENTS

Alongside agreeing the brief with the organisation, you need to ensure that essential aspects of the procedural elements of conducting research are attended to within your research institution. This includes checking if legal contracts are necessary, whether special insurance liability cover is necessary, and the steps needed for ethical approval of the research project. The sort of research that I do includes information about personal characteristics, so requires attention to the constraints of GDPR, a legal Memorandum of Understanding between university and research organisation, safe and secure data storage locations, and safe and secure data transfer arrangements. Sometimes, such as the circumstances of the illustration that I opened this chapter with, data is too sensitive to transfer. All these aspects will form part of your ethics application.

One of the most important elements to consider for your purposes, is if, and how, you will be able to use the data for dissemination and academic publications. This will be specified in the legal contract. My experience is that organisations can be persuaded to allow your analysis for use in publications given assurances of sufficient anonymity and a view of the final draft of your written paper. Along the way then, you are likely to need to agree that they have power to veto your write-up; such is the risk. Happily, this has not happened to me. And given that my research focuses on personal characteristics including individual pay rates, it's a pretty good test.

Not to say that the process has always been straightforward. On one occasion after bidding for a high-profile and super-competitive funded research contract, the university I worked for at the time decided it couldn't meet the insurance requirement of unlimited liability. To be fair, they had raised this possible sticking point during the bid writing process, weeks earlier, but I was of the view that if other universities could meet this requirement so could mine! And I ploughed on regardless. I was on the train home from pitching the bid in the final stage; a face-to-face presentation, when I got the call to say that the final hurdle to the award of the research contract was the matter of the non-agreement on insurance liabilities. And that neither party seemed prepared to shift their position. Faced with a wonderful opportunity disappearing in the final stages, I had to email the university Pro-Vice Chancellor for Research to draw the matter to his attention. Thank goodness, the university changed position and we were awarded the research contract! In the end, we didn't do anything that required a claim on insurance!

CONDUCTING THE RESEARCH

So having spent so long ensuring the preparation stages, the conduct of the research project should be smooth sailing. It's just a question of doing what you have agreed to do. The organisation also needs to keep their side of the agreement. How much support do you need? Are they providing you with access to key research subjects, support from administrative functions, maybe physical or virtual spaces? Are you keeping to key deadlines as agreed in the project plan?

Here again no two research projects are alike. The support required for survey distribution will be different to that needed for participant observation, and different again if you are undertaking a set of interviews. In recent years, in my research projects I have been analysing employee administrative data drawn from the HR information system, which doesn't require a lot of ongoing support once agreements have been reached and data extracted. No matter what your approach is, you should always engage in open communication with the organisation and the stakeholder groups. Prioritise organisation interests, but deep dive into understanding the needs, concerns and expectations of each stakeholder groups.

Always keep tight control over the quality of your research instrument at every step. On one occasion when I was interested in collecting data on possible gender differences in perception of the fairness of the career structure in a group of organisations where I was working alongside the HR department, I was grateful for the help of an administrator to set the research survey in online survey software. I designed it and piloted as per best practice. The same administrator made post-pilot changes. Unfortunately, the final version of the survey was circulated before I saw it and realised that she had omitted to include the gender variable! There was no second chance and the whole effort was wasted. Check, double-check, and check again!

AND WHAT NOW?

The first thing on your To Do List is to check off your obligations to your sponsoring organisation. I usually offer some sort of a bespoke benchmarking analysis of their practice in comparison to other similar organisations. This can be appealing to HR departments who are very keen to understand what their competitors are doing. But this isn't as much hard work as you might think because you can develop a framework that can be applied across organisations just using original data.

Start with a follow-up email sending a personalised thank you that expresses gratitude for the opportunity to work on your project within the collaborating organisation. Keep it concise, but meaningful. Include stakeholders in your email list. Highlight key successes and express your enthusiasm for potential future collaborations. Give them a timeframe for the delivery of your report and stick to that timeframe. Ask for constructive feedback on the deliverables agreed. I have found managers appreciate being asked for their opinion and this can provide you with insight.

Schedule a follow-up meeting to present your findings. After a reasonable period, propose a meeting to discuss the project's long-term impact in the organisation and this might generate future collaboration opportunities.

Maintain contact with the organisations' managers after completing your project. This is crucial for fostering a lasting professional relationship and potentially opening doors for future collaborations. The aim here is to maintain a professional relationship without being intrusive. Show genuine interest in the manager's work and try to be helpful if the opportunity arises. Fortunately, professional social media platforms such as LinkedIn are ideal for this purpose.

The objective is to maintain a positive connection at the very least until you get agreement for your research publication.

REFLECTIONS

Many years on from that chilly experience under the stairs in the East Midlands of England, I reflect on how and why it has made sense to my research career.

Two years later, in 2018 my understanding of NHS pay gaps and how they are founded put me and my colleagues in a super-strong position to bid for the Independent Review into Gender Pay Gaps in Medicine (Dacre et al., 2020) commissioned by the then Secretary of State for Health, the Rt Hon Jeremy Hunt MP and funded by the Department of Health and Social Care. It was a prestigious project, and highly competitive, and we were awarded it. We are now a few years on from the publication of that review, but the benefits of my 2016 investment, which weren't at all clear at the time, keep coming. I have a position on the Gender Pay Gap Implementation Panel, I continue to supply that panel with updates on the trajectory of the gender pay gap (spoiler alert: it's falling) and further analysis on the causes of gender pay gaps. It might seem that I work for the Department of Health and Social Care in an unpaid capacity, but in line with my collaborative approach, in return I continue to have access to very useful data on the medical workforce. Dissemination of my analysis within academic and practice spheres needs to be approved, but for now we're muddling along just fine. And the biggest thrill of all has been to see the outcomes of recommendations of the review adopted (with credit to us) within the new draft contract to all medical consultants in England that brought an end to the 2023–2024 consultant industrial action.[1]

In setting out my collaborative approach to research, I hope that I have highlighted a few key points:

- Be mindful of building in reciprocity in research deliverables. What do you want from the interaction, but also what can you offer in return?
- Quality-assure all stages of your research project; most especially the written 'contract' whether formal or informal. In particular, think about future publications, are you able to use your findings, and in what circumstances?
- Accept offers of help and support, but don't hand over the administration of your precious research instrument without triple-checking it is accurate and complete.
- Train in skills of chairing meetings, or better still, find yourself an experienced chair with a neutral position and political skill.
- Find a reason to keep in touch with key research collaborators and their successors when they (inevitably) move on.

NOTE

1.   https://www.gov.uk/government/news/government-puts-offer-to-consultants
     -to-pave-way-to-end-strikes.

REFERENCES

Bentley, P.J., Gulbrandsen, M. and Kyvik, S. (2015). The relationship between basic and applied research in universities. *Higher Education, 70,* 689–709.

Dacre, J., Woodhams, C., Atkinson, C., Laliotis, I., Williams, M., Blanden, J., Wild, S. and Brown, D. (2020). *Independent Review into Gender Pay Gaps in Medicine in England.* Department of Health and Social Care. https://www.gov.uk/government/publications/independent-review-into-gender-pay-gaps-in-medicine-in-england.

Gibbons, M., Limoges, C., Nowotny, H., Schwartzman, S., Scott, P. and Trow, M. (1994). *The New Production of Knowledge: The Dynamics of Science and Research in Contemporary Societies.* London: Sage.

Kayrooz, C. and Trevitt, C. (2005). *Research in Organisations and Communities: Tales from the Real World.* Canberra: Allen & Unwin.

Lukka, K. and Wouters, M. (2022). Towards interventionist research with theoretical ambition. *Management Accounting Research, 55,* p100783.

23. Where, oh where, is my golden thread?

Vivienne Spooner and Helena Barnard

Both of us have been deeply involved in the doctoral programme at the Gordon Institute of Business Science (GIBS, University of Pretoria) since 2013: Helena as academic head and Viv as programme manager and mentor. We have seen that for new scholars-in-the-making, the process of research often follows seemingly mystical rules and practices. Postgraduate researchers who receive feedback on their written work that the golden thread isn't obvious or worse, not present, can become confused, distressed or bewildered. For the reviewers of these researchers' work it is quite clear if the golden thread has been broken because the logic of the argument is obscure or worse, no longer exists. So, what is the big deal about this golden thread?

The golden thread is a metaphor that refers to the internal coherence of the research. The golden thread breaks, for example, if the research promises an exploration of a new phenomenon – using qualitative language – but quantitative language of hypotheses, variables, effects, or mediation and moderation is used in the research design. Or the research questions in an explanatory quantitative research design can include open-ended questions about the why or how of a phenomenon. Because the research process is, well ..., a process, the various stages require that each part is internally coherent but also that the whole process has integrity between the parts. Adding to the complexity of the process is that the research can often span several years so the ability to maintain the golden thread is vital.

Alongside any research project will be an implicit philosophy which provides guard rails for the research and promotes a systematic approach to the project – the golden thread (see Saunders and Bezzina, 2015 for a fuller discussion on conceptions of research practices). The golden thread can unravel at various stages in the research process. In this chapter we discuss four cases; first two qualitative and then, two quantitative research designs. In all cases, the researchers in the execution of their research – in fact, after they had analysed their results – were challenged to ensure logical coherence throughout their research.

CASE 1: CRAFTING THE FINDINGS SECTION TO PREPARE READERS FOR AN ADDITIONAL THEORETICAL FRAMING

How do communities experience the corporate social responsibility (CSR) programmes of which they are the recipients? Because CSR programmes in their essence recognise that the firm has wider responsibilities in society, stakeholder theory seemed like an appropriate anchor for one of our recent graduates. She decided on a qualitative study and asked communities how they feel about the CSR initiatives in their midst.

Many of her respondents lived in frontline communities, for example, communities who had to be relocated because mining was going to take place where they had lived, or lived adjacent to a manufacturing plant. For these communities, the CSR initiatives were typically understood in terms of justice. They saw CSR initiatives as a form of restitution, sometimes judging them very harshly as not offering sufficient compensation for what they had lost.

Justice theory is well developed, and it was tempting to rework the literature review to make sure that the golden thread was crystal clear. But time was running out for her to submit for examination. Moreover, the line of logic remained with stakeholder theory. Companies are trying to respond as per stakeholder theory, and the (understudied) response of the communities reflected the value of justice theory in relation to these responses.

To make sure that she did not lose the golden thread, our postgraduate researcher's main challenge was in the choices she made in reporting her very rich data. She had to clearly present the main theme of her thesis, that of justice. She had to make sure that she was not distracting the reader by overemphasising other themes. This meant that she had to foreground quotes that mentioned justice, and in her explanations of the quotes that she explained how communities expected the CSR initiatives to offer them restitutive justice.

Our researcher found it hard to leave out so many other themes that were present in her data, but not as significant as the justice theme. She felt that she was building her thesis on only a part of the data, and that other issues were also relevant. But by focusing on the central themes emerging from her data, our researcher could keep the front end of her thesis largely the same as in her proposal, keeping stakeholder theory and the same general research question. Having demonstrated the role of justice in her findings, she could then in the discussion section highlight the importance of justice theory to make sense of the findings.

CASE 2: ADDING TO THE LITERATURE REVIEW TO HOLD ON TO THE GOLDEN THREAD

Another of our graduates had previously worked on housing public-private partnership (PPP) projects, and was interested in the shifts in power in those projects. At first, both parties hold power: local government has land, and the private company has the finances and skills to develop the land. Until the project is complete, the private company, having invested substantial money, is vulnerable to delays in the provision of services. But once the project is close to completion, the power shifts back to the private company.

There was rich literature on power in PPPs, and our researcher went into the field to qualitatively examine how power worked in housing PPPs. The evidence showed that although both parties knew who was the most powerful at any given time, no one ever acted on it. As he worked through his analysis, he realised more and more that the central matter was the duration of time, because there were shifting dependencies over a long period of time. When the time to partnership project completion was very long, there was a need to think differently about power compared to when it was a short-term relationship.

This kind of insight – about the central role of time – seemed incredibly obvious in hindsight. But our researcher had not considered it. Because the golden thread is about making sure there is a clear line of logic, he needed to update his literature review to include scholarship on time. He had to revise the literature review to prepare the reader for the central role of time in the findings section.

He also had to change his research question. His original research question focused only on the role of power, but because his findings showed that the effect of time meant that power faded into the background, he had to make sure that the research question was amended to cover the effects of both time and power.

CASE 3: LETTING GO OF AN IMAGINED GOLDEN THREAD

An ongoing debate in the scholarship on emotional intelligence is whether emotional intelligence really makes any difference to work performance. One of our researchers had set out to answer this question, approaching it in the most rigorous way he could. His whole research design was inspired and powerful. He measured psychometric qualities using established psychometric tests, he differentiated between the different elements of emotional intelligence, and he found a setting, the granting of small business loans, where employees had to make judgements in the absence of clear information. Despite his diligence in both collecting and analysing his data, he found support only for elements that have previously been shown to be significant, and in work that was not done as rigorously as his. He found no support for any of his hypotheses.

His findings were devastating for him. His whole study was motivated by the desire to resolve the debate on whether emotional intelligence influences work performance or not, and it was very hard for him to accept that his hypotheses were not supported. To hold onto the golden thread – for the text to remain coherent – in his discussion section he had to explain that he could not conclusively answer the debate.

He was worried how to communicate that he had made a contribution to scholarship. In his discussion he foregrounded the many contradictory studies, using insights from his own work to (re)interpret those studies. For example, he was able to point out that there was limited variance in the decisions of his respondents. Organisations provide guidelines to reduce variance and increase predictability in outcomes, potentially limiting the opportunities for employees to use their emotional intelligence. Given his gold-standard research design, he was able to propose that companies' efforts to guide (and thus minimise independent) judgement by employees may be one reason why it remains inconclusive whether high emotional intelligence has a positive effect on work performance.

CASE 4: LEARNING BEYOND THE LITERATURE

Another recent graduate had theoretically framed her research on financial inclusion as a part of social inclusion. She built on prior literature to develop the hypothesis that for 'unbanked' individuals to embrace appropriately simplified, mobile banking solutions, they needed both increased financial literacy and increased self-efficacy. She had a very strong field experimental design: her sites in Ghana were far apart so that no contamination could take place between sites. They were all farming communities with similar crops, and gender and age profiles. Communities were offered training programmes in financial literacy, self-efficacy training, both or neither, and then assisted in opening bank accounts. She monitored not only perceptions of having access to banking services, but also how the bank accounts were used.

But although individuals had expressed appreciation for the training, the bank accounts reflected only three people who had actually used their new banking account. Moreover, the people who activated their bank account had all obtained work in the formal sector. Their salary was paid into their bank account but the day after it was paid, they immediately withdrew it all.

She was distraught by her findings. Upon reconciling the objective and subjective sets of data, she realised that in a cash-based economy, financial inclusion involves *not* having a bank account. Cash was used for all transactions.

Those who were paid from the formal sector needed a bank account to receive their salaries, but they needed cash to live in their own community, to buy clothes and food, pay rent and school fees. The financial inclusion literature had not conceptualised financial inclusion at the level of the collective – it has been focused on the individual. Her quantitative findings suggested the need for a substantial theoretical revision.

Writing this up posed a real threat to the golden thread. She decided to keep the whole study as before, and simply report the non-significant findings. She then developed a detailed and quite long discussion chapter, presenting the suggestive evidence of the need to understand financial inclusion at the level of the community, and making strong recommendations for future research.

MONITORING AND MENDING THE GOLDEN THREAD

In both the qualitative inductive theory-building research projects (Cases 1 and 2), the studies began with interesting real-world phenomena. The researchers felt that their contexts mattered to their understanding of the phenomena, in other words, what exactly were the perceptions of communities who are beneficiaries of CSP spend, and in the second study, a curiosity about how power is exercised by the various partners in a PPP.

Their research questions were firmly anchored on how their research participants experienced the phenomena. While an exploratory research process can be highly flexible and not always predictable (Grodal et al., 2021), in both Cases 1 and 2 the research project was executed according to plan. Their surprising and puzzling findings can be expected in qualitative research: scholars opt for qualitative research because phenomena are inadequately understood, which means that scholars often encounter unanticipated findings. But it also meant that the golden thread needed some repair.

For both, it meant a return to the literature. In the study on housing PPPs, the postgraduate researcher had to signal to the reader already in his literature review that time is often a factor in various dimensions of management. In writing about how time is understood in the management literature, he prepared the reader to expect findings that included a time dimension. In the study on community perceptions of CSR spend, it was logical to start with (and keep) stakeholder theory. But in order to mend the golden thread, our researcher had to make sure that the notion of restitutive justice was clearly pointed out in her findings. This laid the groundwork for her discussion and conclusion, where the role of justice theory was foregrounded.

For the researchers who were doing quantitative work (Cases 3 and 4), it was a bigger surprise that their empirical evidence did not support their arguments. Because they were working in a theory testing paradigm, both were wondering if they had done things 'wrong'. But unsupported hypotheses also provide information. By highlighting the diverse views informing their work, and the omissions in extant scholarship, they kept the line of logic through the thesis.

In sum: there is no telling if and when the golden thread of a thesis may break. A relevant brand-new publication may force a shift in the primary goals of the project. Or the interests of the researcher may slightly shift. A first important bit of advice is to not panic if it happens. In fact, it is wise to antici-pate that the plan outlined in the proposal may not work out as hoped for. Even if it did, a research project can take place over many years, and the researcher needs to be constantly vigilant to make sure that the document asks one clear and clearly justified question – and then answers it!

IT IS NOT THE JOURNEY – IT IS THE DESTINATION!

Many scholars are interested in real-world problems. This means there is often an intense and very messy process of finding an appropriate literature to use, of translating the real-world problem into research questions and of developing a research design to help find the answer to the research questions. This itera-tive process to find a tight focus for the research is often marked by false starts and unsuitable or unfruitful lines of inquiry.

Our researchers use a much-repeated mantra 'trust the process', often spoken in hope. The hope is that they will be able to articulate an important research problem, and come up with a robust answer to it, however 'messy' the process may appear to be. While the process must indeed be trusted, readers are not interested in how the process unfolded. Instead, the reader wants to know what question was asked, and how it was answered in terms of data col-lection and analysis, with clear justifications for why those choices were made.

In the research on emotional intelligence, the researcher did not report his consternation at finding his hypotheses were not supported. Rather, he empha-sised the many contradictory findings in how he wrote about the literature. Similarly, the spectacularly non-supported findings in the financial inclusion research project allowed this researcher to develop and communicate new insights about the links between financial inclusion and social inclusion in cash-based economies. In all cases, the reader had little sense of the messiness the researcher experienced as they were making sense of their findings.

This has implications for how researchers should report their research. Specifically, there is no need to report all the mistakes, the blind alleys and the dead ends. In fact, even if the researcher encountered endless headaches until issues were resolved, it is acceptable – advisable! – to submit a final document showing clearly connected lines of logic (see Shepherd and Suddaby, 2017 for their discussion on the importance of narrative in theorising). In short, there is a difference between scientific inquiry – where the scholar is trying to under-stand something – and scientific communication. A thesis is an example of scientific communication, and its purpose is to communicate new knowledge. Communicate the research contribution itself, not its intellectual history.

THE VALUE OF A GOLD-STANDARD METHODOLOGY FOR A GOLDEN THREAD

Many published papers have prehistories that are far more tortuous than one would imagine reading them. Reviewers often ask the authors to change their theoretical framing, to change their research questions, to better focus their contribution, to gather additional data, or reanalyse their data using different methods. All of these suggestions aim to improve the eventual published paper.

Doctoral researchers can expect similar feedback from supervisors, other researchers and (hopefully) from their colleagues – and with the same aim. Research is not simply a process of executing the proposal, because as one develops clearer insights, it may become necessary to consult additional literature or stress-test the emerging insights. In fact, sometimes it can seem as if everything may have to be reworked.

In both the quantitative theory testing studies where the hypotheses were not supported, the robustness of the methodology meant the results that were obtained could not be questioned. In both cases, the methodology had been designed to be the best way of answering the research questions, and executed without any shortcuts. So even though the researchers ended up with unexpected findings, the design of the methodology was so solid that it was possible – for them as much as for any reader – to take their findings seriously. They were then able to develop an argument that pulled through in a logical way despite the argument being one they had not anticipated.

It is unethical to change the findings to tell a better story. If one has concerns about the robustness of the evidence, especially if there are unexpected findings, it may be necessary to gather additional data, or to try other methods or analysis. In all those cases, the aim is to develop a clearer understanding of what is actually happening.

But if one is confident that the methodology was robust and executed with care, the evidence is an anchor. The quality of the methodology means that a researcher can rule out the need to go back to the data process. Instead, the researcher knows that the golden thread must be mended by focusing on the theoretical framing upfront, or on the discussion after the evidence, or both.

This means that a gold-standard methodology is not only a way of getting solid evidence, but also a way to make it easier to have a golden thread.

CONCLUSION

In this chapter we looked at cases where the empirical evidence did not match the expected outcomes. This caused distress to all the researchers, and not least because their unanticipated findings caused them 'more' work. But in each case, it was the ability to rework parts of their thesis in order to keep the golden thread that enabled their contribution to surface. While the methods used to collect and analyse the data, and the empirical evidence obtained cannot be changed in writing up the thesis, we have shown how our researchers could supplement their literature or use their discussion sections to signal new insights. These changes helped them to maintain a strong golden thread. We now turn to our lessons for keeping your project on track.

LESSONS FOR KEEPING ON TRACK

There are three main lessons from these four cases:

• First, the golden thread can break in many ways, and at many points during the research process. This means that ensuring there is a golden thread is not a one-off task, for example, only during the development of the proposal. It has to be a task throughout the development of the doctoral thesis.
• Second, you are allowed (and sometimes required) to rework the thesis in quite fundamental ways to maintain the golden thread. Researchers sometimes seem to believe that they need to represent their research journey as it unfolded, with all the blind alleys and dead ends. Readers do not want to see scholars' intellectual history: a thesis is a product that is judged for what it contains. And it is the courage to write with confidence of what the research has uncovered that signals scholarship.
• However, the empirical evidence is sacrosanct. It may not be adapted because findings threaten the golden thread. Reporting the findings truthfully has to be the heart of the thesis. Our final important lesson is therefore about the value of a well-executed and high-quality methodology. It is the best way of anchoring a thesis.

REFERENCES

Grodal, S., Anteby, M. and Holm, A.L. (2021). Achieving rigor in qualitative analysis: the role of active categorization in theory building. *Academy of Management Review*, 46(3), 591–612. https://doi.org/10.5465/amr.2018.0482.

Saunders, M.N.K. and Bezzina, F. (2015). Reflections on conceptions of research methodology among management academics. *European Management Journal*, *33*(5), 297–304.

Shepherd, D.A. and Suddaby, R. (2017). Theory building: a review and integration. *Journal of Management*, *43*(1), 59–86. https://doi.org/10.1177/0149206316647102.

24. I'm a paper person or maybe not?

Ilenia Bregoli

In my research career I started working with qualitative research during my PhD. At that time, I did not have access to Computer Aided Qualitative Data Analysis (CAQDAS) software to help me in my coding, but from what I read in books and by talking to colleagues who were more expert than me, I understood how to work with pen and pencil. I highlighted the relevant pieces of interviews, gave them codes, kept updating my code book and then copied and pasted within the same file all the excerpts with the same code. It was time consuming, but the reality is that I always considered myself to be a 'paper' person. One of those people that when they buy a new book need to open it and put their nose in between pages to smell it.

During my PhD I really enjoyed coding manually, and for a few years afterwards I never thought that using CAQDAS software was necessary. If manual coding worked for me, why did I have to change? For this reason when I embarked upon a new research project I had one certainty: I would code manually, working on my printed interview transcripts.

However, I wanted to be more 'efficient' and for this reason one day I entered into a nice stationery shop where I bought myself a fancy, brand-new set of 20 coloured pens; some with colour shades that I was not even able to name.

I set to work and started my coding. Each new code had a different colour, nice isn't it? Together with my coloured annotations and codes on paper I was also developing my code book in an Excel file: one column for the code name, another one for the code description and a third with an example of that code. However, at the second interview transcript I was already mixing my colours … perhaps my 'efficient and artistic' coding was not really so efficient. I had another ten interview transcripts to code, each of which consisted of 25 typed pages, so I was starting to worry a little bit. It was time to move on. I felt I was Robert Plant of Led Zeppelin (1969) singing 'Babe, I'm gonna leave you'. I was betraying my manual coding for technology.

The first thing I did when using NVivo was to input the codes I already developed manually. When I started I noticed that the list of codes was growing quickly and by the time I finished adding the codes from four interviews I found myself with 101 codes and I still had to code another eight interviews! Cleaning was the second task I embarked upon, but soon I realised how many duplicates I had and that I had not noticed this while I was coding manually. Although it took some time, at the end of this cleaning I started to better understand my data, and this allowed me to question my ideas more clearly. Furthermore, the fact that I could move easily from one code to another to check what I did, run queries, write annotations and keep memos, all in one place, made me understand how crazy I was to do manual coding.

So what have I learned? Well … I still listen to Led Zeppelin, but apart from this I now recognise that CAQDAS software is helpful. However, before using such software, I believe that it is important to really understand the particular data analysis method. Indeed, my transition from paper to NVivo was smooth because I knew what type of coding I was carrying out and I knew how to do it. Thus, I did not have any particular trauma when I did it. I believe it helps to understand the basics of the data analysis and be comfortable with it and then use such software as a tool to help. Knowing a data analysis method means far more than just being able to use a piece of software.

Needless to say, I now usually code with NVivo, my 20 coloured pens still being used while reading journals. In the end, I still am a 'paper' person, honest!

REFERENCE

Led Zeppelin (1969) 'Babe I'm gonna leave you' [CD track] 6 mins, 42 seconds. *Led Zeppelin*. London: Olympic Studios.

25. A mug of stress

Rohit Talwar

Cardigans aside, there are several clichés that most academics, regardless of their career stage, would agree with. One such cliché involves the reliance on warm beverages. Coffee to be specific. It appears that an academic's life relies heavily on it. Coffee exists as one of the primary sources of magical inspiration that helps one stay up at odd hours, make small talk about writing, showing off that unknown brand of independent coffee … you get the picture.

It is surely only a matter of following tradition, then, that someone chasing an academic career would rely on a healthy supply of coffee, too. If you are like me, you have a coffee mug for all your work desks, including that compact tumbler (made of recycled material, no less) in your backpack to stay on top of your academic pursuits. Your academic training process involves learning all about research, building an argument, writing clearly, etcetera, but no one tells you about the level of caution needed to consume coffee while using your electronic devices. Probably because they expect you to have basic life skills. Well, not if you are me.

It was a rather warm night of July 2016, and I had been working on the world's best research paper in my field, when the cup of coffee on my desk met my hands, and then, in a completely unannounced fashion, slipped off my hands. Gulp. You may call me clumsy; I blame the mug. And my luck. I must have woken up my housemate, for it is quite unlike them to run to my room at 3 am, asking if I had seen a ghost. No, much worse. I had just learned that my beloved computer does not appreciate coffee the way academics do.

I know what you are thinking; surely I had taken a back-up. Of course! Not as often as I should have, though. This is what not following the weekly ritual of backing up can do to you: over three weeks of data analysis and associated writing had gone missing, never to find its way back into my computer again. Nothing aside from the faint but glorious smell of coffee was left. In retrospect, I should have been backing up all my work every day. No, every hour. Paranoia aside, my fellow researchers, please back up your work (aka your heart and soul) as often as you can. Things like that crucial argument you took days to articulate, that transcription along with notes that took more days than expected, those notes from that not-easy-to-access book … all deserve a lot more love. Time is money, they say, and I spent mine reconstructing documents from memory. Fun.

As I type, I have three hard drives, two cloud accounts, and a phone reminder to back-up every night, collectively offering some kind of hope. Here's to never letting go of the habit and enjoying that mug of, er coffee, and being more productive, stress-free.

26. Excuse me … should that comma be there? Dealing with awkward questions

Kenneth Cafferkey

Common convention suggests the PhD viva is the most daunting experience in any researcher's career. Students are constantly reminded of urban myths where an unnamed student in a distant university had a doctoral viva that went on for over a week. The reality, however, is very different; students are usually well versed, well supervised and largely ready for their doctoral defence. The same cannot be said for the first-year progress review; this can be an altogether daunting experience for the PhD student in waiting. Emotions run high, sense of one's ability and self-worth plummets and long sleepless nights define the run-in to the moment of truth. The constant self-doubt is never far away: Am I good enough? Is my idea good enough? Should I even be doing this? This all culminates in the first-year progress review.

When the day of truth arrived I felt physically sick; no kind words of encouragement from my supervisor could help, I felt hopeless. My name was called. I entered. Game time!

I plodded through the early part, safe in the knowledge that questions were spared until the presentation was over; I would get to say my piece before being thrown to the lions. Then out of the blue I walked head first into the most bizarre exchange: a professor from a different department, sitting in the front row, abruptly interjected, 'Should that comma be there?' in relation to a definition. I turned around dumbfounded and read the definition a number of times to myself and responded, 'I don't know, it's not my definition', which seemed to infuriate the professor in question. A lengthy dressing down ensued regarding taking responsibility for my work and implying that my work was substandard (all because of a comma). I wanted to walk out and just quit there and then and the only reason I didn't is that I could tell the room was on my side. I proceeded; needless to say the professor in question had issue with absolutely everything, from what human resource management is, to methodological issues regarding the collection of worker perspectives. I finished the presentation and said with a wry smile, 'You're not a people person, are you?'

I had survived the ambush. All in all, it was a truly bizarre experience; I didn't really end up defending my PhD proposal – it felt more like I was defending myself.

Overall I was buoyed by the whole experience, and the encounter has become a staple in my research methodology teaching: 'Watch out for the commas.'

Note: I have intentionally misplaced a comma in this vignette; be aware if you decide to quote this work!

27. Finding the time to progress your research, and the big lie that you are part of!

Jennifer Kilroy

If this were just a two-line vignette, it would simply read: 'I finished my research project. (But) typed words revealed the hiding places of life's idleness and rhetoric.' It would be designed, first, to let the reader know that there is light at the end of the tunnel: yes, you can actually finish a research project! And second, it would evoke a moment of self-doubt, followed swiftly by a personal affirmation that their life surely has no idle space. And it is this lie, which many researchers tell themselves, that forms the gap for this small tale. One day I learned about this lie, and this is how.

Flashback to September 2013, my favourite GAA football team, namely, County Mayo in Ireland, have progressed to the All-Ireland Final. This is akin to the Super Bowl of the NFL, or the Grand Final of the AFL, or the FA Cup Final at Wembley. Of course, as County Mayo had reached the final three times in the previous ten years and seven times in total since they last won in 1951, it was no surprise to me that they had reached the final. Winning, on the other hand, would be a surprise, as Mayo are rumoured to be cursed to lose until the last member of the 1951 winning team has passed on to the next world. As an evidence-based researcher, this nonsensical (and somewhat morbid) backdrop to the game only strengthens the hopefulness of the occasion for me. If you want to use Google, you can do your own research to find more on the nonsensical curse. Throw into the mix that the game was the usual 3.30 pm on an autumn Sunday, when 80,000 fans (that's a lot in Ireland, by the way) descend on Dublin city and Croke Park stadium. It is 3 pm, and I am just closing down my laptop in a car parking lot near the stadium.

I have just spent two hours analysing my interview transcripts in the comfortable office of my passenger seat (Tip: steering wheel is problematic for laptop use in driver's seat). Also, I should mention the virtual capabilities of my office. I am also communicating with my PhD supervisor via mobile calls and 'WhatsApp' messaging – although I did not learn that medium of communication and data transfer in any research methodology book. My supervisor, despite or perhaps because of being a (born) Everton soccer fan, is reading the summary of the research findings in his now local pub in Co. Galway, Ireland, awaiting to enjoy the tradition of an All-Ireland GAA game on the inevitable large screen television, just over the shoulder of a barman busily tending the Guinness taps. He seems as excited as I am about the transcript findings (though that might be the Guinness). Or it might be the theoretical themes of reciprocity, recounting Gouldner (1960) via WhatsApp, as emergent from the transcripts. Multiple employees give accounts on the interview tapes of going 'above and beyond', or applying discretionary effort (Purcell and Hutchinson, 2007) for the supervisor who treats them well. In addition, the individual variation in frontline manager styles emerges stronger than expected for a single HR system (Kilroy and Dundon, 2015).

Yes, that Kilroy reference is me! The transcript findings found their way into my first journal publication. This moment of actual real-life connection with a literature review journey, as well as having it published, is, by the way, a pretty bright light at the end of that research tunnel! It has revealed some joys of social science research to me, a sort of reflective self-discovery and learning, advancing knowledge in a field for further inquiry, and the resulting practical implication to the lives of employees as we teach the next generation who may too become managers shaping the lives of others. In other words, those countless journal searches and late library nights are not in vain!

Meanwhile, as I close up my laptop, I am delighted with the ingenuity of my four-step plan. Step one was to depart five hours early for Croke Park, in order to miss traffic and to secure parking in the nearby school for the deaf which places me within sprinting distance of the stadium turnstiles. Step two, convert the car into an office to analyse transcripts for research findings chapter, listening to recordings on car radio and reading and typing on my laptop. Step three is to attend the All-Ireland final free of the never-ending researcher guilt. Step four, celebrate historic win! Simple. By 3 pm the entire plan had been a resounding success and all was on track, despite the odd stare off with the car parking lot attendant, as well as the gritty teeth stare to the opposing Dublin supporters, just to say I have got my game face on, laptop and all!

Here was the dilemma that had given birth to the plan. Any Mayo supporter will tell you, an All-Ireland is a full day commitment. You know, by the time you have the Irish breakfast, round up the flags and jerseys, hit the slow road train from west of Ireland to the east, mingle with fellow supporters on Jones' Road outside the game. However, the research deadline for my first ever publication submission was also looming and it seemed kind of important too. So the problem emerged. Miss the game and perhaps miss the most historic sporting event in the GAA for any self-respecting Mayo supporter, meaning I may never go home with pride ever again! Or, go to the game and risk delaying the pilot study beyond the submission date for my first publishable piece of research (in reality, that should read: miss 'another' submission date, again!).

Think, Jennifer, think! Queue the choir of gremlins that feed the lie of busy lives: 'you deserve to go to the game, as you've spent the last month doing data collection'; 'life is too short to be spending it in the library on your own'. The reality was, I had only spent one weekend in the previous month at data collection, and as for the library, it was a daily aspiration but only a weekly reality. In that moment I realised … I was lying to myself. I never actually spent the hours of research that I rhetorically attributed to research. Likewise, attending a Mayo game was never a full day event. The rhetoric of a full day event was in fact a reality of a three-hour drive and a 70-minute game. Uncovering this lie helped me to find four more hours on research on that special Sunday in September. There are always more minutes in the day. We are not perfect. In fact, we are often idly engaged in thoughts of how busy we are. Unfortunately, Step four didn't come to fruition that day, and not any day since. In fact, in 2016, Mayo competed once again and drew the All-Ireland final. The game went to replay, which they lost by a single point. The fans still have hope. That curse is still nonsensical.

REFERENCES

Gouldner, A.W. (1960). 'The norm of reciprocity: a preliminary statement', *American Sociological Review*, *25*(2), 161–78.

Kilroy, J. and Dundon, T. (2015). 'The multiple faces of front line managers: a preliminary examination of FLM styles and reciprocated employee outcomes', *Employee Relations*, *37*(4), 410–27.

Purcell, J. and Hutchinson, S. (2007). 'Front-line managers as agents in the HRM–performance causal chain: theory, analysis and evidence', *Human Resource Management Journal*, *17*(1), 3–20.

PART IV

Getting finished

28. Authorship in action

Kate L. Daunt and Aoife M. McDermott[1]

INTRODUCTION

Research methods textbooks focus on the research process. This is both necessary and important. But for those aiming for or pursuing an academic career, the generation of published outputs is equally significant. Writing for publication is a core part of a sustainable research career – and a successful research project. Authorship informs appointment decisions, retention and confirmation in post, as well as progression and promotion. It can also inform funders' evaluation of the success of the project. Reflecting this, there are an increasing number of useful texts on academic writing and the publishing process. However, what are often neglected, but highly significant for academic careers, are the issues surrounding authorship. Regardless of the type of research relationship – which can range from the dyadic relationship between a student and a supervisor, to the multi-party (and often multi-disciplinary) relationships within large teams – similar issues arise: on what basis to award authorship? In what order? And via what process? Addressing these questions also raises consideration of alternative strategies for acknowledging contributions that may not merit full authorship, and what to do when things go wrong. These can be awkward issues, often left implicit for this very reason.

We were prompted to discuss issues surrounding authorship during a conference. Following attendance at a 'meet the editors' session at the conference, we shared lunch with a group of other delegates. The usual chit-chat followed: where are you from; what are you working on; and where are you sending it? All going well, until someone who turned out to be a junior faculty member piped up from the other side of the table: 'Mmm … I asked a colleague to read my paper. They did, and gave me some helpful comments. But now they keep talking about "our" paper. And now I don't know what to do. Is this normal? How do you know if someone should be an author?' A short period of silence – and some funny facial expressions ensued. They prompted, 'What do you do?' Cue more awkward looks. 'That's like asking someone to share their secrets', said someone down the other end of the table. What can we say – sharing ensued.

APPROACHES TO AUTHORSHIP

Our first contributor [we apologise for the absence of names – but we'd only just met these people, and the conference lanyards all faced the wrong way, as they do!] started by saying that their team worked on the basis of all names on all papers produced from a project. They explained that, in their team, all of the collaborators contributed to the design and conduct of the study – albeit in different ways – and therefore had contributed to the production of the publications. For them, authorship acknowledged the 'combination capability' inherent in getting a research project from early conceptualisation to a final, finished piece. In surprise, someone questioned, 'But what's the incentive to write?', noting that 'in my team, we only put the names of the people who write the paper, on the paper'. Their reasoning was that this led to better overall output – and was fair. The first speaker did recognise the benefits of this, and suggested that ideally all team members would take turns in leading a paper. But they explained that, in their experience, this is not always feasible in larger groups – where there may be more team members than potential papers within a project. They also noted that, realistically within a large group, not all papers come to fruition. As a result, in their view the combination capability, all names on all papers, approach was fair. Despite their debate, both delegates did agree that the lead writer should be the lead author. Happy nodding around the table on this point, from all but one.

The interjection of the dissenter shifted the focus of the discussion from who should be included as an author on the paper, to the order in which their names should appear. With a slight frown, this contributor explained that they took a different approach to the lead writer as lead author – with alphabetical acknowledgement of authorship. There were a few raised eyebrows at that one: 'Do you put in an asterisk to say that all authors make an equal contribution?' someone asked. The response was quick and negative, but accompanied by a laugh. Grinning, the speaker explained that their surname began with a letter earlier in the alphabet than their most common co-authors, so that by and large, this worked quite well for them. One individual noted that their team tried to support early career researchers to be high on the list of designated authors. But they flagged that whilst this was something they had historically done without much thought, they were increasingly aware that their efforts to support capacity-building made it look as if they were consistently a research collaborator, rather than a research leader. They felt that getting the balance right was important for people coming up the ranks.

An opposite approach was also mentioned: that of having the most senior individual – be it the project PI or supervisor – as the lead author. There was heated debate about this. Not just about the idea of seniority as premise for authorship, but also about the difference between a project PI and a supervisor. Inherent in this debate was concern about exploitation and the importance of recognising the intellectual property of PhD students, and balancing this with helping them to develop publishing skills and capacity. A side-debate ensued, with a continuum of supervisory roles in the publishing process evident. This ranged from a view of the supervisor as a paid overseer of a project that belongs to the student, who should be guided to publish in their own right, at one extreme; to a middle-ground perspective on the student as apprentice, who should work collaboratively to develop their publishing skillset; to a view of the student as employee, working as part of a larger (in this instance funded) project, with a need to negotiate their data versus project data upfront, to enable delineation of their contribution and publishing arena. Strong early career voices in the group emphasised the importance of learning how to publish, especially for securing post-PhD employment.

Whilst there was broad agreement (in our non-representative convenience sample!) that the lead author is typically the individual who takes the lead in drafting the paper, or the PhD student on whose data the paper is based, a range of models for allocating remaining places in authorship were evident. In effect, it seemed to be the case that allocating first authorship was relatively straight-forward, but that subsequent ordering had the potential to become a quagmire. The solution advocated by a majority in our small group was to order authors in accordance with the weight of their contribution. All sorted. Until our lovely early career colleague piped back up asking, 'Contribution to the paper or the project? And how do you know what counts as a contribution?', Collective groans all round. Someone pulled out their laptop.

After searching for 'authorship guidelines' they brought up a number of links. Both of us were interested that a number of those having lunch had never looked at such formal guidance. The guidelines brought up on the laptop included the British Psychological Society (BPS, 2011) statement of policy, the British Sociological Association (BSA, 2001) authorship guidelines, a briefing from the Committee on Publication Ethics regarding how to handle authorship disputes (Albert and Wager, 2003) and the University of Cambridge Authorship Guidance (2016). The owner of the laptop did note that there are a lot of medically oriented guidance documents – but that conventions vary across disciplines. The group were interested to see that themes raised across these documents echoed their earlier discussion relating to the premise and order of authorship. Three themes are worth emphasising.

First, the BPS (2011, 1) notes that its members should 'ensure that the contributions of others in collaborative work are accurately reflected in the authorship and other publication credits (including appropriate use of acknowledgements and footnotes)'. The issue of acknowledgements hadn't been considered in our discussion, and our early career colleague raised the potential of using this as a strategy to recognise the contribution of the individual who had reviewed their draft. Second, the BPS (2011) guidance explicitly notes that authorship credit should not be claimed on the basis of status or seniority, but rather on contribution. The BSA (2001, 4) echoes this, noting further that 'Participation solely in the acquisition of funding or general supervision of the research group is not sufficient for authorship. Honorary authorship is not acceptable.' The BPS (2011) also makes specific reference to PhD students, noting that authorship from doctoral work should normally be joint, with the student listed first. However, the level of supervision provided should justify the inclusion of the supervisor (with the implication that, at times, the exclusion of the supervisor may be merited). The BPS (2011) also draws attention to circumstances in which the supervisor may go first. Specifically, these relate to where the student lacks capability to progress the publication, or does not wish to write up their work for publication. Third, again raising an issue not previously noted, the BPS (2011) emphasises that initial agreed authorship may change during the publication process, to reflect different levels of contribution.

This causes us to return to the definition of a contribution – the initial reason our lunch companion began to search for formal guidance on authorship. Although definitions vary, some key commonalities are evident. Here we present and subsequently discuss three perspectives. For the BPS (2011, 1), a broad range of contributions can merit authorship:

> Authorship refers to not only the writing up of the work but also scientific contributions (origination and formulation of the research idea and hypotheses, design of the research, designing and conducting major analysis, and interpreting findings). Lesser contributions (such as designing or building research apparatus, recruiting research participants, data collation and entry, and other administrative duties) should not be considered to constitute authorship, but should merit formal acknowledgement. Where significant combinations of these tasks are undertaken, collaborators should ensure that agreement is reached as early in the research as possible as to whether authorship is merited and on what level. (Fine and Kurdek, 1993, 1146)

Within our lunch group, dismay was expressed by one member, who felt that playing a significant role in data collection should merit authorship. Interestingly, this is an issue addressed within the BSA (2001) guidance. They argue that all those listed on a paper should have made a substantive contribution – explained as comprising intellectual responsibility and substantive work – to at least two of the four main components of the paper. For the BSA (2001), these are: (1) the conception or design of the project; (2) data collection and processing; (3) data analysis and interpretation; and (4) writing substantive sections of the paper. The guidelines further argue that all those listed as authors should have critical input at each point of the review process and should approve the final version of the manuscript. Similar themes are raised under the University of Cambridge (2016) guidance, which states that:

> Normally, an author is an individual judged to have made a substantial intellectual or practical contribution to a publication and who agrees to be accountable for that contribution. This would normally include anyone who has: a. made a significant contribution to the conception or design of the project or the acquisition, analysis, or interpretation of data for the work; AND/OR b. drafted the work or reviewed/ revised it critically for important intellectual content.

Having noted formal guidance regarding the basis of authorship and the nature of a contribution, we return to insights provided regarding the order of authorship. Beyond noting that authorship should reflect the contribution made, and specific guidance regarding students, the order of authors is not explicitly addressed within BPS (2011) guidance. It is, however, within the BSA (2001). They note that the person who has made the major contribution or led the writing of the paper should be first author; that those who have made major contributions should follow (with the size of the contribution determining order); and that remaining contributors should be in alphabetical order. As noted by one of our colleagues, they also suggest that equal contribution by authors can be indicated by a footnote.

Also of interest to the group was the discovery of a document posted by the Committee on Publication Ethics authored by Albert and Wager (2003). In the spirit of prevention being better than cure, the guidance document, aimed at early career researchers, attempts to tackle the often politically charged and personally embarrassing scenario of authorship disputes. Recommending how authors might adopt proactive tactics so as to avoid authorship problems, three key principles are highlighted. These are: encouraging a culture of ethical authorship (and not blindly following precedent); starting to discuss authorship when you plan your research (and continuing these discussions throughout the life of the paper development, keeping written records of decisions); and deciding authorship before you start each article (including communicating and managing expectations). The document also condemns the use of 'gift' and 'ghost' writers. Gift writers refers to authors who are listed as so but have not fulfilled at least two of the four criteria listed above. Ghost writers by contrast are those who have made a significant contribution to the project but whose input is not acknowledged. Usefully, the document (see Albert and Wager, 2003) also provides insight into how to handle authorship disputes and misconduct.

Having reviewed the formal guidance, by way of summary one of the group members noted that the guidelines seemed to be a helpful way to depersonalise conflict. In their view, common to all was discussion about 'expectations, obligations, accountability and integrity'. They then directly addressed the early career faculty member, noting that there are different bases for awarding authorship. In the circumstances described, the speaker felt that the early career researcher's colleague hadn't made a sufficient contribution to merit authorship, although they could, if the feedback merited it, be given an acknowledgement. The speaker also advised that the author continue to refer to 'my' paper!

AUTHORSHIP: EXPECTATIONS AND OBLIGATIONS

In our research we look at exchange relationships, respectively examining customer–employee interfaces and employment relationships. Like all relationships, including authorship ones, issues relating to the expectations and perceived obligations of all parties arise. Within authorship relationships, key points around which expectations are likely to occur are:

- the basis for inclusion as an author on papers;
- the premise on which the order of authors is determined, and by whom.

These expectations can arise and exist implicitly, if not formally addressed. Based on the experiences of those in our group, problems are likely to occur where expectations are implicit, and differences in perceptions don't become apparent, or resolved, early in the process. The longer it goes on, the harder it seems to be. Consequently, communication is key. Formal authorship guidelines provide a basis for discussion when starting new relationships or projects. For each project and paper, being upfront and honest regarding individuals' own expectations, time and ability to contribute is paramount – as is building in opportunities to revisit relative contributions and author ordering.

Like anything worth having in life, negotiating co-authorship isn't always easy. However, here we add a personal note to the discussion – and an advocacy of its benefits. We both really enjoy co-authoring. For each of us, co-authors have served hugely significant roles in developing our research skills, and our careers. Aspects of academic life can be lonely and trying. Working with others to see a project through from conception to completion can be a great source of fun and reward. A good co-author isn't just someone who you want to spend time with: they should challenge you. Co-authors provide deadlines that focus progression. They enable conversations about theoretical framing and data analysis – helping make tacit connections explicit. For us, co-authoring with others has developed our individual capacities to write, helped to enhance the quality of our work, and our enjoyment in the process. It has also enabled us, in turn, to mentor others in this process. Everyone, regardless of their level of seniority or time spent as an academician, can enjoy, learn and benefit from co-authoring. It is the fuel that propels academic and individual development.

Being clear about expectations and obligations in this most common, and critical, of academic relationships can support enjoyable, enduring and productive writing relationships.

LESSONS

- Have a clear understanding of the basis of authorship at the start of a project and each paper within it.
- Contemplate who merits authorship and what order of authorship best represents each individual's contribution.
- Don't be afraid to communicate, discuss and debate. Ask questions and don't blindly follow authorship traditions or conventions.
- Revisit authorship and ordering of authors throughout the key milestones of an article's development, including the review and revision process. If needed, formally document any agreed changes.
- Be accountable. Authorship represents a responsibility. Ensure all co-authors sign off on the content of the paper at each stage of the writing and publication process.
- Leave egos at the door and actively manage your own expectations and the expectations of others. Who is responsible for what and by when? Agree on the process that needs to be followed by each co-author to bring the paper to fruition. It's good to talk.
- Use formal guidance notes to guide and depersonalise conflict. Don't let problems or misunderstandings fester, face them head on.
- Last and not least, act with integrity and enjoy co-authoring.

ACKNOWLEDGEMENTS

We acknowledge the input of our lunch companions to the ideas shared in this chapter. As they made a substantive contribution to the development of the ideas therein, we would ideally have afforded them authorship – but we don't know their names.

NOTE

1. Authors in alphabetical order. Each author contributed equally to the writing process. In addition, one contributed a packet of posh biscuits. The other ate most of them.

REFERENCES

Albert, T. and Wager, E. (2003), 'How to handle authorship disputes: a guide for new researchers', Committee on Publication Ethics (COPE) Report, pp. 32–4.

British Psychological Society (2011), Research Board Statement of Policy on Authorship and Publication Credit (July), accessed 10 November 2016 at http://www.bps.org.uk/system/files/images/statement_of_policy_on_authorship_credit.pdf.

British Sociological Association (2001), Authorship Guidelines for Academic Papers, accessed 22 November 2016 at https://www.britsoc.co.uk/media/21409/authorship_01.pdf.

Fine, M.A. and Kurdek, L.A. (1993), 'Reflections on determining authorship credit and authorship order on faculty–staff collaborations', *American Psychologist*, *48*(11), 1141–7.

University of Cambridge (2016), Guidelines on Authorship, accessed 11 November 2015 at http://www.research-integrity.admin.cam.ac.uk/research-integrity/guidelines-authorship.

29. 'Will I ever be good enough?': Using feedback constructively

Amanda Lee

I'M JUST NOT GOOD ENOUGH

Wondering if my writing is ever going to be good enough has been a perennial theme throughout my academic life. Writing convincingly and articulately is a highly skilled craft, and like all skills, it takes time, practice, and patience to master. From my experience, practice was undoubtedly the key. In my attempts to produce work of reasonable quality, I remember thinking, 'What's the point in writing if I don't have anything to say?' However, I soon learnt that that even if you don't think you have anything to say, write anyway. I found that once I begin writing, I start thinking, creating, reflecting, and critiquing, all of which ultimately contributes to and supports my writing.

My doctoral research spanned six years, with the added complexity of being a part-time distance learner and full-time working mum. Six years prior to embarking on my doctorate I had completed a Master's degree and considered myself to be reasonably articulate in respect of my writing skills. However, all that changed when I became a doctoral student and received detailed written feedback from one of my supervisors. Even though this happened several years ago, the memory of how utterly stupid and useless I felt is still vivid. I was upset and confused, because I had already received some encouraging feedback from my other supervisor. Thankfully, I had a very close colleague and friend in whom I could confide, so my first response was to call her up and tell her how I felt. She was also a full-time working mum and studying part time for her doctorate, so I knew she would understand my situation. As a part-time student researcher, I found the support of colleagues, friends, and fellow students was, and is, incredibly important. For me, the doctoral road was very long, often lonely, introspective, and frequently all-consuming. The knowledge that someone else was going through the same trials and tribulations was a comfort and reassurance to me. The first piece of advice my colleague offered was to capture my feelings in that moment, so I wrote them down.

From the beginning of my doctoral studies, I kept a reflective research journal in which I recorded my thoughts, feelings, experiences, and observations. These related both to the subject of my research, as well as my own introspective reflections. This extract from my journal captures my feelings and state of mind on receiving this feedback:

> Feeling rather fed up this evening. Received feedback on my managerialism chapter in the post today and although comments were very constructive it made it clear to me that I have such a long way to go. I am getting so tired, work is very demanding at the moment, yet I am aware of how much more time I need to spend on my research. It isn't just time, its useful time. It really struck me that work produced for my doctorate can't be just good enough, it has to be much better than that, it has to make a difference and it has to matter. At the moment I feel as though it is all far beyond me and unachievable. I really hope this feeling passes soon as it is affecting my motivation and I am finding excuses as to why I shouldn't just get on with it.

Perhaps this extract strikes a chord with you, if so, I hope it reassures you that you are not alone. On the other hand, if you have not been on the receiving end of such feedback it may help to prepare you for such an experience. The good news is things will, and do, get better. It is all part of the steep learning curve synonymous with postgraduate research. That journal entry was written towards the end of my first 12 months. Working full time I found it incredibly difficult to juggle the demands of my job, doctorate, and family and regularly felt guilty that I was not devoting enough time to any of them, but particularly my doctoral research. When something had to give, it was invariably my research. As I read through my supervisor's comments, I came to the realization of what is required to produce a body of work considered to be of doctoral level and, especially significant for me, how (and how much) to write. I had previously sent short pieces of written work to my supervisors, but their feedback had been sparse. Looking back, this was because I hadn't actually written anything of substance for them to comment upon.

A few weeks after receiving this feedback I attended a conference where my supervisor was chairing a developmental paper session. It was difficult (not to mention a bit scary), but I told him how I had felt when I received his feedback, and I was surprised at his reaction – in a good way. He was genuinely concerned that I had been so upset by his comments and this was clearly not his intention. He explained that whilst my written work was good, his role was to help me make it even better. I was very appreciative of this; it cleared the air and helped me get things into perspective. He also told me I needed to write more, but as I have already indicated, I was fully aware of that. Talking frankly to my supervisor was beneficial, and if you find yourself in a similar situation, I strongly recommend you do this, but maybe after a few days when you have given yourself time to fully digest their feedback and see things more objectively. It was also a learning experience for my supervisor who, because of this experience, told me he is more reflective and considered in the way he gives feedback. Although his students still say his comments don't pull any punches!

After six years, as I reached the enviable final stage of writing up my thesis, I looked back on my journal entry, and it seemed as though I was reading about someone else. It was only with the benefit of hindsight I could see how far I had come. I felt as though I wanted to reach out to my earlier self and tell her everything would be all right in the end. The successful completion and award of my doctorate is testament that it was. As my research and writing developed, I became accustomed to receiving critical feedback and was better prepared both emotionally and practically. I also got to know my supervisors' own idiosyncratic styles, likes, dislikes, and expectations. This helped me cultivate a clearer sense of what they believed I could achieve. However, this was not necessarily compatible with estimations of my own ability, which were somewhat lower. Another recurring theme throughout my professional and academic career, and to some extent my personal life, has been the notion of Imposter Syndrome (Bothello and Roulet 2019). I am still convinced that someday, someone, will find out that I don't have a clue what I am doing, or know what I am talking about. Indeed, it is my association with this phenomenon that led me to the title of this chapter. That aside, I do acknowledge that by the time I had written the first full draft of my thesis, I could see the extent to which my writing had improved. But, had it not been for the honest, frank, comprehensive, and critical feedback received from my supervisors, I do not believe this would have been the case. So, I suppose what I am saying is, it hurts like hell at the time, but it really is worth the pain!

ACTUALLY, I THINK I MIGHT BE OK

Towards the end of my second year, I was writing more, though not as regularly as I would have liked. Despite my efforts to write 'little and often', the demands of my job and family often precluded this. So, I would block time out in my diary and use annual leave to enable space for concentrated thinking and writing. As the volume of my written work increased, so did the frequency and depth of the feedback I received. By this stage, I had developed a strong relationship and bond with both my supervisors and in some cases I was able to anticipate their feedback. For this reason, I would often include my own notes and comments in drafts to show them my thought patterns and plans for how I thought the writing of my chapters should progress. This process worked very well for me, and it also made it much easier to respond to their feedback. The following are some journal extracts written when I was working on a peer-reviewed journal article on which my supervisors were second and third authors:

> Feedback received from first supervisor and main comments were that I needed to inject a more nuanced picture into my narrative. But overall, she felt it was a rich and interesting discussion. Obviously, feeling more anxious about second supervisor's comments.

A day later I received feedback from my second supervisor:

> Feedback received from second supervisor and the paper, together with both sets of comments, is pasted in my journal. Second supervisor wanted me to include more quotes/comments that I've observed and beef up the conclusion considerably.

What I find interesting to note in these journal extracts (as opposed to my earlier example) is that the focus is on summarizing what I need to do, rather than how I was feeling. Nevertheless, the first extract above does reveal I was more apprehensive waiting for my second supervisor's comments.

Within the paper were numerous comments, suggestions, amendments, additions, and deletions from both supervisors, but by now I was much better equipped to deal with and respond to them. I did this by systematically working through each point, making the necessary modifications, and detailing my response in writing for my supervisors. I realized as I was doing this, I was honing skills that would be needed to respond to other academic peer reviewers outside of the comfort zone of my own supervisors.

Ultimately, the paper we were working on was accepted for publication and this was a high point in my doctoral studies. As first author I had to respond to the journal editor's comments and I drew heavily on my experiences of responding to my own supervisors' feedback:

> Worked hard on getting the amendments done (with advice from my first and second supervisors). It was time-consuming, but a very worthwhile exercise and it was a learning curve for me as it was the first time I have written back to an editor with my responses. For my sake (as well as the Journal's), I sent back one draft with all amendments, another showing all the track changes and a separate document detailing all our responses to the copy editor's comments. I am really excited about seeing my first publication in print and it is a vindication that my doctorate is worth doing.

The final 12 months of my doctorate was spent analysing my data, revisiting, reviewing, and updating earlier chapters and writing up later chapters and my introduction. By now, I had begun to think of myself as a competent writer and this really struck home when I received feedback from my supervisors on my revised literature review chapters. In contrast to comments on my earlier work, they really didn't have much to say. My first supervisor responded only by email pointing out a few typos but was happy with the content and quality of my work. My second supervisor (the scary one) only made seven comments and most of these were for clarification. For the first time, I didn't need to make any substantial changes or amendments in response to their feedback. I felt really good when my second supervisor told me in person that when he read my updated literature review chapters, he could see that 'I had got it'. This gave me a burst of confidence and a real spur to get on with writing up the remainder of the damn thing!

When I was ready to send the first full draft of my thesis to my supervisors, I still felt apprehensive about their feedback (that never completely went away), but I was also incredibly relieved that this day had finally come. Furthermore, because I had been sending them written work throughout the whole process, they had already seen and commented on much of it. I can't stress enough how important it had been to send work to my supervisors for feedback and comment, and as I said at the start of this chapter, I have done this from the beginning. However, every supervisor/supervisee relationship is different and unique and learning how to manage your supervisors, and nurture your relationship with them, are other skills you need to develop. I consider myself very fortunate to have had the supervisory team I did, but this relationship is two-way, and I was always ready to take their advice and act upon it.

After submitting my first full draft I was genuinely surprised by how quickly my supervisors came back to me, although I realize this may not be the case for all doctoral students. Nevertheless, I do recommend asking your supervisors how long you can expect to wait for feedback on written work. On this occasion, I can honestly say I was pleasantly surprised by their feedback: Yes, I still had work to do, amendments, additions, and corrections to make, but their positive comments really gave me a lift. However, because this time the comments were few, and not in as much detail as I had been used to previously, I had several questions for my supervisors. I was no longer afraid to challenge them or ask for clarity or on the feedback they gave me. As I have mentioned previously, talking to supervisors about my concerns, feelings, and any difficulties I was having was essential. This also fostered mutual trust and respect within the supervisory relationship.

I responded to my supervisors' comments by email, carefully going through each of their points one by one, explaining my rationale and asking for more information and clarity where needed. I also followed this up with telephone and Skype conversations, so I was absolutely clear about what it was my supervisors felt I must do. That was in July 2016, and I spent every spare moment of the summer (including my holidays – much to the disgust of my long-suffering family) making the necessary amendments and adjustments to my thesis. By early September, my amended full draft was sent to my supervisors.

For the next few days, I waited with bated breath. I was due to see my second supervisor at a conference the following week and I knew he would want to discuss my latest attempt. He was full of smiles when I saw him and said, 'Have you read my email?' I hadn't, and for a split second I had a feeling of dread. This soon passed when he told me, 'Well, in my view its ready to submit.' I felt euphoric, six years' work and I was nearly there! If you had told me I would be in this situation even one year ago, I would not have believed it. Every doctoral student experience is unique, but for me, much of my thesis came together in the final six months. This was a culmination of the preceding months and years of work and slog, combined with the unstinting support, guidance, and constructive criticism of my supervisors. I could not have done it without them and for that I will be eternally grateful. But, and there is always a 'but', it is *my* thesis and *I* had to do the work. This included sending regular drafts to my supervisors, accepting their feedback in the spirit in which it was offered, and acting on their advice. I always asked if I didn't understand – and even when I thought I did – as I knew they were driven by the desire to help me improve and enable me to craft my work to be the best it could be.

LESSONS FOR KEEPING ON TRACK: DEALING WITH FEEDBACK CONSTRUCTIVELY

In this final section I present a list of Dos and Don'ts, based on my own experiences. I have listed the Don'ts first, as from my perspective these were some of the feelings I experienced when first receiving supervisor feedback. From discussions with other doctoral students, I now realize such feelings and reactions are normal, and you are not alone, but you can develop the resilience to face them.

Don't:

- Take feedback personally, even though it is intensely personal to you. Your thesis is your creation, and it is a natural reaction to defend your work. Indeed, being able to defend your work is an important skill to develop.
- Ignore or dismiss supervisor feedback. Their comments are intended to help you hone your craft and develop as a researcher and writer.
- Use feedback as an excuse not to write.
- Use feedback to beat yourself up, or to think you are stupid, or not good enough. *You are not stupid,* and *you are good enough*, but you have to learn how to do it.

Do:

- Write down, or audio/video record how you feel and reflect on why you feel this way. This can really help to consolidate and make sense of the situation and the feedback.
- Talk to someone unconnected with your thesis. This could be a fellow student, colleague, friend, or family member. They will not be emotionally attached to your thesis in the way that you are.
- Sleep on it. Give yourself time to digest the feedback and go back to it a few days later. Make notes on the comments from your supervisor(s) and how you can address them.
- Arrange a meeting with your supervisor(s). Talk to them about their comments and your reactions to their feedback. Ask questions to clarify exactly what they mean and what you need to do.
- Once you are clear about what you need to do to improve your work, systematically work through each comment and make the necessary amendments. Make a note of the amendments you have made.
- Keep earlier versions of your work, clearly labelled by date and version.
- Agree a timescale with your supervisor(s) for submission of your written work and stick to it.
- Write every day if you can – little and often soon mounts up. Some supervisors like to see small chunks of work on a regular basis, whilst others prefer complete chapters. Set the ground rules with your supervisor so you both know what is expected.
- After a few weeks (or months), go back and reflect on your initial thoughts and feelings. With the benefit of hindsight, you will appreciate how far you have come and how you have developed as a researcher.

REFERENCE

Bothello, J. and Roulet, T.J. (2019). The imposter syndrome, or the mis-representation of self in academic life. *Journal of Management Studies*, *56*(4), 854–61.

30. Grasping roses or nettles? Losing and finding ourselves in research projects

Kiran Trehan, Alex Kevill and Jane Glover

> All the world's a stage
> And all the men and women merely players
> They have their exits and their entrances
> And one man in his time plays many parts
> (William Shakespeare, *As You Like It*, Act II, Scene VII)

INTRODUCTION

Developing, maintaining and sustaining research projects have become almost obligatory within research arenas. The aim of our chapter is to illuminate and explore the relationship between emotions, politics and disappointment in developing and maintaining research projects. We elucidate the lived reality of undertaking research projects as turbulent, volatile and an emotional endeavour. Using illustrations from our own experiences in the field, we develop three distinct in-depth accounts as 'scenes' to describe the dynamics that underpin research projects whilst also making connections between reflexivity, emotions and disappointment. We highlight how messy and complex keeping research projects on track can be. Our chapter it is not written up 'straightforwardly' as a description of what happened but is an attempt to reveal the shadow side of finding, securing and maintaining research projects by three researchers' different trajectories in their academic careers. We end with our reflections and with lessons learnt for our own practice as researchers.

SCENE 1: AN EARLY CAREER RESEARCHER'S MUSINGS

So there I was, sitting in a small plain meeting room, eating sandwiches and cakes, and celebrating my successful PhD viva with my supervisors and internal examiner. Four and a half years of blood, sweat and tears – and let's not forget the support of my wonderful supervisors – had got me to this point. Finally, I was living the moment that I had pictured in my mind for so long! I had the ticket to my future career in academia and my mind basked in idyllic

images of numerous journal papers flowing from my PhD study. I had successfully completed my first research project – my PhD – and it felt good! Now it
was time to sit back and enjoy the fruits of all my hard work …

… Fast-forward 18 months and here I am. A full-time lecturer, loving my
job, yet frustratingly finding those journal papers are not quite as forthcoming
as I had assumed. Time constraints have become my nemesis, intent as they
are on starving me of my research endeavours. Exciting research ideas regularly give way to my increasingly familiar resignation that most of them will
never materialise. My nemesis is winning the battle it seems. And now, all of
a sudden, I am being encouraged to get involved in my next research project!
Furthermore, I sense that the more significant and impactful it is, the better!

A small tremor of anxiety ripples through me and culminates in an overwhelming sense of exasperation. Surely, I should be concentrating on getting
publications from my previous research study, shouldn't I?! Why embark on
another project when I don't even have time to make the most of the previous
one? How can I possibly make time, within my already packed schedule,
to undertake a new research project to the high standard I would demand
of myself? Whilst such concerns flow through my mind though, they live
awkwardly alongside a sense of enticement and excitement that I feel about
embarking on a new challenge. After all, who wouldn't want to be part of an
interesting, significant and impactful research project if they got the chance?

But where would I start? What would I, as an early career researcher,
know about this? What, if anything, could I bring to the table? Will this be
the point at which my self-perceived shortcomings as a researcher finally
become evident to others? The thought of engaging and working with others in
order to generate real impact both excites and terrifies me in reasonably equal
measure. I feel lost in a sea of unknowns. I wonder particularly about how to
establish links with relevant stakeholders outside of academic circles. This
was challenging enough during my PhD study when trying to establish and
maintain relationships with reasonably small numbers of research participants,
each of whom had little vested interest in my research. A larger scale project,
I am sure, would likely include a more diverse range of stakeholders – academic, organisational, governmental, interest groups etc. – each with different
motivations and vested interests, and each needing to be satisfied and kept
on board with the project. This seems to promise an unappealing labyrinth of
politics and tension that require navigation – do I really want to be involved in
this? How does one even start to navigate such politics and tensions in order
to deliver impact from a project? And at a much more functional level, how
do I even make contact with these stakeholders in the first place to bring them
on board? Do I call them? Can I find somebody who can help get me a foot in
the door?

And what about funding? Who do I seek funding from? How do I seek it? I know that funding applications require a thorough and well-considered research proposal, which likely requires a lot of the groundwork – particularly bringing stakeholders on board – to be done before funding is even assured. And ultimately, all of that groundwork could surely be for nothing if funding is not gained. I wonder to myself how one possibly deals with the disappointment and anguish of facing such a rejection, knowing that all of the hard work and hours dedicated to the bid have essentially been futile.

My mind then switches to that word that we so often hear when talking about research projects – impact. What does impact really mean? Surely all research is impactful in some way, so is impactful research determined by achieving a certain threshold of impact? If so, what is the threshold and how does one go about achieving it? Surely different project stakeholders will have different perceptions of what impact means to them so is it really possible to achieve impact in all stakeholders' eyes or do the views and interests of some stakeholders matter more than others? Most frighteningly of all, what if I promise impact and then can't deliver it? That doesn't even bear thinking about!

These doubts and anxieties become lessened to some degree by the realisation that I could, first of all, seek an opportunity to work as a reasonably junior member of a large research project team. Yes, this sounds a promising compromise! It could surely help me gain much needed experience whilst absolving me of some of the responsibility that I currently feel ill-equipped to take on. But yet nervousness begins to overwhelm my short-lived comfort. Do I really want to be subject to unequal power relationships with those leading the project? Could they drive my future research direction too much? Could I really bring myself to stand up to them if I feel that I need to? I also wonder about how one spots an opportunity to join a good research project team and how one initiates their integration into the project. It seems obvious that I should join a project that I am truly interested in but what if such a project does not present itself? What impact would that then have on my career and, if that happens, should I just take part in any old project whether I am interested in it or not?

Then my immediate next steps suddenly become clear to me. It's time to seek advice from colleagues more experienced in developing and maintaining research projects …

SCENE 2: A POSTDOC'S TRIALS AND TRIBULATIONS OF SECURING (OR NOT) FUNDED RESEARCH PROJECTS

In this section I share with you my reflective life experience of projects, and trying to seamlessly move from one project to another (quite the romantic dream when you read my story). I completed my PhD post changes to university funding in the UK so with little in the way of lectureships at the time I pursued a research career, I found I had more flexibility on research contracts, and because I was restricted to a specific location for family reasons, I found myself not actively pursuing teaching and research posts. My life working on projects started whilst I was doing my PhD; my supervisor at the time asked me if I would like to work on a project, and naturally, as I was self-funded I leapt at the opportunity to earn some money. I would, however, recommend this with caution as you become distracted from your PhD and get used to earning money. There is a certain amount of willpower and dedication required to return to full-time studies again but that's another story.

So I obtained my first working project and it was in an area related to my PhD – small business and innovation. I think I was extremely lucky with the person who was my line manager for this project, I was treated as an equal and based on experiences I will detail later on, he was a total dream to work for. I learnt a lot on this project and improved my research skills. Having done this short stint, about eight months, I returned to my doctoral studies but managed to secure a few hours work doing follow-up work on the project (I also took on teaching work to bolster my income).

A few months before finishing my PhD I secured another short-term project at the same university but in a different department. Maybe not the best decision, but you can't live off fresh air. I think this prolonged the agony of actually finishing my PhD along with the fact that three months before PhD submission we had a house fire which turned everything into turmoil. Anyway, this project, on innovation, was an enlightening experience. I was working for what could only be described as a lovely, old school professor (due to retire) and two younger recently appointed academics, one was very quiet and relatively easy to work for, the other somewhat different to my previous experiences – his view of a researcher was someone to do all the hard work, write the papers so that he could be lead author and bask in the glory with minimal effort. This changed my previously somewhat romantic view that all line managers were like my first one. The key reflections when things go wrong is be careful in terms of the ideas you share; we have no way of securing intellectual property, so ideas for funding research projects can easily get hijacked; and only share these with someone you trust and someone you really want to work with and build a research agenda.

So by this point, I was becoming quite apt at juggling many different projects but still hadn't got used to the fact that short-term projects are often intense (people seem to expect more in less time …) and no sooner have you started one, you are trying to find the next one. This also has implications for creating your own research agenda and developing your own area of expertise so you either end up working on your own research in your spare time, which

I did and found myself working 50 hours plus a week. I didn't mind at the time; I was younger, ambitious and I wanted to succeed and saw this as a way to do that.

Then with another stroke of luck a part-time position became available working with my original line manager. I was overjoyed and couldn't wait to start working with him again, and this was the start of a great role working on different projects either full or part time for the next four years. These were four great years I was able to take the lead in my areas of expertise (qualitative research methods) and complement my line manager (who was as I describe him a die-hard quants man), and it worked. I was allowed to freely manage projects so long as I delivered, I was encouraged to publish, to apply for internal departmental funds (which I managed to win twice), and to look for grants that we could apply for. To me this was what a working academic/researcher partnership should be like; we applied for two external grants, but sadly were unsuccessful. I was also heavily involved in his bid to create a research centre at the institution, which got funded. This was a highly productive partnership; in this time we had six publications, and I had four publications from my own research (which I was encouraged to do as well as others under review). I have never been as productive again in my career nor been as encouraged as I was by this line manager. But as the saying goes, all good things come to an end ... and it did ... My line manager phoned me one day and said, 'I need to tell you something (deathly silence) ... I'm leaving and moving to another institution ...' I was speechless, totally gutted, I felt like my whole world had been swallowed up by a black hole and that I was about to be deserted for a life working for egotistical academics who are only concerned with their own alter-ego and prestige. To be fair, my line manager did say that if I wanted to go, he would try to take me with him, but I couldn't. So my academic knight in shining armour, a complete role model for all line managers, was leaving. I think for my career that was the single worst day, it changed my future direction.

The key thing to note about this working relationship was that I will happily work with him again (and do – we currently have papers in review and also papers to write). He is the only line manager I have had who I would actively seek to work with in the future. The reason for this is, he helped me a lot in my early career, and I believe my path would have taken a different turn had he not left. The institution was not impressed one of their best performing academics (in terms of grants and publications) was leaving. Because I had worked solely with him they were not bothered about trying to keep me on and so I was faced with a (short) spell of unemployment.

This very point signalled a change in my luck in terms of securing back to back projects whether they were full or part time. I had to change my view and learn to cope with disappointment, the stress of being unable to find projects that were longer than a couple of years, and whilst that sounds like a long time, it really isn't. As you have to start looking for the next one at least nine months before your current project expires. I'm sure this would have been easier had I not been restricted to a particular location but that was a life situation that I had to cope with.

I found part-time work again back at the institution, for some of this time, I also worked part time at other institutions to keep myself in full-time employment. I found some of this time quite stressful as during one point I was working on five different projects across two institutions. This was some of my least productive time and I often felt constrained and in some cases (unlike my first line manager) I felt that people didn't trust my judgement. For example, having spent months doing a literature review to identify gaps in the literature and a potential paper, this was ignored – you feel really deflated especially if you put your heart and soul into something because it is interesting. As a word of caution, as a female researcher, my experience has taught me to be cautious and never, I really mean never, question a male professor who requires constant reassurance of their excellence – well not if you want a good reference or a job somewhere else!

However, I did meet another academic on this project who reminded me of my first line manager, and I have, over the years developed a good working relationship with her and she is the only other person I have actively sought to secure funding with and publish with. Maybe one day we will secure that all important large grant and I can bask in my own glory.

During my time of short-term projects I have been presented with obstacles and barriers when trying to apply for external funds, unless I have been lucky enough to have a supportive line manager. Even here, when we submitted two applications that progressed through stage one of review, and then after hours of hard work producing full proposals, we were not awarded anything. Over my somewhat erratic research career I have found there to be, in some institutions, a protectionist type philosophy where I think that young ambitious researchers who question the status quo are not actually something that the institution wants (ironic given that we are taught to be critical and reflective in undergraduate and postgraduate studies). I think that to be successful in securing external funding you need to have some luck, and a very supportive line manager where your work resonates with theirs in such a way that you can legitimately make the suggestion that you should be a co-investigator! Otherwise as someone on short-term contracts moving between institutions, unless you secure that all important permanent position, I have found that it is virtually impossible to apply for external funds.

I'm still, now, stuck on short-term projects and would love to secure something full time for three years or so just to have that bit of stability and security to allow me to pursue a particular research agenda and win funding for projects of my own! The best advice I can give to anyone is I think you need to be prepared that life will throw many obstacles in your way, you may have luck on your side, but if you don't, you have to persevere. I've found the more you want something, the less likely it is you get it – I think you subconsciously put pressure on yourself, so as hard as it may be, try my philosophy of expect nothing every time you try to secure a project and then you'll find one day you land a project totally unexpected, not really what you wanted, but you end up enjoying it and it provides you with opportunity.

In terms of managing projects themselves and trying to find the next one, all I can say is you have to know exactly what YOU (nobody else) want to achieve from that particular project. By this, I mean if you see a project that you wish to work on be clear about the reasons why. Is it the topic, the people you will be working with, the institution and then where does this get you (if times are desperate I appreciate anything will do … but even then you should carve out what could the benefits be for yourself even if to simply learn)? You need to be adept at spotting opportunity and being entrepreneurial.

In summary, my experience of projects, managing projects and looking for projects is one of ups and downs, getting one's hopes up only to come crashing down again (and again) but my hope is that my strategy of being savvy, very selective as to who I will work with, and sheer grit determination will mean that one day I WILL get that large grant and that 4* Journal paper. I can look back and think: it may have been hard work, I may have been taken advantage of, but who cares if I achieve my goal …

SCENE 3: RESEARCHER TURNED PROFESSOR – GRASPING ROSES, OR IS IT NETTLES?

And so to the final scene, how does the story end? Is it a tale of tragedy, as is Julius Caesar, or is it a tale of triumph such as Henry V? The next illustration illuminates the emotional and political labour required to secure and maintain a research project:

I lie in bed, its 6:30 am. Far too early to be getting out of bed on a cold morning, not quite winter yet, there's still a chill in the air. I spy out of the window, dreary day. I haven't slept well, but there it was as I jumped in the shower, the familiar feeling in the pit of my stomach. I'm excited and anxious about a significant project meeting with key stakeholder from the Finance, business, policy and academic community. The stakes are high and we only get one chance to get it right! I feel out of my depth and the initial excitement turns to fear. I remind myself why I had yes to co-directing the project, I wanted to learn and be part of an exciting opportunity. I mused as the warm water of the shower washed over me, not wanting to get out, but I must as I muster the energy for the meeting ahead with trepidation.

On the surface of it, all looks great and exciting – how often to do you get the [highly influential] people together in the same room for 24 hours to work on a major research project. There is an edge of anxiety that I can feel and sense in the room between us (the team) – a conflictual edge that I have not experienced before. I'm intrigued and curious about what's going on but now's not the time to raise it so I stay focused on the task as we prepare for the arrival of our guests.

Our partners begin to arrive and we each play our part yet there is no script ... It is interesting to observe the roles we take on ... [Our administrator] does the meeting and greeting – checking everybody in – making them feels like old friends that have come round for dinner, introducing the newcomers so that feel part of the group. Another colleague is warm and engaging ... There's a good buzz about the place. Dinner goes extremely well ... The newcomers are vocal and have made an impression; there is an interesting tension building behind the friendly and relaxed façade presented by some members and the challenges by new members.

The evening ends, we have a quick debrief in preparation for tomorrow. It's 11.45 pm we are all tired, that edge I mentioned earlier is still there. We should be on a high. We have everyone's commitment and buy-in. Actually we have much more than that, we have access to some of the most powerful resource holders and gatekeepers and they want to engage with us. It feels genuine, authentic and hugely exciting, so why is the team so flat? This is the thought I'm left with as I head to my room.

My reflections are that managing and keeping research projects on track requires particular types of collaboration, leadership and facilitation which are imaginative, passionate, experiential and action related. My own recollections are flooded with a myriad of emotions, fear, anxiety, excitement, limited understanding of all the political processes were at the start anxiety provoking, however, the lived experience of enacting interdisciplinary research has been an incredibly rich endeavour. Extending the reach, reflecting and refracting light opened up my growing curiosities to not just talk about interdisciplinary research as an academic exercise but to endeavour to work with the struggle, fears and insecurities that come from a place of not knowing to a place of unlearning and re-learning. Working on the project has enriched my knowledge and my passion to stray from the narrow confines and alleys of the academic community to travel through wider streets and borders because when combined with passion, rigour, evidence and the commitment of others to make a difference, a difference that matters, nothing is more powerful than working in an interdisciplinary team with all its trials and tribulations.

CONCLUDING REFLECTIONS

Our collective narratives have attempted to offer a glimpse in the life of a researcher attempting to broker and navigate their way through complex dynamics in the lives of research projects when things do not go quite to plan. What it does not do is tell the whole story ... research projects are not without their risks, those big moments of self-doubt, frustrations, anguish alongside moments of laughter, hope, excitement and imagination. Our illustrations highlight the need for commitment, criticality, openness to risk, the ability to speak about the unspoken and question the systems, structures and institutions in which research is crafted, maintained and disrupted ... And as the journey begins:

- Always be true to yourself and what you eventually wish to be known for in the world of research.
- If someone looks after you, such as a line manager, then maintain that relationship, and in time you will be able to repay them.
- Be prepared for utter disappointment but master the art of bouncing back and learning from that experience.
- Try not to take things to heart if someone doesn't like what you've done, ask how it should be improved.
- Be opportunistic – always look for things such as external funding, internal institutional funding and projects to work on and don't be afraid to give it a go.
- Never settle for the path of least resistance.
- When you come close to selling out, reconsider.
- Do not be afraid to take the occasional risk.

31. The problem with peer review … they say as if there's only one problem …

Keith Townsend, Adrian Wilkinson, Andrew Timming and Rebecca Loudoun

Fortunately for the authors of this chapter, there will be no 'peer review' process. It's not that the peer review process is bad, it's just … well … it has some problems. All four of us are very fortunate in that we have managed to publish extensively, primarily in the management and associated fields, but one of the frustrating parts of our careers has been the unevenness of the peer review process. This does cut both ways: sometimes the process has torpedoed what we considered excellent articles, but we would also need to acknowledge that uneven peer reviewing has also helped some weaker papers to creep across the line. We have never complained about those – and to be fair, we try hard to not complain when things don't go our way either. We write this chapter to give the early career researcher some insight into the experience that we will all face in the current social science context – the peer review process. It's fair to say that it can be sometimes peculiar.

There have been significant changes in publication pressures over recent decades. These include: the quantification of research 'quality' (e.g., impact factors, citation counts, h-indices), changes to university funding based around publication quality and impact; an increase in the number of academics per-forming research; work intensification of research scholars' roles; structural changes in publishing houses and their approach to academic research; journal ranking lists; and more.

These changes mean that the publication process (not the research process) provides for a different experience in the current era. Sometimes we feel like skilled craftsmen of the pre-industrial era seeing changes towards factory-based working and the incoming mass production era, but our work-places are not changing to meet the demands placed upon us. Although careers are built upon publishing, for the most part editors do not get paid for editing the journal nor are they provided with a time allocation by universities. Rarely do academics receive administrative support for the editorial role, but universi-ties are very keen to know that we have editorial roles to support the university accreditation process. Equally, the peer review process is the foundation of the academic publishing system yet an academic does not receive monetary reward for it and it rarely counts towards their workload allocation or annual performance reviews.

SO WHERE DOES PEER REVIEW FIT IN?

In historical terms, peer review is relatively recent. Al-Mousawi (2020) provides an overview of the peer review system tracking the first use of a 'referee' back to 1817, but editorial judgement of publication 'worthiness' as early as 1665. But it wasn't until the mid-1990s that the peer review process became ubiquitous. And for the modern-day social scientist, the process goes a little something like this. After designing and completing your research project and writing up your journal articles, you submit your toil to a journal where the first hurdle is an editor. If that hurdle is cleared, the editor sends your de-identified article to between two and four 'experts' in the field who are expected to read your work and decide whether it is appropriate for publication. They send their reviews back to the editor to make a judgement – typically one of three outcomes – rejection, minor revisions or major revisions.

And here is where things start getting a bit weird. All of us have published widely, but also been editors of journals and reviewers for many articles. So, we can speak from experience as authors, editors and reviewers when we say that not all reviewers are actually 'experts' in the field. Not all reviewers seem to actually read the articles that they are sent in great detail. And not all editors adequately consider the reviewers' comments, indeed, many do not read the paper either. But we face the reality that it's our job to perform research *and* publish our findings, so we keep working through an imperfect system.

The following are examples of experiences and comments that we have received in the reviewing process that left us scratching our heads. We hope the more experienced readers of this chapter will nod their heads knowingly, and the less experienced readers will endeavour to help us collectively lift the standard of the peer review system for future researchers:

- **Rogue editors and hidden reviewer comments.** After recently submitting a paper to a high-profile HRM journal, the Associate Editor (AE) screened it and decided that it was worth sending out for review. The paper was a Study 1 (quant) and Study 2 (qual follow-up). We acknowledged the limitations of Study 1 and designed Study 2 to address them. In the first round three reviews came back: minor revisions, major revisions, major revisions, and none of the suggestions seemed too onerous. Finally, we had received a good set of reviews! However, the AE decided that s/he would only accept a revision with further data collection, that is, Study 3! None of the reviewers had suggested this and they were overwhelmingly positive.

We appealed the decision to the Editor in Charge (EiC), explaining that the AE should have desk rejected it if s/he thought more data were needed and pointed to the three sets of positive comments from the reviewers. Our appeal was rejected, and we were told that one of the reviewers provided 'confidential' comments to the editor that justified his/her decision. Of course, we had no access to these hidden comments, so there was no way of verifying one way or the other.

In a similar vein and, unfortunately, from the same journal we had the following experience:

- **Eight months in review, minor comments and rejected.** After eight months in review, the author contacted the editor of the journal and the response was that there were difficulties with finding reviewers. Approximately six weeks later the article was rejected despite what the authors thought was one very positive review with limited and very manageable rewrites required. In fact, the reviewer stated that 'The findings of the study ... is important for this sector and is important for the HR process research.' The reviewer continued, 'Good luck with the revisions of your article.' Yet the article was rejected and when the authors contacted the editor, we were told that 'The reviewer had sent me comments in private' and that 'the article is at a very early stage at the moment'. The delicious irony here was that we sent this article largely unchanged to a higher-ranked journal where it was published (and is tracking quite well with citations!).
- **Reject and resubmit to minor revisions on same submission.** In 2019 an article with a PhD student as the lead author was submitted to a mid-ranking journal. The article received an unusual but increasingly common 'reject and resubmit', which, given the context, the authors were not unhappy. The authorship team took the advice of the reviewers and editors to the best of their ability and prepared a detailed response document along with the revised article. Some months after submission the article was returned with a 'minor revision'. The reviewer also noted that 'the revised manuscript presents a clearer contribution sufficient for publication'. Not surprisingly the authors were pleased with this result and set about addressing the minor issues in the revised manuscript. One author noted that something did not add up – there seemed to be a disconnection between the minor revision requests and the revised article. After logging in to the online system the author realised that the PhD student had made a mistake and uploaded the original version of the document rather than the revision. This means that exactly the same version of an article was given a 'reject and resubmit' followed by a 'minor revision' by the reviewer and editor. We chose not

to point this out to the editor and accepted the minor revision decision. We felt it was the right decision ...

- **Two PhD students, two different results.** We made two submissions to the same high-ranking journal during the same week. Both articles had a PhD student as the lead author and similar co-authors. Both articles held similar merit, however article 1 was returned with a very negative single review with comments like 'Generally the findings are not that surprising and hence, I don't feel that the contribution is significant enough to warrant publication'; this article received a R&R. Some weeks later article 2 was returned – also only receiving one review which was very positive. The authors considered the comments as they related to the submission and predicted that it was about 4–5 hours of work to address. The reviewer also finished this review with 'Best of luck with your revision'. Article 2 though was rejected. If there was a modicum of consistency with editorial decisions, the outcomes for these two articles ought to have been reversed – article 1 review was quite negative with many days' worth of re-working required, while article 2 review was very positive and with very few changes.

- **Desperation for referees leads to strange referee comments.** Occasionally there are comments from reviewers that seem so peculiar that they are almost impossible to address. For example, in one article the reviewer commented: 'Why did you choose 2 companies from the same public sector? I would have thought choosing companies from different industries may at least allow the author/s to tell a different story.' Well, we were astounded by that brilliant insight! Of course, if we chose different companies we would have told a different story because the data collected would likely have been different! However, the study was designed to identify similarities and differences within similar organisations. Surely the fundamental role of reviewers is to provide a critique of the study that is before them, rather than suggest that a different study should have occurred.

If we thought the review process wasn't hard enough, when you start doing multi-disciplinary or multi-method research the problems increase!

- **Don't use 'paradigms' or you'll confuse readers.** A 2010 submission to a cross-disciplinary journal was titled 'Can the high-performance paradigm contribute to healthcare management'. The article was rejected, and two comments stood out as peculiar. The first was that the article had little to offer because 'high performance work systems were not a real thing, just something pushed by textbooks or consultants'. At the time, the key high-performance research works (Huselid, 1995; Appelbaum et al., 2001)

had more than 3000 citations between them (and more than 21,000 citations by the time this chapter is published). The second comment which we
found peculiar was that 'the author/s should not use paradigm in the title
because it will confuse people'. When writing for a readership operating
within the tertiary education sector, the notion that people will be confused
by 'paradigm' is alarming.

- **The perils of multi-disciplinarity.** One author's 2019 book, *Human
Resource Management and Evolutionary Psychology: Exploring the
Biological Foundations of Managing People at Work*, was never intended
to be a book. After writing several articles linking evolutionary biology and
human resource management, and regardless of the quality of those articles
(and I maintain that they are scientifically sound and make an original
contribution to the literature), they were repeatedly rejected from HRM
journals because they were viewed as 'biology' and they were repeatedly
rejected from biology journals because they were viewed as 'HRM'. In
short, taking a truly multi-disciplinary approach leaves authors in 'no
man's land', especially given that most journals are grounded in specific
disciplines.

- **Ideological bias.** This one is impossible to prove, but my suspicion is
that articles that challenge orthodox thinking are rejected out of reviewer
and/or editor bias. One of the authors wrote a paper looking at 'voice
discrimination' in relation to attractiveness, race and gender. In other
words, are managers more likely to listen and act on the suggestions of
more attractive, white and male employees? The empirical results showed
a huge attractiveness effect (managers ignore less attractive employees and
listen to more attractive ones), but no race effect and an opposite gender
effect (managers are more likely to listen to women than men). I explained
these race and gender effects as likely down to social desirability bias (no
one wants to admit that they discriminate against women and non-white
employees), but this result is not consistent with the intersectionality narrative. Would it be too provocative to wonder whether the attractiveness of
reviewers play into their evaluations of attractiveness papers?

The next few examples demonstrate that many editors unfortunately have a
'form letter' that they do not adequately tailor for the letter to the authors. This
can be incredibly frustrating because it provides the academics with the sense
that the process is not given an appropriate level of attention:

- **Employee voice article rejected because it was unsuitable.** Throughout
late 2018 we had developed an article that had an employee voice focus
and submitted to a journal that not only had we published employee voice
articles in previously, but the journal's website shows 230 articles on

employee voice have been published. We received a single sentence desk reject with the phrase 'in light of the appropriateness of your manuscript for our journal' as the only reason provided for rejection. Again, we can pleasingly say this article was accepted elsewhere and is doing quite well with citations.

- **Your article is neither international nor HRM.** On two occasions we have received rejections from a journal for international research on HRM. We are not claiming that our articles should have been accepted, but the process provides feedback that does not align with the submissions. For example, one article was about performance management systems in Singapore, and the other was about HRM systems in Pakistan. On both occasions there was a standard line in the rejection letter suggesting we pay attention to the scope of the journal as it requires submissions to be HRM with an international focus.

Now these are just a handful of examples from decades' worth of involvement in the reviewing process. We could provide enough comments to fill this whole book. Importantly, we want to make the point that this chapter is not designed to just whine and complain (but hey – we are human, we whine a little bit) because we aren't getting our work published – that's not the case at all. As we mentioned earlier, we have all published widely but that doesn't preclude us from recognising problems within the system.

Some of the problems that we think are occurring due primarily to time constraints and workload pressures are that good-quality expert reviewers are not available to do as many reviews as the system requires, thus many early career researchers are reviewing articles that they do not have expertise in and they do not have a great deal of experience in the review process, so they are approaching the review process with that inexperience. The editors' workloads are so great that they find themselves counting reviews rather than making judgements on the quality of the reviews.

SO AS A NEW RESEARCHER, WHAT ARE THE LESSONS OR TAKEAWAYS FROM THESE HORROR STORIES?

The first is to have faith in your work. Generally, if you have done good research, it will find a good home but it may take time and you will have to be patient. Second, is not to take comments personally. The referees may be experts although that does not guarantee a fair review as some experts are inclined to use the review to show they are so much smarter than you or you really should have done a project they wanted you to do rather than the one you did. Sometimes the reviewers may be generalists offering non-expert comments. So don't take it personally, it's about the work and the process.

Third, rejection is not failure. Even the very best scholars get rejections. We often joke that we've been rejected from the best journals in the world. As Rousseeuw (1991, p. 41) stated:

> It is commonly known and a constant source of frustration that even well-known refereed journals contain a large fraction of bad articles which are boring, repetitive, incorrect, redundant, and harmful to science in general. What is perhaps even worse, the same journals also stubbornly reject some brilliant and insightful articles (i.e., your own) for no good reason.

Keep in mind, there is almost always something in the comments which will help you improve your work. Whatever the expertise or experience of the reviewers, they are providing you with FREE comments and feedback. See what can be done with them even if you are not going back to the journal. It is a rare article that cannot be improved with feedback. Don't see a rejection as a rejection – look at it as a revise and resubmit ... elsewhere.

Fourth, keep in mind that experience does help. Over time persistent researchers get better at dealing with journals and editors and perhaps become more sanguine ... Until that point you need to ensure you have good support around you. These can be your supervisors or senior researchers who might not be at your university. They can provide you with good advice and see your travails in a wider context.

Now from the other side, reviewers, please – take your job seriously and remember you don't have to change the article. You are not an author, you are being asked to see if you can find ways to make the article that was submitted better. You are not being asked to convince the authors to write the article that you would have written. And try to be kind and respectful.

Editors, we know it's a thankless task and we know that you are probably overworked like the rest of us. But there are things that you can do to make the process better. Like being transparent about comments from reviewers that aren't in the reviews; reading the article to see if the reviewer comments match the submitted article; and removing ridiculous comments from reviews before they are sent to the authors.

Finally, we have lived the experience from all sides. We know that it's not easy and we know that we aren't rewarded for effort. So, we offer this chapter to help new researchers to understand the uneven system that we work within and to encourage all involved to be better at what we do.

REFERENCES

Al-Mousawi, Y., (2020) 'A brief history of peer review'. https://blog.f1000.com/2020/01/31/a-brief-history-of-peer-review/#:~:text=The%20beginnings%20of%20peer%20review%20as%20we%20know%20it%20now&text=This%20process%20was%20based%20on,for%20the%20invention%20of%20refereeing.

Appelbaum, E., Bailey, T., Berg, P. and Kalleberg, A.L. (2001) 'Do high performance work systems pay off?' In Vallas, S. (Ed.) *The Transformation of Work* (*Research in the Sociology of Work, Vol. 10*). Bingley, UK: Emerald Group Publishing, pp. 85–107. https://doi.org/10.1016/S0277-2833(01)80022-4.

Huselid, M.A. (1995) 'The impact of human resource management practices on turnover, productivity, and corporate financial performance'. *Academy of Management Journal, 38,* 635–72. http://dx.doi.org/10.2307/256741.

Rousseeuw, P.J. (1991) 'Why the wrong papers get published'. *Chance: New Directions for Statistics and Computing, 4*(1), 41–3.

32. My research journey in the offline and online world of social media

Samreen Ashraf

INTRODUCTION

Colleague:	You know, I was just thinking about how different researching is nowadays with social media everywhere. I started way before all this digital revolution.
Me:	Oh, really? That must have been a whole different ball game. How did you manage your research at the time?
Colleague:	Well, back in my day, it was all about dusty library shelves, printed journals, and phone calls to fellow researchers. We didn't have the luxury of a quick Google search or a LinkedIn group for academic discussions.
Me:	That sounds challenging. How did you keep up with the latest research trends and connect with other researchers?
Colleague:	It was a slower process, for sure. Conferences and workshops were the main avenues. You had to physically attend to network and stay updated. It's amazing how social media has changed the game, connecting researchers globally at the click of a button.
Me:	I can't imagine not having those tools at my fingertips. How do you think it has changed the way we do research?
Colleague:	Well, it's made collaboration easier and information more accessible. But there was a charm in the slower pace too – gave us time to reflect. The digital era has its perks, but sometimes I miss the quieter, more deliberate rhythm of the pre-social media research world.

These excerpts are from various conversations I had with a colleague of mine who had completed his PhD almost four decades ago. Returning to academia after all these years, he was surprised to see how much social media changed the way we do research. On his return, he was amazed to see how the research world has moved on, especially with the interventions from social media.

This compelling insight became the starting point for my reflections, highlighting the evolving perceptions surrounding social media in the world of research. In today's world, you can't really ignore social media, instead, it has become imperative to harness its potential for our benefit.

But let's not pretend everything is perfect. Social media has its good and not-so-good sides. Come along with me as we explore how social media and research work together. There's a lot to talk about, but I will keep it short and sweet. So, keep reading to find out about the different experiences and things I've started to figure out while navigating the world of research in the digital age, although, I still have a long way to go. In the following sections, you will find my observations on the ups and downs of using social media for research through my lens. I will share the importance of looking at social media as an enabler and a tool to help us in our respective journeys – keeping in mind its downsides.

I will start the chapter by highlighting some of the positives of using social media in our research journeys, that is, DOs and later I will delve into some of the potential negatives of using these platforms, that is, DON'Ts. Let's go.

DOs

You Are Not Alone (Learning from Each Other)

Doing a research project can feel like a crazy ride with lots of ups and downs. It's like being on a roller coaster without being able to see where you're going. But here's the cool part – on social media, you can connect with others who understand the ride you're on.

In the world of research, some tasks can be tough. It's like trying to find your way in a big jungle. Social media can be a guide, like a helpful compass. Whether you're stuck on tricky statistics or feeling unsure about your methodological choices, someone out there has been through the same situation.

Imagine this: it's late at night, and you're drowning in books and papers. Suddenly, you see a post from another researcher going through the same struggle. You realize you're not alone! Social media is like a friendly oasis in the middle of the hard times of research.

I was struggling to decide on a viable methodological approach for my research project. I wanted to opt for a mixed methods approach to make my research not only exploratory but also broad enough to generalize the findings. But in one Twitter (referred to now as X) interaction with a fellow researcher, I realized the problem of using mixed methods due to the scope and the limited time frame for my research. Hence, I decided to use only an exploratory design for my research. So, my fellow researchers, remember this – social media isn't just for fun pictures and updates. It's like a toolbox full of shared experiences that can turn your solo research journey into an adventure with others. So I will recommend:

Top Tip: As you work on your research project, don't forget to reach out to your online friends. Whether you need advice, want to celebrate your successes, or just need a virtual hug during tough times, social media could be a map guiding you through the unknown areas of academia.

Self-awareness (for Self-improvement)

While using social media you are also made aware of your skills as a researcher and how you could improve them. It shows you different viewpoints, even though it can be a bit confusing/misleading. But it helps to prevent us from having unrealistic beliefs, especially about our own self.

Reflecting from my personal experience, I initially felt myself lost in the complex world of research and critical thinking. It was tough, and I wished for someone to guide me. Little did I know that this guidance would come from tweets, likes and connections.

I stepped into the worlds of X, LinkedIn and Instagram – a few friends that opened doors to a place where people connect and work together. With a click and a tweet, I found myself talking to other researchers. It was like a digital marketplace of ideas, and I really wanted to be part of it. As I talked with others on these platforms, something amazing happened. We shared ideas that not only made me think differently but also showed me how I might approach aspects of my research. Suddenly, I wasn't just a researcher; I was part of a lively conversation about the heart of undertaking research. Meeting with different points of view was eye-opening. It was like having lots of teachers, each giving me a new perspective on my own work. This helped me see the wide world of research and understand where I was doing well through opening myself to a variety of viewpoints and my areas of improvement. It also signposted me to a variety of useful reading materials and research articles through which I could refine and improve my skills.

With time, I also realized that social media wasn't just a place to show off my accomplishments. It was a tool to help me get better at research, to find areas where I could learn and do things better. One big discovery was about how I might do research and think critically. The talks and experiences shared on social media were like a quick class on getting better at these things. The shared wisdom online became my guide, showing me ways to improve that I wouldn't find in textbooks. With this new awareness, I started working on improving my research skills. I took courses, got advice from the online community, and started to realize that it all takes time, needs patience and continued work. Some of the feedback I got online became important in my academic journey. Though I would also like to share a word of caution here. Amidst the great advice one can find online, there is also a chance of drowning in the sea of advice which might not work for you and your research project. For example,

in one of these online interactions, I came to know about conducting systematic literature review for my project. I was fascinated by this information and
had started considering it for my project, only to realize later that I did not have
enough time to learn the skills required to conduct a systemic literature review
considering the tight deadline to complete this project. Therefore, I had to drop
this idea and complete my project following the traditional literature review.
So, the advice on its own was good but did not suit my situation and project.
Another important factor to consider here is the authenticity of the sources we
use to gather information and online advice. Instead of utilizing information
from any and every source, we need to identify the authentic sources. I was not
always successful in that, but I tried.

As the story goes, my research skills improved. I wasn't just figuring out
academics; I was growing as a researcher. Social media, once thought of as
a distraction, became a way for me to learn more about myself and grow
professionally.

Top Tip: Social media has the power to help you in your academic journey.
Join conversations, make connections and let the online world be the mirror
that helps you see the researcher inside you.

Accountability (Setting Goals, Deadlines, Self-discipline)

You might be curious about why I'm discussing the positive impact of social
media when it's often seen as a giant distraction, especially when it comes to
meeting deadlines, achieving personal goals and maintaining self-discipline.
Well, let me shed some light on how using social media can be a valuable ally
in setting and sticking to goals.

As an early career researcher, diving into the world of research is like
embarking on a solo adventure. You face the highs and lows all on your own.
For me, it wasn't any different. Juggling research projects simultaneously
along with managing other roles of academic life (teaching and admin)
demands clear goals, realistic deadlines and the self-discipline to stay on track.
For example, conducting a literature review for one project, participating in
grant writing for the second project and collecting data for a third project
while managing teaching responsibilities. Yet, in the whirlwind of full-time
academic jobs, maintaining focus can be a challenge. Some people excel at
keeping personal goals without external help, but that isn't always the case
for me.

Remember having a study buddy in school? Well, I found a similar role for
social media in my research journey. I started sharing my plans online, looking
at fellow researchers for goal-setting techniques and insights into how they
maintain discipline to achieve their goals. Social media became my support
system, a place where I could connect with like-minded individuals. We shared

our short-term goals, and when one of us went quiet, a friendly nudge would follow. It's like having a virtual study partner, someone to check in on your progress and bring you back on track if you've veered off.

In this digital community, I started to find inspiration and motivation from peers. We exchanged ideas on how to tackle challenges, shared our successes and kept each other accountable. Social media transformed from a potential distraction into a valuable tool, a friend cheering me on in my research endeavours.

Top Tip: Treat social media as a supportive (and sometimes) critical friend and see the wonders for yourself.

I vs Us

As researchers, the success of our projects hinges on how well we convey our findings through writing. No matter how groundbreaking the research may be, without effective writing and presentation, it might not be considered a true success. One common challenge that writers face globally is the notorious writer's block, a hurdle that becomes even more formidable when you're just starting your research journey and navigating the complex paths of your projects (Bastug et al., 2017).

In one of those challenging moments, I discovered a few X accounts where researchers candidly shared their struggles with writing, collaborating with others and finding their unique voice. This revelation sparked an idea, inspiring me to create my own online writing community.

I decided to announce to my social network that every Thursday morning, I would dedicate two hours to writing on Zoom, inviting anyone interested to join me for a free writing session. These sessions were designed exclusively for writing, and here's how the structure unfolded:

a. Brief Introduction (1–2 minutes): Members shared their names and a quick overview of their research projects.
b. Goal Setting: Each participant articulated a focused and realistic goal for the two-hour session.
c. One-hour Writing Session: A dedicated hour for focused writing.
d. Comfort Break: A short break to relax.
e. Continuation of Writing: Resuming the writing session.
f. Progress Sharing: Ten minutes before the end of the session, participants shared their progress.

Certainly, not every session was a huge success, but this initiative provided me with a valuable opportunity. It not only helped me establish writing discipline but also allowed me to learn from my online research peers. For example, being a self-proclaimed multitasker, I learnt that focusing on one task at a time (instead of trying to do many at once) can be immensely helpful in efficient writing. Secondly, I also learnt the power of accountability, having peers around you (be it virtual or in person) brought a different kind of motivation. I felt accountable to my peers and therefore I found myself more productive knowing that I would be reporting back on my progress. Finally, it was also helpful to share our struggles with each other, find solace in each other, share the challenges we might be facing in that moment and seek help/advice from the fellow writers right there and then. It was more than just a writing community; it became a supportive space where challenges were embraced, and progress was celebrated.

As I said earlier, it was not a success always but the sessions which did work well helped us to overcome writer's block. Because it became a collective effort, proving that a shared commitment to writing goals can transform challenges into opportunities for growth. My online writing community became a testament to the power of collaboration and discipline in the, often solitary, world of research.

Top Tip: If you are struggling with something, take the initiative yourself, ask, and see the magic.

DON'Ts

Up until this point, you might be thinking that despite all the criticism of social media (Baccarella et al., 2018) how come I have only gone through the positive side of this medium in my research journey. Well, hang on, in my honest reflections, the next sections share some of the potential downsides of social media.

Offline vs Online Identities

Knowing the drill – you scroll through your social media feed, and you see your fellow researchers posting about their achievements. It's all smiles, conference glamour and high-quality journal victories. They are sharing their 'tips' to remain focused, stress free and successful. But let's peel back the layers and explore the reality that often hides behind those gleaming screens.

Beyond the fancy online world, things change. I have seen some fellow researchers who seem happy online but who are dealing with sad feelings in their real lives. Complaints about having 'no life' echo in the real-life corridors. The aspects they reveal online show sometimes their lives can be difficult.

So, what's the deal with this dual identity? Well, here's the real deal, social media is like an art gallery where we tend to display the best parts of our lives and leave out the regular or tough times. It's not always easy, and our fellow researchers face their fair share of challenges during their academic journey. Life is not always perfect, and it is okay to have some tough moments, even as researchers.

Although, we might think about being authentic and genuine on social media, that is not always the case. Considering the public nature of social media where everyone is free to express their opinions, be it good, bad or ugly, we tend to worry about these and the judgements they may bring about our personal views. Thus, we tend to pretend which, as a result, impacts on our authentic selves negatively. This tendency to pretend has been the topic for discussion in various studies in the recent past for its potential impact on one's mental wellbeing (O'Reilly, 2020). So, you are probably wondering how I deal with it.

Top Tip: My top tip to handle the online and offline worlds of social media is about keeping the real perspectives. Let's try to not forget about the actual stories, the difficulties we deal with and the real nature of our academic journeys, which varies for each one of us. So, less judgement and more empathy!

Sea of Information

'Ever find it easy to gather all the articles you need for your research?' I was asked by my colleague ... (continuing our conversation from the introduction).

'Why would you say that?' I replied, genuinely surprised.

His response shed light on the stark contrast in our research journeys: 'You live in the era of the internet and social media. During my PhD, I had to find all the required information by visiting the library, searching for books, hunting down the right articles, reading through them, and deciding if they were relevant to my work or not.'

However, what my colleague didn't realize was that the easy access to information, which he saw as a massive resource and an 'easy way out', could be an overflow of information making researchers overwhelmed and posing a significant hindrance in completing research projects on time.

If you're anything like me, you can relate to the challenge of having too much information and numerous choices. It makes the task even harder as you strive for perfection rather than completion. The desire to include everything to make your research shine leads to a loss of focus. You keep broadening your scope until you eventually need to narrow down to your main topic to operationalize and collect empirical data. But by then, time has slipped away, and deadlines are looming. This situation is commonly referred to in the literature as 'information overload', where excess information makes it difficult for researchers to sift through the noise and identify relevant sources (Eppler and Mengis, 2004). This challenge is intensified by the constant stream of updates and the rapid dissemination of information. What to do in this situation? Here is my 'top tip' to overcome this challenge:

Top Tip: At the start of your research journey, spend plenty of time understanding your aim and objectives; what are you really trying to investigate and find out? Once you decide on this, keep your search of social media limited within these boundaries. Keep focused and ignore anything and everything which does not serve the purpose for your research and, trust me that will help you to save a lot of time and produce positive results.

Doing It All at Once

In the world of social media, looking at the highlight of others' lives makes us believe that everyone around us is living their absolute best life. It is a common feeling. You start getting this vibe that you need to do it all, and maybe a bit more, just like your social media pals. But here's the deal – that kind of thinking piles on unnecessary pressure to be a superhero who conquers everything at once.

For instance, you might see a friend jetting off to a research conference, being offered speaking opportunities, succeeding in getting their research paper published in a top-tier journal or preparing research grant applications. The list goes on. Yet, amidst this social media showcase, it's easy to lose sight of the unique journeys of our fellow researchers. We forget about the networks they've built, the hard work they've poured in and, perhaps most crucially, the life they lead beyond academia.

There are plenty of studies which have discussed the same issues at length (Huang and Fan, 2022). Healthy competition can be a catalyst for learning from one another, but the moment it transforms into an unhealthy obsession, it's time to stop. So, what is my top tip for this challenge?

Top Tip: Keep your eyes on the prize by staying focused on your personal and your life goals. Regularly reminding yourself of the broader picture helps put things into perspective.

Who Else Is Like Me?

Okay, so you might be thinking, 'Wait a minute, isn't this contradicting her earlier point about our similar experiences on the social media?' Well, hold on, because here's the twist. The quest to find someone similar to yourself can be challenging. This became evident to me during my academic journey. Let me tell you a story. Picture this – I packed my bags, left my home country and landed in the UK for an MBA and subsequently a PhD. Now, you'd think with all the social media connections I have built over time, finding a buddy with a similar story would be a piece of cake. Surprise, surprise – not so much.

Despite being plugged into this vast social media universe, finding someone who had a similar background and journey turned out to be trickier than playing hide-and-seek in the dark. I was scrolling, clicking and swiping, but where were my academic soulmates? It's like this weird feeling of isolation crept in. I was on a quest to find someone whose story ran parallel to mine. And let me tell you, it was not easy.

And here's the moment of truth – it makes you question the whole façade of social media. You start wondering, 'Hey, I thought this was supposed to connect me with my tribe!' But no, sometimes it feels like social media missed the memo on finding your doppelgänger.

So, here's the scoop – the quest for someone just like you on social media might hit a few bumps. It's not always easy. But guess what? That doesn't mean you're alone in this. We're all trying to figure out this crazy maze of social media together, even if our stories aren't carbon copies. After all, who said finding your academic twin was going to be easy? So my top tip is:

Top Tip: Focus on the similarities among your fellow researchers instead of differences. These might not be immediately apparent but become visible with time.

LESSONS FOR KEEPING YOUR PROJECT ON TRACK

My research journey in the offline and online world of social media has been a nuanced experience. While social media has undoubtedly transformed the way we connect, collaborate and share, it's essential to approach it with awareness. Recognizing the dual identity, acknowledging the challenges and focusing on the positives can help researchers make the most of this dynamic digital landscape. It's a journey of continuous learning, adaptation and finding a balance between the benefits and pitfalls of social media in the pursuit of academic excellence.

Concluding the above discussion, here are some of the lessons I have been learning (which is still work in progress) to keep my research projects and academic career on track and hope you will find them useful too:

- **Stay Connected:** Don't go solo! Reach out to your online friends when you need advice, want to celebrate or just need a virtual hug during those tough research times. Social media can be your guiding map through the unknowns of academia.
- **Harness the Power:** Social media isn't just for scrolling – it's a powerful tool for academic growth. Join conversations, make connections, and let the online world be the mirror reflecting the researcher within you.

- **Treat It as a Friend:** Consider social media your supportive (and some-times critical) friend. You might be surprised by the wonders it may unfold when you embrace it with an open mind.
- **Take the Initiative:** Feeling stuck? Be the driver of change! Take the initi-ative on social media, actively seek solutions and watch the magic happen.
- **Balance Online and Offline Lives:** Juggling your virtual and real-world existence? It's complex, but let's not forget the real stories and difficul-ties we face. Choose empathy over judgement in our diverse academic journeys.
- **Define Research Boundaries:** Set the stage early! Understand your research aims and keep social media searches within those boundaries. Trust me, it can save time and produce focused results.
- **Keep Your Eyes on the Prize:** Amidst the academic chaos, don't lose sight of your personal and life goals. Regular reminders of the bigger picture help to maintain the perspective.
- **Seek Similarities:** Instead of focusing on differences, embrace the simi-larities among fellow researchers. Over time, these commonalities become more visible and foster a sense of community.

REFERENCES

Baccarella, C.V., Wagner, T.F., Kietzmann, J.H. and McCarthy, I.P. (2018). Social media? It's serious! Understanding the dark side of social media. *European Management Journal*, *36*(4), 431–8.

Bastug, M., Ertem, I.S. and Keskin, H.K. (2017). A phenomenological research study on writer's block: causes, processes, and results. *Education+ Training*, *59*(6), 605–18.

Eppler, M.J. and Mengis, J. (2004). The concept of information overload – a review of literature from organization science, accounting, marketing, MIS, and related disci-plines. *The Information Society: An International Journal*, *20*(5), 1–20.

Huang, X. and Fan, P. (2022). The dark side of social media in the workplace: a social comparison perspective. *Computers in Human Behavior*, *136*, 107377.

O'Reilly, M. (2020). Social media and adolescent mental health: the good, the bad and the ugly. *Journal of Mental Health*, *29*(2), 200–6.

33. Scribble, leave it, type it, change it

Mark N.K. Saunders

In spring 1975, John Lennon, co-lead vocalist and rhythm guitarist of 1960s pop group The Beatles, was interviewed by Francis Schoenberger. During the interview Schoenberger (1988, p. 71) asked the question 'How do you write your lyrics?' Lennon responded:

> I just scribble on a bit of paper, you know. And then leave it in a sort of pile. And when it begins to be more interesting, I venture onto the typewriter and type it out. And the typewriter adds things, too. I change it as I type it. It's usually the third draft when I get to the typewriter. Depending on how easy it came. If it just all came, it's just like 'write it and type it.' But if it's a general song, I'll type it a few more times. But the final version is never until we've recorded it. I always change a word or two, at the last minute.

Lennon's answer is similar to many researchers when asked 'How do you write?' When we start to write about our research, we initially make notes (either by hand or electronically), then leave these for a while before working further. We subsequently refine our notes on our laptops, developing them over time into some semblance of what we refer to as our first complete draft. Like Lennon's initial song lyrics, this is redrafted at least a few more times, and we continue to refine it up to the moment the finalised draft is submitted.

My conversations about writing with colleagues and postgraduate researchers invariably focus on how difficult we all find the process. We discuss how we spend what can seem like hours (or even days!) staring at our laptop screens: typing a few words, editing these words, re-editing these words, believing they are rubbish and sometimes even deleting them. This is our reality of writing or rather, as Becker (2020) emphasises, re-writing. Writing and re-writing are difficult because, the process forces us to make our thoughts clear.

Some years ago Keith Townsend (the co-editor of this volume) and I wrote a paper on sample size in qualitative interviewing which we gave the working title 'How many are enough?' This paper, eventually published in the *British Journal of Management* (Saunders and Townsend, 2016), had begun life as a conversation over an early morning cup of coffee whilst overlooking the Brisbane River. During our conversation, which was wide-ranging, we discussed the seeming lack of advice about the number of qualitative interviews that were likely to be sufficient when conducting research; a question we were often asked.

On the basis of this conversation we decided we should undertake a critical literature review of the extent and nature of advice actually available (rather than just moaning about an apparent lack) and, if very little had actually been written, undertake a piece of research to establish the sample size norms for published organisational and workplace research articles. We searched a range of online databases finding very few articles offering advice, and no empirical research on sample size for organisation and workplace studies. We made notes of our findings from the literature and decided to answer our question 'How many are enough?' by looking at researchers' reported practice. We began reading and recording how sampling had been undertaken in articles published in ten journals, analysing 798 articles and identifying 248 studies using qualitative interviews. We then began refining our notes from the literature reviewed and, along with the initial analysis findings, began writing the first draft of our paper.

Some 22 draft versions later we submitted our first potential output, a conference paper. Whilst 22 drafts are undoubtably a great deal of re-writing, each version had represented a significant improvement over the previous one; the process of refining helping us to get our ideas clearer. Although our paper was accepted by the conference, the reviewers made suggestions for improvement, which we addressed before presenting. Unsurprisingly our audience, comprising mainly people with an interest in research methodology, highlighted a number of flaws in our arguments. As we began to address these, we realised we had written responses to some of these flaws in our earlier drafts. Fortunately, we had kept them all!

Following four further versions our paper was submitted, and we were relieved that the editor sent it out for review. Our three anonymous reviewers, and the editor, felt that the paper required substantial revision. We redrafted the paper, going through eight further versions. Our penultimate version had been shown to two colleagues who were constructively critical, suggesting further improvements which we made. Believing we had now addressed the reviewers' comments fully we resubmitted the 34th draft! Whilst one of our reviewers was now happy with our revised paper, the other two felt more revisions were needed. Following a further seven versions we felt ready to resubmit the paper again. This time the reviewers' comments were more favourable, but further revisions were still needed. We both worked on redrafting the paper exchanging five further versions, again asking colleagues for critical feedback. The version we resubmitted was accepted.

Keith and I despite (or probably because of) the number of years we have been academics have learned that for our arguments to be clear and our writing to meet the standard required by journals we need to redraft our work numerous times. We have learned that constructive critical feedback by others improves our writing; drafts having been commented upon by conference reviewers, colleagues, three journal reviewers and the journal editor. Finally, we always keep earlier versions of our papers in case we need to go back to them.

REFERENCES

Becker, H.S. (2020). *Writing for Social Scientists: How to Start and Finish Your Thesis, Book, or Article* (3rd ed). Chicago, IL: University of Chicago Press.

Saunders, M.N.K. and Townsend, K. (2016). 'Reporting and justifying the number of interviews participants in organisation and workplace research'. *British Journal of Management*, 27(4), 836–52.

Schoenberger, F. (1988). 'He said, She said'. *Spins*, October, 29–32, 70–2.

34. 'I'm over it …'

Peter J. Jordan

This is a phrase I have often heard repeated by students and less so by academics. It emerges in a number of situations, with the most common being prior to the submission of a doctoral thesis. That said, I have also heard it said during data collections, when writing articles for journal submission and (surprise, surprise) sometimes from supervisors when supervising research students.

So what does this mean?

I think there are plenty of interpretations, from 'I have done the best I can', to 'I am sick of this project', to 'close enough is good enough', to 'I am not going to be told that this work could be improved any more' (fragile ego), to 'there is nothing wrong with my work' (narcissism), to 'I am never working with these people again'.

I used to have a view that doctoral students were never close to the submission if they did not tell me they were 'over it'. Then I would keep them working at it for a few more months to achieve a quality they were proud of and suggest they submit. I have never had a student fail or require anything other than minor revisions on this basis.

That said, there are only a couple of times in around 30 years in academia when I have actually said this myself. When submitting my doctoral dissertation, my memory (which probably gives me a false heroic status to protect my ego) is that there were times when I said, 'Let the examiners find any mistakes and I will fix them' – but I can't remember a time during my PhD when I was 'over it'. This is the same with my current research streams. I am never 'over' my research. Indeed, I find it a bit weird (or lucky) that someone pays me to do something I love doing and find endlessly interesting.

'Over it' denotes to me a loss of passion about the topic or the task. If you say it too often, it might mean an alternative profession is in the offing. Indeed, in preparing this piece, I reflected on the students who I have supervised as doctoral students and those who were most prone to the 'I'm over it' statement. All of them have taken career paths outside academia. Some have had very successful careers, in a broad range of professions, but not as a researcher who is passionate about or who simply enjoys their research and writing.

So next time you tell your supervisor or colleagues that you are 'over it', take a step back and figure out what you mean. You might want to be a bit more specific about what you are over. If you say it all the time to the point where those you work with are 'over' hearing you're 'over it', enjoy taxi driving or whatever you are passionate about. Life is too short to spend time doing things we are constantly 'over'.

35. The skill of bouncing back: a toolkit for developing resilience in academia

Mollie Bryde-Evens and Rebecca Beech

> The oak fought the wind and was broken,
> The willow bent when it must and survived –
> (Robert Jordan)

In an academic landscape that continues to ask more and more of scholars, with increasing metrics to be measured and expanding standards to be met, developing resilience is more critical now than ever before. As academics, we must master the skill of bouncing back from adversity; of moving forward not just despite of but in virtue of the challenges we face (Yang et al., 2022). Like the elastic band that returns to shape after being stretched and contorted, we as academics must strive to be supple and quick to recover. However, in our experience, to truly develop resilience we must go beyond simply returning to our former shape. Rather, we must view the challenges we face as an opportunity to reach a new and ultimately improved form, having learned something about ourselves or our professional environment along the way. It is this proactive, dynamic and engaged version of resilience, which centres on the ability to adapt, learn and progress when faced with challenges (Brendan et al., 2023), that we discuss in this chapter.

We begin the chapter by outlining our context for developing resilience. Next, we turn to consider how we have prepared for resilience. Following this, we discuss ways in which we have responded with resilience. Finally, we end with a summary of some key lessons that we have learned on developing resilience that we wish to share with others.

OUR CONTEXT FOR DEVELOPING RESILIENCE

Resilience can be developed through a range of life experiences. In this chapter, we explore resilience through our personal experiences of the UK higher education sector and the many challenges that we as academics face. Through this context we discuss the hardships we have experienced and how we overcame these by applying our coping mechanisms. For instance, we discuss resilience in relation to receiving feedback on our research, the review process, leading research teams, managing teaching commitments and experiences of working with others.

PREPARING FOR RESILIENCE

For us, resilience involves how we react in challenging situations and, as such, it seems to require lived experiences of hardship. However, in our experience, developing resilience ought not to begin at the first sign of a challenge. Rather, we have found that there are actions we can take and decisions we can make to better prepare ourselves to be resilient so that, when we are exposed to distressing situations, we are well placed to respond.

Vulnerability

One of these differentiating factors is the skill of vulnerability. Although vulnerability may be overlooked by some as a skill, we find that allowing ourselves to be vulnerable, particularly in relation to research, teaching and learning, has helped us to develop resilience in these areas. As academics, we often face many difficulties throughout our careers such as having our work rejected for publication or being unsuccessful in a grant application.

When faced with such challenges in the past, we have been required to make a decision regarding vulnerability. We could either allow ourselves to be vulnerable by engaging in the challenge, thus risking what could feel like failure, or we could avoid the situation altogether and seemingly avert disappointment. Early in our academic roles, our response was to shy away from such ventures as it was better, we reasoned, to avoid the risk of adversity and perceived failure that could follow. However, from our experience we have learned that it is only by allowing ourselves to be vulnerable, by facing the fear and by choosing to expose ourselves to challenges, regardless of the potential outcome, that we can hope to progress and move forward.

An example of when we have progressed through practising vulnerability was when we submitted a proposal to present at an international conference in America and to be considered for a prestigious award at this conference. Putting time, effort and care into writing the application was daunting as we had to accept the fact that we might not be successful. By putting ourselves forward, we opened ourselves up to fail and, hence, we allowed ourselves to be vulnerable. In this instance our application was successful, and we learned that when we choose to avoid vulnerability we may safeguard ourselves from failure, but we also avoid the opportunity to succeed.

Of course, it is not always the case that practising vulnerability leads to an obvious and immediate success. For example, we have experienced challenging paper revision processes including six rejections on a particular paper.

Each time that we have recrafted the paper and resubmitted it to a journal for review we have been required to embrace our vulnerability. Despite the initial feeling of failure that we experience each time the paper is rejected, the experience is still valuable as it provides us with an opportunity to practise and develop our resilience.

Therefore, even when the outcome is seemingly negative, practising vulnerability fosters our progression as each challenge and perceived failure develops our resilience. Hence, as much as resilience does demand a certain kind of strength, in our experience, that strength is born out of our willingness to take a chance, to risk failure and to embrace our vulnerability, whatever the outcome may be.

A Positive, Growth Mindset

When faced with a hurdle so high that we begin to doubt ourselves and that requires resilience, it is important that we adopt a positive, growth mindset. An example of a hurdle we have faced is receiving our first journal review on a paper which highlighted numerous areas for improvement. This led us to question our ability and understanding. Initially, instead of acting on the feedback and editing the work to address the reviewers' comments, we concentrated on the negative aspects of the comments. Rather than viewing the comments as constructive, we used the perceived negativity as a reason to stall the progress of the paper and to procrastinate. However, after attending a publishing workshop at our place of work, we experienced a shift in mindset. During the event, senior academics shared their experiences of publishing and the setbacks they had faced and, particularly, how they had adopted a positive mindset when reviewing feedback from editors. This fresh perspective from the senior academics, that focused on how we can use feedback to strengthen our work, helped us to initiate a positive mindset.

This example reflects that, when faced with a challenge, two types of mindsets can emerge. Firstly, we can respond by focusing on the error and negativity of the situation. In this case, the challenge is an ordeal that may take much mental and physical processing to overcome. This type of mindset is limiting and often restricts our ability to grow and develop. From a short-term perspective, we are prevented from tackling the issue at hand and our thinking processes may become stuck, leading to us being unable to move on and accept making changes. An alternative mindset, a positive, growth mindset, is one where we take time to absorb the feedback and to view it as an opportunity for development. For us, adopting a positive, growth mindset in relation to receiving feedback involves reading the feedback, reflecting on this by ourselves and with others, and then creating action points of how we can use the feedback to develop our work.

In relation to the previous example, when a positive, growth mindset was adopted, we were able to view the reviewer's feedback as an opportunity to learn and grow as researchers. The feedback encouraged us to think about our research with an improved academic understanding and enabled us to develop our work. For instance, when revising the paper, we deepened our understanding of the theoretical concepts used, repositioned our rationale to evidence rigour and demonstrated a greater contribution to knowledge. Hence, a positive, growth mindset, that seeks to flourish from difficult experiences and that views challenges as an opportunity to improve, is key to developing our resilience as academics.

Resilience in Others

In previous sections we have alluded to a 'self-help' approach to developing resilience which includes looking within yourself to find strength. However, resilience can also be built by reaching out to and learning from others. This, we have found, is particularly useful when dealing with imposter syndrome. As imposter syndrome can impact our mindset and particularly how we feel about ourselves and our work; we have found that it can be difficult to remain positive and practise resilience when experiencing this. We have found that when we are struggling with imposter syndrome a useful way to remain resilient is by reaching out to others and learning from how they demonstrate resilience.

An instance where we learned from and were inspired by others' resilience was when our funding bid to deliver a workshop with a colleague was rejected. Initially, we felt overwhelmed by the feedback. We felt it confirmed our anxiety that we are not good enough and we wanted to disregard the proposal. Instead of choosing a positive mindset and learning from the experience, we perceived the feedback negatively and were not prepared to learn from the suggestions given. That was until speaking with our colleague about the rejection and the insights they had taken from this. Our colleague reflected constructively upon the feedback whilst sharing their past experiences of rejections, which inspired us to see the feedback in a different light. Their resilient attitude on how the proposal could have been improved and their encouraging guidance on making future bids together deepened our comprehension of responding positively to adversity and learning from the experience.

As well as observing and learning from the resilience of other academics, we have also developed resilience through conversation with friends and family. For instance, when we first started working in academic roles after completing our doctorates, we struggled to juggle our research alongside our teaching responsibilities, and this led to us feeling overwhelmed. From speaking to loved ones, we learned more about their experiences of approaching a new challenge in life and how they had weathered each storm. This demonstrated to us that there is a great deal we can learn about resilience from our personal networks that can be applied to our experiences in academia. Resilient techniques that we learned from our family and friends that we applied to develop our own resilience included starting new hobbies to help us relax and adopting reflection and mindfulness.

RESPONDING WITH RESILIENCE

Once we have prepared for resilience, we must then engage with the arguably more challenging demand of responding with resilience when faced with adversity. In our experience, this is concerned with the time that precedes a challenging encounter, that requires action and in which resilience physically is or is not exhibited. Through our experience, we have learned that there are several ways we can take an active role in our resilience response thereby ensuring that, when we do face the challenges that will inevitably come, we are able to respond with resilience.

Practising Resilience

As we have already seen, resilience can enable us to adapt to challenging situations, cope with stress and embrace change. Resilience helps us to navigate the ups and downs of academia, ensuring that we do not get stuck in a negative mindset or succumb to the many pressures that come our way. However, from our experience, resilience is not something that we can expect to develop on its own accord. Instead, developing resilience demands our active participation, consistent effort and continual practice. As the saying goes, 'practice makes perfect' and this, we believe, applies to resilience.

From our experience, we have found that when practising resilience, it can help to adopt a 'fake it until you make it' mentality. When a challenging situation occurs, we sometimes struggle to interpret the experience as an opportunity for growth and we cannot see – or we do not wish to see – how to learn from it. For us, this is typically the case when the situation is emotionally charged, for instance, when we are deeply invested in a project or when, perhaps for external reasons such as issues in our personal life, we feel more sensitive. In such circumstances we have found that we can and should practise resilience, even if that means initially faking a resilient response.

For example, amidst positive feedback in our module evaluation feedback, we received some more constructive feedback that could be perceived negatively. Upon reading the feedback, we felt defensive, and we did not see the feedback as a fantastic opportunity for self-development. For a multitude of reasons, a genuine resilience response seemed unattainable in that moment.

However, despite not truly feeling resilient, we acted as though we were, and we feigned what we considered to be a resilient response. For instance, we verbalised that we felt positive about the feedback to ourselves and to others even when that wasn't wholly true. We have found that feigning a resilient response to a negative experience such as this has enabled us to visualise ourselves being resilient which, in turn, helped to transform a negative and unhelpful inner narrative into a more positive one. Thus, we have found that this 'fake it until you make it' approach to practising resilience is a powerful way to develop resilience when a genuine resilient response seems out of our grasp.

Sharing the Load

Research is often viewed as an independent and lonely activity: a single person's pursuit to achieve a deeper understanding and to enrich current thinking. In the past, we have adopted the perspective that we must deal with challenges independently as asking for help might be perceived as a weakness. For instance, when starting a new job at the start of our academic career, we did this to demonstrate to our peers and line managers that we were confident leading on tasks. However, our experience has taught us that taking this view is problematic for two reasons. Firstly, our work as academics need not be an independent pursuit as collaboration is key to developing excellent research. Secondly, attempting to manage everything on our own can be a major inhibitor to developing resilience.

We have found that sharing the load with others, whether that is discussing the emotional burden of the challenge we are experiencing or sharing the physical workload that is involved in the said challenge, is particularly useful. This is particularly helpful for early career academics such as ourselves as we may be less well versed in dealing with failures – if these are indeed failures. That being said, the importance of sharing the load is also relevant for academics of all career stages. For instance, as we have progressed in our roles to adopt leadership responsibilities, we have further learned the importance of sharing the load through, for example, delegation of workload and not saying 'yes' to everything.

Furthermore, sharing the load is important as we have found that resilience is more difficult to exhibit when we are tired and burned out. This is because the factors required to develop resilience, such as those discussed in this chapter, require great effort. Sharing the load ensures that, when we do face challenges, we have the strength to respond resiliently. An example of when we have shared the load was when we allocated specific roles amongst our research team, rather than taking them all on ourselves. In this scenario, we were able to lighten what might have been an overwhelming burden and, in doing so, invited different perspectives, highlighted new ways of thinking, and freed up our emotional, mental and physical capacity to deal with any challenges that arose.

We learned that strong communication, a sense of trust and a positive rapport between colleagues is crucial for sharing the load. When such a relationship and camaraderie is established, sharing the load allows us to be open to others' thinking and provides a safe space to share our own doubts with the purpose of inviting others' suggestions and support.

Being Selective with Focus

Another key aspect of developing our resilience has been ensuring that we are selective with our focus. Whilst we should certainly not ignore the adversity or the negativity that we experience, it is important that we direct our efforts to the aspects of the situation that we can change. Being consumed by factors that we cannot control can lead to stagnation and can stifle our opportunity to develop resilience, as we find ourselves rooted in what can feel like an unmovable situation. However, in these cases, we have found that we are never really stuck but instead, we are focusing on that which is stuck. Shifting our focus to what we can control can present a brilliant opportunity to rewrite the narrative and practise some of the key elements of resilience previously discussed, such as adopting a positive, growth mindset.

For example, when we first applied to undertake doctoral study, we experienced rejections from numerous funded PhD opportunities. Our first response was to feel downhearted and negative and to concentrate on everything that went wrong with our application. Mostly, we focused on the decision-makers in the process and why they didn't deem our application a success. However, we found that in these moments we had to remind ourselves that we could not change the panel's response to our interview and thus, there was little to no point focusing on that aspect of the experience. Instead, what we could influence was our reaction to their response.

Rather than directing our focus and expending our energy on circumstances that we had no control over, we chose to be selective with our focus. This involved focusing constructively on the feedback we received to determine what we could learn from the situation and what we could feed forward. For instance, when the response from our application included that we needed a more comprehensive understanding of the existing research in our proposed area of study, we chose to direct our efforts on addressing this requirement. That meant taking time away to engage in further reading and widen our knowledge base so that, when we did apply for a different role, we did so as more developed scholars.

Notably, ensuring that we are selective with our focus when faced with adversity is significant because, as we have seen from the discussion so far, preparing for and practising resilience takes substantial work and commitment. Thus, being selective with focus and investing our time and efforts into those factors that we can affect is important as it ensures that we have sufficient energy to practise and ultimately develop resilience.

Reflection

To keep moving forward in our careers, we have had to engage in reflection. Crucially, self-compassion and mindfulness ought to be central to our self-reflections. We have found that we must confront our past experiences without judgement, even – or especially – when reflecting on situations where we know we could have responded more resiliently. By being mindful, we can remind ourselves that challenges are an inevitable and essential part of life as an academic and that our worth and value are not determined by our ability to easily overcome challenges. This perspective, that involves noticing and taking stock of our feelings and reactions towards the experience and practising being kind to ourselves, has encouraged us to continue learning from our experiences and developing our resilience.

Reflecting on each challenging experience, whether it is an unwelcome response from a member of our teaching team or a rejection from a conference, has allowed us to learn and make positive changes for the future. For instance, after we have faced difficulties we have reflected on whether we interpreted the experience personally or whether we were able to respond to it objectively or whether we focused more on the negatives of the situation rather than the potential positives. In this way, reflection gives us a second opportunity to focus on and practise the different elements outlined in this chapter that are central to developing resilience.

One challenging experience that we have had to reflect on was when we struggled to engage and recruit participants to take part in our research. As their involvement was essential to the progression of our research, it was frustrating that participants were not willing to engage, and the challenge made us question and doubt the future of our project. However, through reflection, we identified areas of our own behaviour and research practices that could be improved. In this instance, our reflection led us to determine that the way we were approaching potential participants could be improved, as could the information we were sharing with them. This reflection allowed us to get a better understanding of the strengths and weaknesses of our approach which, in turn, led to us improving that approach and, ultimately, finding the participants we needed to progress the research.

Hence, by engaging in reflection and by critically considering our reactions to past challenging experiences, we have been able to identify moments when we have been too quick to react, have taken the challenging experience to heart, or have failed to see the path ahead. Through reflection we have addressed these problematic, resilience-inhibiting responses so that, when faced with similar challenges again in the future, we are able to respond more positively.

LESSONS WE HAVE LEARNED ON DEVELOPING OUR RESILIENCE

Our short summary offers a list of key learnings that we wish to share with others and that we believe, when adopted, can assist individuals in their development of resilience. The order reflects that in which we discussed them, rather than a suggestion of importance or priority.

- Allow yourself to be vulnerable and put yourself out there, despite the perceived risk of failure.
- Adopt a positive, growth mindset when embarking on ventures that might require resilience.
- Observe resilience in others and learn from their example.
- Actively practise resilience, even when that initially requires a feigned resilient response.
- Share the mental and physical load through building trusted, strong networks and collaborations.
- Be selective with your focus by being attentive to the positives as well as the perceived negatives and prioritise what you can change.
- Reflect compassionately on each challenging situation.

REFERENCES

Brendan, A. Rich, Nina S. Starin, Christopher J. Senior, Melissa M. Zarger, Colleen M. Cummings, Anahi Collado and Mary K. Alvord (2023). Improved resilience and academics following a school-based resilience intervention: a randomized controlled trial. *Evidence-Based Practice in Child and Adolescent Mental Health, 8*(2), 252–68.
Yang, S., D. Shu and H. Yin (2022). 'Teaching, my passion; publishing, my pain': unpacking academics' professional identity tensions through the lens of emotional resilience. *Higher Education, 84*(2), 235–54.

36. I have left the country, but the project continues

Stefan Jooss

Academic labour markets are truly global, and our roles allow us to potentially work in many different contexts and places around the world. For those of us who have the privilege, mobility, and flexibility, opportunities come up to move institutions and countries. Of course, these moves cannot be perfectly timed and planned, and as we leave one country, we often continue working on our ongoing research projects.

For my most recent move from Ireland to Australia, I was thinking about what needed to happen to ensure success and completion of existing research projects and commitments. Doing some desk research, the recommendations I got were sensible but barely scratched the surface of what relocation experiences entail; I was told to plan ahead, stay organised, and utilise technology to collaborate virtually. In terms of my research projects, I tried to get a good overview of my role (leading, supporting) and the stage of each project (early discussions, data collection, write-up of papers). Prior to my move, I also assessed priorities, for example, upcoming deadlines for submissions or revisions of work.

Having empathetic research collaborators was a great help, but of course they needed to be made aware of my relocation. Once I had signed my contract and the decision to move abroad was final, I reached out to my collaborators to inform them of my move. As we had more open conversations, we considered our timelines and potential disruptions. I updated my collaborators on progress made, acknowledged limitations, and shared any challenges faced.

I had to admit that relocations are not easy and consider a range of potential challenges. Even though I enjoyed the move and being in my new home, adjusting to the new surroundings took more time than I initially expected. I needed to tackle logistical issues, consider social integration (i.e., meeting new people and making friends), and make work, career, and cultural adjustments. I had to remind myself every now and then of the personal impact of moving and that, despite my best planning efforts, relocation was inevitably eating into my research time, for example, when house hunting for several months. At times, this meant postponing data collection and analysis, asking journal editors for extensions, or delaying initial submissions of papers.

Working across multiple time zones was also a learning curve. This certainly required more consideration of schedules, with colleagues being in various countries around the globe. With some collaborators, we decided to schedule morning and evening calls. With other collaborators, who were spread globally across four time zones, we decided to do the bulk of our work over emails, using online documents, and meeting at annual conferences. While I initially committed to late evening meetings on any day of the week, I learnt that I had to say 'no' to regular Friday 8 pm (or later) meetings for a healthier work-life balance. However, working across time zones also provided our team with the ability to work continuously when we were under time pressure; as one team member wrapped up their day, another team member stepped in – that was a real positive.

Being in Australia means acknowledging the vast distances and my research collaborators and I had to accept that connecting virtually was the meeting norm. Nevertheless, I have been trying to meet up with my collaborators at conferences, and I now see those events primarily as great opportunities to (re)connect in a face-to-face setting. We are also connected on some social media channels, and we drop each other casual messages here and there which means there is a bit of a conversation beyond the research itself. Ultimately, this helps us to stay in touch and maintain the human element in our collaborations. Going forward, I will also consider funding opportunities for research exchanges and visits which will also help me to maintain existing relationships and research projects.

37. To Dean, or not to Dean, that is the question

Jenna Ward

This vignette is an illustration of how taking up a senior academic leadership position poses an existential threat to research, relationships and reputation. Based on my own experience of being a mother, research-focused academic and a Dean, I offer insights, reflections and some critical questions for those who are either in, or considering taking up, a senior leadership position whilst maintaining a research career. The chapter will not present research as a scientific, linear process that follows logical and clearly defined stages to completion but instead will focus on the often chaotic, fraught and frustrating reality of keeping research projects on track; in and amongst real life.

INTRODUCTION

I was ambitious, not in a greedy, egotistical way, but for me, success allowed me to prove to myself that I was capable of more, that I was just as good as others. I come from a working-class background in the Midlands. I was first to go to university in my family. My parents' work ethic was unprecedented and I subconsciously emulated that. By the age of 10, I was cooking family meals, doing the laundry and spending hours cleaning the house. I had no hobbies and did no extra-curricular activities, but I loved to read. By the age of 15, I had read every Jane Austen novel and was beginning to fall in love with Dickens. I was good at most subjects at school (excluding those that were practical or artsy). I was predicted straight As and opted to take on more subjects just for fun!

Despite a stellar academic record, I had no idea what I wanted 'to be'. I did not set out with a plan, a great support network or even a role model or mentor. My journey to where I am now, Dean at a teaching-intensive university, a mother of two daughters (aged 10 and 2) and a passionate and committed researcher has been a process of becoming. In this chapter, I hope that my experiences will offer others points of reflection, to perhaps consider things that we often choose to exclude or find difficult to share.

I have tried to be as candid as possible throughout but recognise that this is my very personal experience. In no way am I making recommendations or suggesting that how I have navigated my career, made decisions or chose to manage my own work-life balance are the 'right ones'. They have worked for me so far, but I will also illustrate how I have had to stop, reflect and recalibrate on a number of occasions. What I hope to illustrate is how I came to understand myself as a research academic, a mother and an academic leader and how I have learned over time that none of these things are mutually exclusive.

BECOMING ... A RESEARCHER (TEACHING SEVEN MODULES AND WRITING A PAPER)

My PhD was conferred at aged 25 and I took up my first academic post straight after. I loved teaching but found research more challenging. Academic research is a long game. No quick wins, no short cuts. I was at a teaching-focused university so, I had the choice not to pursue research. I had a good job, taught and/ or led seven modules and worked with a great bunch of early career academics. However, having completed my PhD at a research-intensive university, the expectation from my supervisors and from myself was that I needed to publish. 'A real academic is someone who publishes in world-leading journals ... right?' In 2012, my first co-authored paper in the journal *Social Science and Medicine* was published.

That paper was predominately written in between teaching semesters. It was hard work, I was honing my academic voice and navigating the dark arts of the peer review process. Once published, I felt I had proven to myself and everyone else that I was capable of publishing and teaching. That paper was proof that I had *become* a 'proper academic' ...

Not quite ... my first real attempt at publishing post PhD had been a relatively easy affair. One round of review and we successfully published in a world-leading journal. Not all of my publications have followed the same trajectory.

Becoming a researcher is about learning to accept rejection. I now appreciate the research process for its ability to humble and keep me grounded. It is also incredibly frustrating, fraught with bias and largely a labour of love. At one point, I remember having five papers rejected in the space of a year. I thought my research career was over and I would make the choice to focus on teaching. I felt my work was irrelevant, that I was not capable of writing to the required standard and that I had no purpose in academic research. Fast forward 18 months and all but one of those papers are now published in highly regarded peer review journals.

That experience inspired me to set up a WEResearch tradition when I became Head of Research for the Department of Work and Employment at the University of Leicester. When a colleague had a successful publication, we had a celebratory research seminar, but the authors had to present the story of how the publication had come into being. They were asked to focus on and share the realities of the research process. This very often involved rejections, disagreements with reviewers and prolonged periods between idea generation and publication. We focused on what we could really learn from one another about the realities of 'success'. Not all publications come as easy as my first. Navigating the rejections, reflecting on reviews and building positive supportive networks are really important parts of *becoming a researcher*.

BECOMING ... A MUM (AND WRITING A RESEARCH BOOK)

I gave birth to my first daughter at the age of 30. At that point I was a Senior Lecturer living alone. How would I cope with being a solo parent? Holding down a job? Paying a mortgage? Being a good mum? Cooking, cleaning, washing? When would I walk the dog?

The question about how to be a good mum was much bigger for me than I had realised. My own mother had stayed at home to raise me and my two sisters. She took in work at home but was always with us. We did not go to childcare, which was a fairly typical situation in the mid-1980s in the UK. However, that shaped my own view of what being a good mum looked like. I thought I needed to be at home as much as I could. I thought it was me who needed to do everything and be everything for my daughter. This led to me feeling incredibly guilty about needing to go to work.

My financial situation meant that despite being a first time, solo parent I could only take six weeks maternity leave. In the UK, you are only legally entitled to the first six weeks at full pay, beyond that, maternity pay and policy can differ depending on your employer. The year before I had applied for a research sabbatical which I was successful in securing but delayed its start to dovetail with the end of my maternity leave. I secured the sabbatical on a book proposal for Routledge that was predominately based on my PhD and subsequent publications. So, after just six short weeks at home getting to know my tiny newborn and my new self, as Mum, I returned to work with the not so small task of co-writing a research monograph!

The sabbatical gave me flexibility over my time. A whole semester without teaching meant that I could control my own diary and my own time. I went out into the field and collected empirical data, talking to prison guards, doormen, veterinarians and teachers. If my daughter had been awake in the night, I could have a slower start to my day. If she went to bed a little earlier, I would sit at my desk. Yet, despite my very best efforts, running a house and looking after a newborn was more time consuming than I had ever imagined. At the end of my sabbatical, the book was not ready for submission. My co-author convinced me to contact the publisher to push back the deadline. I hated this idea. To me it was defeat. I had never missed a deadline in my life. Why couldn't I meet the deadline just because I had a baby?

The publishers were very amicable, and we agreed a new deadline for three months' time. I was surprised how easy it all was and there was no sense of disappointment or condemnation but instead a supportive approach to bringing the project to fruition. This helped me come to terms with the decision, yet I was determined not to need to delay again. We made some tweaks to some of the proposed chapters which reduced the need for further empirical data without compromising the vision and contribution of the text and we set out to meet the new deadline. *I realised I needed to be flexible and be confident to ask questions and renegotiate where and when I needed to.*

Those final three months were the toughest. I was back to teaching and marking and there was very little time in the working day to do anything on the book. If you are anything like me, I need to immerse myself in research, I cannot be productive without at least two cups of coffee, an hour of warming up and copious amount of reading and re-reading to get myself back into the headspace of my own academic imagination and craft. And so, the reality was that I wrote at nights. As soon as I put my daughter to bed, I ate dinner at my desk, I wrote and wrote into the night, and I only stopped for the night feeds. There were many times during that period where I had just three hours sleep a night. But I had a routine. If I worked crazy late one night, I went to bed at 7 pm the following night. I knew I had to recharge. I still wanted to be a great mum, but I was determined to meet that deadline too (Hochschild, 1989).

Writing *The Dark Side of Emotional Labour* (Ward & McMurray, 2016) was not just a wonderful academic achievement, and still one that I am proud of, but it was a process that redefined what being a good Mum meant to me. I learned to understand that my daughter needed more than me. Being a good mum meant ensuring we were not entirely dependent on one another. I managed to find the most wonderful childminder. She lives 20 minutes in the opposite direction to work but that drive every day was worth it. To know that my daughter was happy and surrounded by love meant that I stopped carrying around the guilt of going to work. The guilt of chatting with colleagues or not being 100 per cent productive every minute that I wasn't with her. This was a total liberation. It gave me back my academic identity and a greater semblance of control over my own career choices. I realised that she loved being at the childminders and I loved being at work. Learning how to re-evaluate deeply held beliefs, appreciate the importance and value of work to well-being and develop new depths to my own resilience were important for me *becoming a Mum.*

BECOMING ... A DEAN (TO RESEARCH OR NOT TO RESEARCH)

It was 2020, mid-pandemic. I had been Associate Dean Learning & Teaching for three years. We had navigated the transition to online learning, and I was surviving the lockdown with a seven-year-old bouncing off the walls. At that point I was receiving 250 emails a day. I could barely keep up and certainly could not afford to take a day off. The workload was crushing and the demands to home school, social distance, entertain and get enough exercise were all getting too much. I wanted to take some downtime but there were too many staff and students relying on me to make decisions and keep things moving. Despite all of this, I was happy. I loved the job and the team I worked with. I still taught a little and had managed to keep interesting research projects moving forward, albeit slowly.

At that point I started to receive emails from head-hunters. There was one in particular that was persistent to say the least. The emails led to phone calls which led to Zoom meetings, until finally I was in the recruitment process. Coventry University was a fast-moving, innovative institution that had defied all odds by climbing the rankings a few years before. It had a reputation for being ambitious and creative.

My first year as Dean at Coventry was a fully online experience. I sat at my desk every day meeting new people and trying to understand how things worked, what made people tick and how I could be of use. I was now line managing 13 members of staff who directly reported to me. I managed a significant budget, larger than some FTSE500 companies and had to lead and navigate a variety of complex strategic changes and people-related issues. The culture at Coventry was very different to what I was used to. Research was not in every academic's contract, in fact there was an institutional move to encourage staff to specialise in either teaching or research.

My natural disposition as a critical management studies academic was to resist leadership, to encourage debate and resistance and collective action. How could I be the Dean and continue to recognise and value these activities? (Brown et al., 2021) I tried to offer forums for engagement and open discussion, hosted research seminars and supported staff development opportunities but this was a very different environment to that which I was used. So, what did this mean for me?

Initially I sat at my desk in my smart jacket with slippers and fluffy socks under the desk. Then, as the restrictions eased, I started to go on to campus. People were shocked. I was 36, a woman and Dean of one of the largest undergraduate-providing faculties in Europe. My face did not fit. I was very conscious of perceptions, of how I needed to navigate this new landscape in which I found myself. I am not the type of person to wear a dress, nor to wear a suit. I tend to dress in black jeans, boots and to pop on a jacket if the occasion requires it. Smart casual might be the most generous way to describe it. In research circles, this type of attire is entirely acceptable. I quickly learned, however, that my research publications, my impact case studies, the way I dress and my experience as a research academic were no longer as important as they had been. This felt very strange.

Approximately 18 months into my tenure as Dean, I started to feel a little lost. I realised that when you meet the Dean you want an answer to a resourcing question or clarity on a policy. Had the long nights, the hours and hours of reading and writing to develop a research career been in vain? Did I want to give up my research entirely in order to be a Dean? Was that what being the Dean required of me? I was at a crossroads ... to Dean, or not to Dean?

I could continue to let my research rest or 'sleep' to use Shakespeare's term. To be honest I had secretly enjoyed not having to navigate the third reviewer, to bid for funding and meet writing deadlines. Being the Dean had allowed me to 'end the heartache, and the thousand natural shocks' born by the process of research. However, just as Prince Hamlet describes, I was caught in a purgatorial state. I am an academic researcher, but I am also a Dean. If I was going to make any sense of my own identity, I had to carve a new path. So, I began to look at re-engaging with my research. I read half-finished papers from years before, ordered new books and it did not take long until I was enthused again. I went to a couple of research conferences and bumped into people who had known me before I was Dean. This was re-energising, I realised I could perhaps find some way of doing both things, but it would require a whole different approach.

I must admit that I am far from bossing it (as my daughter and her friends would say) but I am starting to get a better balance. After three years as Dean, I know the institution. I know who to contact, how to get things done, what will and will not fly. I now try to use the time I would have been doing those things engaging with my scholarship. *I have made a commitment to myself to write at least one thing every year. This might sound very small, but it is a realistic commitment that I have managed to exceed. This feels good.* Writing book chapters, like this one, is an important part of me continuing to engage in academic writing and thinking. I attend research conferences and make a purposeful effort to present, be present within my scholarly community and contribute to the network of knowledge dissemination.

I have also found that *working with organisations on consultancy research tends to utilise retrospective knowledge in action in new contexts as opposed to developing new theoretical insights or findings.* In this respect, it is much less time consuming and can be done in a slightly more transactional way.

Purposefully plotting out realistic amounts of time and using holes in calendars are so very important for developing a healthier balance between research and administrative duties. I now work less in the evenings because I put myself under less pressure. That is not to say that I do not work long hours or spend too long worrying about decisions I've made or where I am going next. I also use international travel and conferences as dedicated spaces for reading and writing. Away from the children and the routine of daily life I try to use my time carefully. I spend less time socialising, perhaps drinking a little more than I should and regretting the things I have not done and more time using the available time I do have to get things done! Research for me is about intellectual stimulation, giving back, being part of my academic community and being a grounded, engaged and authentic academic leader. Understanding the importance of my research identity has been an important part of me *becoming a Dean.*

BOX 37.1 KEEPING MY RESEARCH ON TRACK: A DAY IN THE LIFE OF DEAN/MUM/PROF.

'Muuuuum! Is it waking up time yet?'

That is C, my two-year-old. It's 5.30 in the morning and she is ready to start the day. It's still dark outside but my feet hit the floor knowing that I need to muster the energy for another packed day.

As I stand in the kitchen drinking my tea, the TV is on in the playroom and the children are already eating breakfast. I scroll through my calendar on my iPad. Today is Clearing. This is when school children get their results and make final decisions about which university they want to attend. For an institution like mine, Clearing is one of the most significant days of the year.

After taking laundry from the machine, replying to five or so emails and deleting a tranche of spam, I wrangle the children into the shower, make packed lunches, pack school bags, feed the dog, put the slow cooker on and leave the house for 7.30 am.

Another cup of tea and some breakfast in the car. I get onto campus for 8.30 am. I head straight for the 'basement' from where we run the Clearing operation. We have provided breakfast and refreshments for the team. I say hellos, get stopped by a couple of people asking when we expect to release next year's budget and then head up to the office.

Staffing and Resourcing Committee, followed by a 1-2-1 with a direct report, a Senior Leadership Team meeting and then my video call pops up in the corner of my laptop screen. I answer, reluctantly. 'Can you come and shoot a TikTok to help boost Clearing numbers?' That is the request.

I scramble trying to make sense of the ask. I hate social media; I dislike technology and I have certainly never been on TikTok. I have no choice but to say yes, I am the Dean! I head off dutifully to shoot my TikTok video, which apparently generates 40 new calls from prospective students, so deemed worth it in the end.

No time for lunch so nibble on some nuts and dried fruit in my bag to keep me going. I pop down to the basement again to ensure I am visible to the Clearing teams. They don't need me to make decisions, but I want them to appreciate that I value their efforts. Back up to the office for another four back-to-back meetings. Budgets, marketing, registry and planning for graduation. I add to my to do lists all the actions and do my best to delegate throughout.

It's 4.30 pm – I get back in the car, hoping that the traffic will not be too bad as I head for the childminder at 5 pm. I collect the two-year-old and drop her back home. Collect my ten-year-old and take her to a two-hour football training session 40 minutes away. In the car, in the quiet I look at my to do list. The overwhelming urge to open the laptop and start ticking off some of the quick wins descends on me but I know that I have time blocked out tomorrow morning for exactly that task. Tasks that I can do sat in the team office whilst I am chatting to others and being a present Dean.

Instead, I pull out a stack of research papers that I have printed out. I know it is not environmentally friendly to print stuff, but it is the only way I can work. I like to highlight, to annotate, to doodle and to engage physically with the knowledge in front of me. I am writing a paper on the experiences of working as a funeral director. I have read what feels like hundreds of articles but still I am reluctant to start writing. This always happens to me. So, I read more ... but I know this is my process and privilege of becoming.

By the time I pull the car on the drive it is almost 9 pm. I'm tired and hungry. I eat, put on my Pjs and commit to reading a chapter of a PhD thesis that I am examining before I go to bed.

I am a Mum of two girls, a Dean and a Research Professor and I wouldn't have it any other way.

LESSONS FOR KEEPING YOUR RESEARCH PROJECT ON TRACK

1. If you have caring responsibilities, find help, support or provision that you are entirely comfortable with. Drive a little further, pay a little more if you can. It will be worth it in the long run.

2. Academic research needs to be a passion rather than a task. There are plenty of alternative ways in which you can work at a university and be an academic without needing to be a researcher. Be kind to yourself, there are plenty of options.
3. Be flexible. This applies to your own goals, your working hours and your expectations. Do not be afraid to negotiate.
4. Match time you have available with the tasks you must do.
5. Get started! We can often become paralysed or procrastinate in fear that we cannot meet our own high expectations. Just get started. It will make you feel better.

REFERENCES

Brown, A.D., Lewis, M. A. and Oliver, N. (2021). Identity work, loss and preferred identities: a study of UK business school deans. *Organization Studies*, *42*(6), 823–44.
Hochshild, A.R. (1989). *The Second Shift*. London: Penguin.
Ward, J. and McMurray, R. (2016). *The Dark Side of Emotional Labour*. London: Routledge.

Index